Oxford Business English

Essential Business Grammar & Practice

Michael Duckworth

OXFORD
UNIVERSITY PRESS

OXFORD
UNIVERSITY PRESS

Great Clarendon Street, Oxford OX2 6DP

Oxford University Press is a department of the University of Oxford.
It furthers the University's objective of excellence in research, scholarship,
and education by publishing worldwide in

Oxford New York

Auckland Cape Town Dar es Salaam Hong Kong Karachi
Kuala Lumpur Madrid Melbourne Mexico City Nairobi
New Delhi Shanghai Taipei Toronto

With offices in

Argentina Austria Brazil Chile Czech Republic France Greece
Guatemala Hungary Italy Japan Poland Portugal Singapore
South Korea Switzerland Thailand Turkey Ukraine Vietnam

OXFORD and OXFORD ENGLISH are registered trade marks of
Oxford University Press in the UK and in certain other countries

ISBN-13: 978 0 19 457625 3
ISBN-10: 0 19 457625 6

Printed in Spain by Gráficas Estella

ACKNOWLEDGEMENTS

*The publishers would like to thank the following for permission to reproduce the
following photographs:* AKG Images p 129 (Pravda); Alamy pp 11 (M.Hamilton),
26 (Elizabeth Whiting & Associates), 29 (Palace ticket/E.Farrelly/Adams
Picture Library), 29 (tower/Mooch Images), 35 (wasteland/geogphotos), 35
(tower blocks/D.Burke), 49 (olympic village/Elmtree Images), 51 (D.Gowans),
55 (foodfolio), 97 (weather/A.Sherratt), 97 (supermarket/A.King), 97
(city/B.Horisk), 99 (Ibiza/Debbie Bragg), 127 (geogphotos), 129
(bridge/M.Zylber); Auto Express Picture Library p 101 (Mitsubishi); Corbis pp
14 (H.Spichtinger/Zefa), 24 (skyscraper/D.M.Allan/Travel Ink), 41
(J.Ferrari/epa), 49 (swimming pool/M.Bicanski/Zuma), 49
(stadium/Y.Karahalis/Reuters), 49 (railway/C.Garratt), 49 (olympic
park/M.S.Yamashita), 58 (Freud/A.Woolfitt), 59 (P.Wojazer/Reuters), 113
(W.Deuter/Zefa); Empics p 89 (PA); Getty Images pp 18 (George/L.Quail), 24
(stairs/A.Garcia), 33 (Annie Saunders/D.Lees), 33 (Ken Lo/Chabruken), 33 (Uma
Jensen/J.Toy), 88 (O.Wolberger), 97 (food/I.O'Leary), 97 (buses/M.Harwood), 99
(Paxox/J.Bayne/Robert Harding World Imagery), 101 (Peogeot/P.Le Segretain),
101 (Aston Martin/B.Vincent), 129 (Morse/Hulton Archive), 129 (winter
oympics/Hulton Archive/Topical Press Agency); The Kobal Collection p 58
(Psycho poster/Paramount); NASA p 129 (astronaut); Panasonic Consumer
Electronics UK p 139; Punchstock pp 18 (Juanita/PhotoDisc Red), 18
(Martin/Brand X Pictures), 29 (Doge's Palace left/S.Allen/Brand X Pictures), 77
(M.Rakusen/Digital Vision)

Illustrations by: Adrian Barclay p 7 (cities); Mark Duffin pp 8, 9, 29, 44, 58, 96,
100 (perfumes), 103, 109, 117, 130; Julian Mosedale pp 34, 64, 70, 86, 91;
Carol Seatory pp 17, 21, 22, 41, 54, 65, 74, 104, 107, 114 (keys), 125
(managers), 145; Paul Stroud pp 19, 45, 61, 76, 100 (towers), 102, 116, 125
(Sunlight), 132; Harry Venning pp 6, 7 (ID card), 42, 67, 87, 94, 106, 111, 114
(cars), 146;

*The authors and publisher are grateful to those who have given permission to reproduce
the following extracts and adaptations of copyright material:*
p 75 'How to nail a job interview' from www.ehow.com. Reproduced by
permission.

Sources:
p 27 www.hp.com
p 39 www.eurostar.com
pp 59 & 99 www.news.bbc.co.uk
p 59 www.dailystar.com
p 101 www.geneva.cars.msn.co.uk
p 113 www.clipper-ventures.co.uk

With special thanks to Isobel Fletcher de Téllez.

Contents

Grammatical words 5

1 *to be* (1) 6

2 *to be* (2): questions and negatives 8

3 *have* and *have got* 10

4 Present simple (1) 12

5 Present simple (2): questions and negatives 14

6 Questions 16

7 Present continuous (1): *I am doing* 18

8 Present continuous (2): questions and negatives 20

9 Present simple or present continuous (1) 22

10 Present simple or present continuous (2): actions and states 24

11 Past simple (1): regular verbs: *I worked* 26

12 Past simple (2): regular verbs: questions and negatives: *Did I ...?, I didn't ...* 28

13 Past simple (3): irregular verbs 30

14 Past continuous: *I was doing* 32

15 *Used to: I used to do* 34

16 Future (1): *I will* 36

17 Future (2): *I am doing* 38

18 Future (3): *I am going to do* 40

19 Future (4): *I am going to do, I will do,* or *I am doing* 42

20 Present perfect (1): *I have done* 44

21 Present perfect (2): questions and negatives 46

22 Present perfect (3): *already, yet* 48

23 Present perfect (4): *for, since* 50

24 Present perfect (5): present perfect or past simple 52

25 Present perfect continuous: *I have been doing* 54

26 Passive (1): *is done, are done* 56

27 Passive (2): *was done, were done* 58

28 Ability and permission: *can, could* 60

29 Requests and offers: *Could you ...?, Shall I ...?, Would you like me to ...?* 62

30 Suggestions: *Why don't you ...?, Let's ..., What about ...?* 64

31 Advice: *if I were you, should, ought to* 66

32 Uncertainty: *may, might* 68

33 Obligation (1): *must, mustn't, needn't* 70

34 Obligation (2): *have to, don't have to, can't* 72

35 Imperative: instructions and directions 74

36 Zero conditional: *if you work ..., you get* 76

37 Conditional 1: *if you work ..., you will get* 78

38 Conditional 2: *if you worked ..., you would get*   80

39 *-ing* or infinitive (1)   82

40 *-ing* or infinitive (2)   84

41 Verbs + infinitive   86

42 Adjectives: *-ing* and *-ed*   88

43 Adjectives and adverbs (1)   90

44 Adjectives and adverbs (2)   92

45 Adverbs of frequency: *always, sometimes, never,* etc.   94

46 Comparing adjectives (1): *older than*   96

47 Comparing adjectives (2): *more modern than*   98

48 Superlatives: *oldest, most expensive*   100

49 *too* and *not ... enough*   102

50 Pronouns and possessives: *I, me, my, mine*   104

51 Reflexive pronouns: *myself, yourself*   106

52 Relative pronouns: *who, which, that*   108

53 Articles (1): *a, an, the*   110

54 Articles (2): *a, an, the*   112

55 *this, that, these, those*   114

56 Nouns (1): countable and uncountable   116

57 Nouns (2): countable and uncountable   118

58 Nouns (3): singular and plural   120

59 *some* and *any*   122

60 *something* and *anything*   124

61 *much* and *many*   126

62 Numbers (1): large numbers, dates   128

63 Numbers (2): decimals and fractions   130

64 Prepositions (1): place and direction   132

65 Prepositions (2): time   134

66 Prepositions (3): noun + preposition, preposition + verb, preposition + noun   136

67 Prepositions (4): adjective + preposition   138

68 Prepositions (5): verb + preposition   140

69 Expressions with *make* and *do*   142

70 Expressions with *have* and *have got*   144

71 Expressions with *get*   146

72 Expressions with *give* and *take*   148

Appendix 1 – Spelling rules   150

Appendix 2 – Irregular verbs   15

Answer key   15

Progress tests   17

Progress tests – Answer key   19

Index   19

Grammatical words

Adjective An adjective tells us about a thing or person. For example:

I've got an expensive car.

In this sentence, *expensive* is an adjective.

Adverb An adverb tells us about a verb. For example:

I work carefully.

In this sentence, *carefully* is an adverb.

Articles The words *a*, *an*, and *the* are articles.

Bare infinitive (see **Infinitive**)

Conditional 'If' sentences are called conditionals. For example:

If you come tomorrow, Mr Jones will see you.
If I had more time, I would go on holiday.

Consonants These letters are consonants: *b, c, d, f, g, h, j, k, l, m, n, p, q, r, s, t, v, w, x, y, z.*

Continuous (see **Simple and continuous**)

Infinitive This is the basic form of the verb, with *to*. For example:

to be, to have, to work, to go

Sometimes we use an infinitive without the word *to*. We call this the bare infinitive. For example:

My boss lets me use his car.

In this sentence, *use* (not *to use*) is the bare infinitive.

-ing form This is the form of the verb that ends in *-ing*. We use the *-ing* form after some words. For example:

I enjoy meeting people.

In this sentence we use the *-ing* form *meeting* after *enjoy*; we don't use the infinitive form *to meet*.

Modal verb This is a small group of verbs that often come in front of other verbs: *can, could, may, might, should, ought to, need, must, will, would*. For example:

I can speak French.
I might see you tomorrow.

Negative and positive A negative is a 'no' sentence:

I do not work in London.

A positive is a 'yes' sentence:

I live in London.

Noun A noun is a thing or a person. For example:

an office, a book, a car, a boss, a manager

Object (see **Subject and object**)

Passive and active In an active sentence we say what somebody does. For example:

Maria runs the department.
Henri posts the monthly report on our website.

In a passive sentence, we say what happens to something or someone. For example:

The department is run by Maria.
The monthly report is posted on our website.

Preposition Prepositions are words like *at, by, for, from, in, on, to, up, with*. They often tell us about time and place.

I live in Madrid. (place)
I start work at 8.30. (time)

Pronoun A word like *I, you, he, she, it, we, they* or *me, him, her, us, them.*

Relative clause A clause (a part of a sentence) that begins with a word like *who, that*, or *which*.

I know a man who works for Intel.
Here's the invoice which has all the figures.

Short form When we are speaking we often use short forms of verbs. For example:

I am >	*I'm*
It is >	*it's*
We have >	*we've*
They have >	*they've*
You are not >	*you aren't*

In writing, the letters missed out are replaced by '.

Simple and continuous Tenses can be simple or continuous. Continuous forms use *to be* and *-ing*.

Present simple:	*I work*
Present continuous:	*I am working*
Past simple:	*I worked*
Past continuous:	*I was working*

Subject and object Many sentences have a subject, verb, and object. The subject is the person (or thing) who does the action. The object is the person or thing that the action happens to. For example:

Subject	Verb	Object
I	*broke*	*the photocopier.*
My boss	*wants*	*the report.*

Tenses Tenses are forms of the verb that help to show what time we are talking about. For example:

I go to the office every day.
(Present simple tense for everyday actions)

Please don't disturb me. I'm working.
(Present continuous for something happening now)

I worked hard last week.
(Past simple tense for the past)

Verb Action words like *come, go, work, buy, sell*, etc., or state words like *be, seem*, etc. For example:

I come to the office at 8.00 every day.
When do you go home?
I am the department secretary.
This invoice seems wrong.

Vowel These letters are vowels:
a, e, i, o, u.

1 to be (1)

ⓐ Form

Look at the table:

I am late.	*He is late.*	*We are late.*
You are late.	*She is late.*	*They are late.*
	It is late.	

Look at the pictures:

Here I **am** with my family.
We **are** on holiday in Greece.

I **am** Hans Larsen.
I **am** 28 and
I **am** from Munich.

This is Herr Eisen.
He **is** my boss.

This **is** Frau Peters.
She **is** my assistant.

This **is** our Head Office.
It **is** in Frankfurt.

Here **are** my colleagues.
They **are** at a conference.

Hans, this is for you. You **are** the Employee of the Year.

Thank you! You **are** very kind.

ⓑ Short forms

When we speak, we often use the short forms *'m*, *'s*, *'re*:

I am	*I'm*	*He is*	*He's*	*We are*	*We're*
You are	*You're*	*She is*	*She's*	*They are*	*They're*
		It is	*It's*		

I'm Jose Antonio. I'm a production manager. I'm from Spain.

1 **Form**

Complete the sentences with the words in the box.

| ~~you~~ | he | she | it | we | they |

1 Adam, you are in my group today.
2 Paula and I are old friends. _____ are in the Export Department.
3 Yoshi and Takashi are on a business trip. _____ are in Kuala Lumpur.
4 Please do not use the photocopier. _____ is broken.
5 This is Sara. _____ is the Human Resources Manager.
6 George is an accountant. _____ is from Lucerne.

2 **Form**

Look at pictures 1–6. Answer the questions with *is* or *are*.

    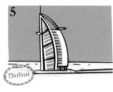 

1 Where is Herr Moser? He is in London.
2 Where is the conference? It _____ .
3 Where are Pierre and Marie Montaigne? They _____ .
4 Where is Señora Cordoba? She _____ .
5 Where is the Burj Al Arab Hotel? _____ .
6 Where is Hasan Jamil? _____ .

3 **Short forms**

Complete the dialogue with *'s*, *'m*, or *'re*.

Security: Stop, please! What's your name, madam?
Anna: I ¹ 'm Anna Rikardsdottir.
Security: And you, sir?
Mark: My name ² _____ Mark Andersen. I ³ _____ a new trainee.
Security: Your ID cards, please. Thank you. Are you from the IT Department?
Anna: No – we ⁴ _____ from Accounts.
Security: OK. You ⁵ _____ free to go.
Anna: Thank you.
Security: You ⁶ _____ welcome.

Look at the notes and the sentences about Juan Ramirez. Then complete the information and sentences about you.

Curriculum Vitae	
Surname	Ramírez
First name	Juan
Nationality	Spanish
Age	28
Status	Single
Occupation	Engineer

1 His name is Juan Ramirez, and he is from Spain.
2 He is 28 and he is single.
3 He is an engineer.

Curriculum Vitae	
Surname	....
First name	....
Nationality	....
Age	....
Status	....
Occupation	....

1 My name is ....
  ....
2 I ....
3 I ....

2 to be (2)
questions and negatives

ⓐ Questions

To make questions we change the word order of the subject (*I, you, he,* etc.) and verb (*am, is, are,* etc.). Look at the table:

Am I late?	*Is he late?*	*Are we late?*
Are you late?	*Is she late?*	*Are they late?*
	Is it late?	

A: *I want to talk to Petra. Is she here today?*   B: *No, she is on a course.*
We can also use make questions with *where, when, who, why, how,* etc. (See Unit 6.)
A: *How are you?*   B: *I am very well, thank you.*

ⓑ Negatives

We make negatives with *not*. There are long forms (*am not, is not, are not*) and short forms (*'m not, isn't, aren't*):

I am not/'m not late.	*He is not/isn't late.*	*We are not/aren't late.*
You are not/aren't late.	*She is not/isn't late.*	*They are not/aren't late.*
	It is not/isn't late.	

A: *Are you from Paris?*   B: *No, I'm not from Paris. I'm from Lyon.*

ⓒ Short answers

Look at the questions and the short answers:

Are you from England?	*Yes, I am.*	or	*No, I'm not.*
Am I late?	*Yes, you are.*	or	*No, you aren't.*
Is your boss here today?	*Yes, she is.*	or	*No, she isn't.*
Are we late?	*Yes, we are.*	or	*No, we aren't.*
Are they here?	*Yes, they are.*	or	*No, they aren't.*

! We use long forms in *yes* answers.
wrong: A: *Are you from Spain?*   B: *Yes, I'm.*
right: A: *Are you from Spain?*   B: *Yes, I am.*

① Questions

Put the words in the right order.

1 the/Is/open/bank ?   A: *Is the bank open?*
                        B: No, it isn't. It is shut.

2 the/on/same/flight/we/Are ? A: _____?
                             B: No, we aren't – we're on different flights.

3 Mme Strens/Is/free ?   A: _____?
                        B: No, she isn't – she is in a meeting.

4 Is/conference/in/July/the ?   A: _____ ?

     B: Yes, it is.

5 they/in/Are/Tokyo ?   A: _____ ?

     B: No, they aren't – they are in Kyoto.

6 late/I/Am ?   A: _____ ?

     B: No, you aren't. There's lots of time.

② Negatives

Read the questions. Make answers from the notes.

1 A: Good morning. Can I speak to M Marechal, please?

   B: sorry/he/not here today. He/at a conference.

     I'm sorry, he isn't here today. He's at a conference.

2 A: Good afternoon, can I speak to Miss Téllez?

   B: afraid/she/not free at the moment. She/in a meeting.

     _____ .

3 A: Hello, can I speak to Mr Ramiro or Mr Sanchez?

   B: sorry/they/not in the office today. They/in London.

     _____ .

4 A: Can I come to the office on Saturday?

   B: afraid/we/not open on Saturday. We/open from Monday to Friday.

     _____ .

③ Short answers

Read the questions. Complete the answers.

1 A: Is the food good here?   B: *Yes, it is.*

2 A: Are the Sales Managers away?   B: No, _____ .

3 A: Are you and I on the same flight?   B: No, _____ .

4 A: Is Anna from Spain?   B: Yes, _____ .

5 A: Is that man from IBM?   B: Yes, _____ .

6 A: Are you the Manager here?   B: Yes, _____ .

OVER TO YOU

Make questions from the notes.

1 your boss/American?   *Is your boss American?*

2 your boss/from Iceland?   _____ ?

3 your Head Office/in London?   _____ ?

4 you/a doctor?   _____ ?

5 you/from Paraguay?   _____ ?

6 you/married?   _____ ?

Now answer the questions. Write true answers.

1 _____ .

2 _____ .

3 _____ .

4 _____ .

5 _____ .

6 _____ .

3 have and have got

ⓐ Form (positive)

We make *have got* by using the verb *to have* and the word *got*. There are long forms (*have got*, *has got*), and there are short forms (*'ve got*, *'s got*).

I have got time.	*I've got time.*	*We have got time.*	*We've got time.*
You have got time.	*You've got time.*	*They have got time.*	*They've got time.*
He/She/It has got time.	*He's/She's/It's got time.*		

We often use the short form when we are talking:
  A: *What's the problem?*   B: *I've got a headache.*

ⓑ Form (questions and negatives)

Look at the table of questions and negatives:

Questions	Negatives	Questions	Negatives
Have I got time?	*I haven't got time.*	*Have we got time?*	*We haven't got time.*
Have you got time?	*You haven't got time.*	*Have they got time?*	*They haven't got time.*
Has he/she/it got time?	*He/She/It hasn't got time.*		

We make short answers with *has, have, hasn't, haven't*:
  A: *Has Jenny got the letter?*   B: *Yes, she has.*
  A: *Has Ben got the key?*   B: *No, he hasn't.*
  A: *Have you got a degree?*   B: *Yes, I have.*
  A: *Have they got a London office?*   B: *No, they haven't.*

ⓒ Use

We use *have got* to talk about possessions:
  My boss loves cars. He has got a Ferrari, a Porsche, and a Jeep.
We can also use *have got* with other situations:
  I've got a problem.   *I've got a headache.*   *I've got an idea!*   *I've got a lot of work.*

Note: In American English and in written English, *have* is more common than *have got*. The short forms are *do, does, don't, doesn't*. (See Unit 5.)
  The Hitachi Group is Japan's largest employer. It has over 320,000 employees worldwide.
  A: *Hi, do you have any donuts?*   B: *Yes, we do.*

❶ Form (positive)

Complete the dialogues with *have got, 've got, has got,* or *'s got*.

1 A: Are you feeling OK?   B: No, not really. I **'ve got** a bad headache.
2 A: Why do you want Frau Frisch?   B: Because she _____ the keys to the store room.
3 A: Is it a big bank?   B: Yes, it is. It _____ branches all over South-East Asia.
4 A: Can you and Lars solve the problem?   B: Yes, I think so. We _____ some good ideas.
5 A: Why is there another meeting?   B: Ms Arnoux _____ some important news.
6 A: Where can I get the information?   B: Talk to Rohani – she _____ the latest figures.
7 A: Can you deliver next week?   B: No, I'm sorry. We _____ a problem with our suppliers.
8 A: Can you speak any foreign languages?   B: Yes, I _____ a degree in French.

② Form (questions and negatives)

Complete the sentences with *have ... got?*, *has ... got?*, *hasn't got*, or *haven't got*.

1 Jason is unemployed – he *hasn't got* a job.
2 I like the PC, but *has* it *got* any good software?
3 The printer's fine – the problem is that it .... any paper.
4 They're in trouble because they .... any new orders for next year.
5 .... we .... any catalogues, or shall I order some more?
6 OK, let's have a meeting. .... you .... any time tomorrow?
7 You can't apply for the job because you .... the right qualifications.
8 Freya, I need to check those sales figures. .... you .... them?

③ Use

A client is phoning a conference centre for information. Complete the dialogue with the correct form of *have got*.

Lara: Hello, Astor Park Conference Centre.

Mark: Hello, this is Mark Jensen from Lumina Systems. We're looking for a place for a conference next year, and [1] *I've got* a few questions. First of all, can you tell me about the conference rooms? [2] .... you .... any big rooms for 100 delegates?

Lara: Yes, we [3] .... We [4] .... one room for 180 people, but if that's too big, we [5] .... two more for 60 people each.

Mark: That sounds fine. What sort of facilities [6] .... you .... in the big conference room?

Lara: It [7] .... a PA system, microphones, a projector, an OHP – most things, I think.

Mark: How big is the hotel?

Lara: The hotel [8] .... 40 double rooms and about 10 single rooms. They're very nice – they [9] .... satellite TV, air conditioning, mini bar, coffee-making facilities, and so on.

Mark: That sounds good. And what about sports? [10] .... you .... a gym?

Lara: No, we [11] .... a gym, but there's a swimming pool and a golf course.

Mark: That's sounds great. Can you send me some information?

Lara: Yes, of course. [12] .... you .... one of our latest brochures?

Mark: No, I [13] ....

Lara: OK, we [14] .... some new ones in – I'll send you one today.

Mark: Thanks very much.

VER TO YOU

Talk about one thing that you *have got* and one thing that you *haven't got*.

1 housing   *I've got a flat in London, but I haven't got a house in the country.*
2 electronic goods ....
3 transport ....
4 software ....
5 clothes ....
6 sports equipment ....
7 qualifications ....
8 family ....

4 Present simple (1)

ⓐ Form

The present simple is usually the same as the infinitive. With *he*, *she*, and *it*, the verb ends in *-s*:

I work	He/she/it works	We work
You work		They work

Remember that the verbs *to be* and *to have* are irregular:

to be:	*I am, you are, he/she/it is, we are, they are*
to have:	*I have, you have, he/she/it has, we have, they have*

ⓑ Spelling

Look at the way these verbs change:

Ending in *-x, -ss, -ch, -sh, -o*		Ending in *-ry, -ly, -dy*	
I fix	*He fixes*	*I try*	*He tries*
I miss	*He misses*	*I study*	*He studies*
I watch	*She watches*	*I carry*	*She carries*
I finish	*She finishes*	*I worry*	*She worries*
I do	*It does*	*I fly*	*It flies*

For spelling rules see page 150.

ⓒ Routines

We use the present simple to talk about routines and things we do every day:
*Ken Smith is a commuter. Every weekday he **drives** to the station and **takes** the train to London. When he **arrives**, he usually **walks** to the office, but if the weather is bad, he **gets** a taxi.*

ⓓ Facts

We use the present simple to talk about facts and things that are always true:
*Reuters is the world's news agency and **supplies** news to international media organizations. However, most of its revenue **comes** from the business sector, and it **provides** information to financial organizations and companies around the world.*

PRACTICE   **① Form**

Say if the sentences are right or wrong and correct the mistakes.

1 My assistant looks after our website.   right
2 You ~~speaks~~ English very well.   wrong   speak
3 My brother live in Japan.
4 All my colleagues agrees with me.
5 We manufacture parts for helicopters.
6 The new catalogue look very nice.
7 Pierre and Jean works in Paris.
8 Frau Müller wants to talk to you.

2 Spelling

Complete the sentences with the correct form of the verbs in brackets.

1 Anna *studies* (study) every evening at home.
2 This _____ (fix) software problems automatically.
3 My boss _____ (fly) to the States once a month.
4 My deputy usually _____ (go) to trade shows in Europe.
5 Pierre usually _____ (finish) work at 6.30.
6 Hans never _____ (watch) TV because he is too busy.
7 This part of the engine _____ (mix) the petrol with air.
8 My boss _____ (try) to make sure that meetings finish on time.

3 Routines

Complete the text with the correct form of the verbs in the boxes.

A DAY IN THE LIFE

OF ANNABELLE HENDERSON, PRESENTER OF THE SATELLITE TV SHOW

*fashion*today.

| listen   read   ~~start~~   watch |

Annabelle Henderson, presenter of the hit TV show *Fashion Today*, [1] *starts* her work even before getting to the studio. She usually [2] _____ breakfast TV or [3] _____ to the radio, looking for new stories. On the way to work she [4] _____ the papers to see if there is any fashion news.

| have   open   arrive   reply |

When she [5] _____ at the studio, she [6] _____ a coffee and then [7] _____ her emails. After deleting all the spam, she [8] _____ to the important messages.

| have   make   talk   work |

Annabelle [9] _____ with a team of TV journalists who [10] _____ reports about top fashion events. They usually [11] _____ a meeting in the morning and they [12] _____ about the latest stories.

| go   tell   spend   come |

She often [13] _____ the afternoon away from the studio. Sometimes she [14] _____ to fashion shows, and at other times the designers [15] _____ to the studio and [16] _____ her about their latest clothes.

| be   enjoy   work   say |

The show [17] _____ on every evening, so everyone [18] _____ really hard. But Annabelle [19] _____ that it's a team effort, and they all [20] _____ it.

4 Facts

Complete the text with the correct form of the verbs in brackets.

Pixar [1] *is* (be) a film company that [2] _____ (make) cartoons such as Toy Story and Finding Nemo. The company [3] _____ (employ) about 750 people, mainly IT experts, and it [4] _____ (use) its own software to create movies.

The company's profits [5] _____ (come) from sales of cinema tickets, and it [6] _____ (distribute) its films through Walt Disney. It also [7] _____ (sell) DVDs of its films. Steve Jobs, the co-founder of Apple Computers, [8] _____ (own) 53% of the company.

OVER TO YOU   Write true sentences about the topics below.

1 your job   I work for _____ .

2 your home and family   I live _____ .

3 your free time   In the evenings, I _____ .

4 your company   My company _____ .

5 Present simple (2)
questions and negatives

PRESENTATION

a Questions

We make questions with *do* and *does*:

Do I work?	*Does he/she/it work?*	*Do we work?*
Do you work?		*Do they work?*

A: *Do you work on Saturdays?*   B: *Yes, I work every weekend.*
We can also make questions with *when, where, why, who, how*, etc. (See Unit 6.)

b Short answers

We make short answers like this:

Positive	Negative
Yes, I do.	*No, I don't.*
Yes, you do.	*No, you don't.*
Yes, he/she/it does.	*No, he/she/it doesn't.*
Yes, we do.	*No, we don't.*
Yes, they do.	*No, they don't.*

A: *Do you live in Germany?*   B: *Yes, I do.*
A: *Do you live in Berlin?*   B: *No, I don't. I live in Munich.*

c Negatives

We make negatives like this:

Long form	Short form
I do not work.	*I don't work.*
You do not work.	*You don't work.*
He/She/It does not work.	*He/She/It doesn't work.*
We do not work.	*We don't work.*
They do not work.	*They don't work.*

In many Muslim countries, people work on Sundays, but they do not work on Fridays.

We often use the short form when we are speaking:
A: *Where's Jack?*   B: *I don't know.*

1 Questions and short answers

Make questions and short answers from the notes.

1 you/speak Chinese?   A: Do you speak Chinese?
B: No, I don't. I only speak English and French.

2 you/work for Sotheby's?   A: _____?
B: _____ . I work in the Fine Art Department.

3 your boss/travel to New York a lot?   A: _____?
B: _____ . He hates travelling, so he sends me.

4 your colleagues/like the new office?   A: _____?
B: _____ . They all say it's great.

5 you/work at weekends?   A: _____?
B: _____ . We only work Monday to Friday.

6 your company/operate in Europe?   A: _____?
B: _____ . And it operates in the USA too.

2 Negatives

Complete the sentences with the negative form of the verbs in the box.

| advertise   come   give   know   ~~sell~~   use   want   work |

1 Microsoft is in the software business – it doesn't sell computers.
2 Anna comes in two days a week; she _____ here full time.
3 I'm sorry, but we _____ discounts over 20% on our top ranges.
4 I can't phone Ella because I _____ her new number.
5 No, Max _____ from the USA – he is Canadian.
6 We have lots of commercials on the radio, but we _____ on TV.
7 The meeting isn't very important, so if you _____ to come, that's OK.
8 Now that we have email, we _____ the fax machine much.

3 Review

Say if the sentences are right or wrong and correct the mistakes.

1 My boss ~~don't like~~ long meetings.   wrong doesn't like
2 Do you want an appointment next week?   right
3 I doesn't like the room I am in.   _____
4 Miss Aniston is a vegetarian – she don't eat meat.   _____
5 Do your colleague like the new design?   _____
6 Does you want to ring the office?   _____
7 I don't have the figures with me.   _____
8 Does he travels to France often?   _____

Make questions from the notes. For each one, write a true answer.

1 you/work on Saturdays?   Q: Do you work on Saturdays?
A: No, I don't. or Yes, I do.

2 you/live near the place you work?   Q: _____?
A: _____ .

3 you/come from Spain?   Q: _____?
A: _____ .

4 you/speak Arabic?   Q: _____?
A: _____ .

5 you/work for yourself?   Q: _____?
A: _____ .

6 you/drive to work?   Q: _____?
A: _____ .

6 Questions

a Yes/No questions

With most verbs (except *to be* and modals like *can, may, will,* etc.) we make questions in the present simple with *do* or *does*:

Questions	Short answers
Do I/you/we/they work ...?	*Yes, I/you/we/they do.* or *No, I/you/we/they don't.*
Does he/she/it work ...?	*Yes, he/she/it does.* or *No, he/she/it doesn't.*

! We do not begin a question with a verb like *work, go, meet,* etc.
wrong: A: *Live you in America?* B: *Yes, I live.*
right: A: *Do you live in America?* B: Yes, I *do*.

b Wh- questions

We can also make questions by using question words:

Asking about:	time	place	people	things	reason	manner
Question word:	*When?*	*Where?*	*Who?*	*What?*	*Why?*	*How?*

When do you get to work?   *What do you want to eat?*
Where is your Head Office?   *Why is Mr Morin at home?*
Who do you work for now?   *How do you turn this machine off?*

! We use *who* in questions to talk about people and companies.

c Common questions

Look at these common questions:
How do you do? We say this when we meet someone for the first time.
    A: *I'm Norman Clifton. How do you do?* B: *How do you do? I am José Solano.*
How are you? We say this to ask about someone's health.
    A: *How are you?* B: *I'm very well, thank you.*
What do you do? This is a question about someone's job.
    A: *What do you do?* B: *I am an accountant.*
What is ... like? We ask this when we want someone to give a description.
    A: *What is New York like?* B: *It's big and crowded, but it has some nice parks.*

1 Yes/No questions

Read the sentences and correct the mistakes.

1 ~~Live you~~ in Athens?   Do you live
2 Does you pay your staff for overtime?   ....
3 A: Do you like curry? B: Yes, I like.   ....
4 Does your colleague wants to see the contract?   ....
5 Come you from England?   ....
6 Is he want to come to the meeting?   ....
7 A: Are you live here? B: Yes, I do.   ....
8 Does American companies pay well?   ....

2 *Wh-* questions

These people are meeting for the first time. Make questions from the notes in the box. Match them with the answers.

where/you/come from?	why/you/like big cities?
what/be/your mobile number?	when/the next talk start?
who/you/work for?	~~when/we/finish today?~~
how/you/spell your name?	

1 When do we finish today?   After dinner, I think.
2 _____ ? B – J – O – R – N.
3 _____ ? 07974 979974.
4 _____ ? 2.15.
5 _____ ? I think they are exciting.
6 _____ ? Madrid.
7 _____ ? I work for Banco Santander.

3 Common questions

Complete the dialogue with the questions in the box.

Who do you work for?	~~How do you do?~~	What's it like?
How is he?	How do you do?	What do you do?

Mary: Hello, I'm Mary Knowles. ¹How do you do?
Laura: ²_____ ? I'm Laura Croft.
Mary: Nice to meet you, Laura. ³_____ ?
Laura: I'm a journalist. I'm with *The Times*.
Mary: Oh, I know lots of people there. ⁴_____ ?
Laura: For Rupert Jones – he's the head of the Business Section.
Mary: Oh, I know Rupert – he's an old friend. ⁵_____ ?
Laura: He's very well.
Mary: Good. You must say hello to him from me. Now, I don't know much about the
       Business Section. ⁶_____ ? Is it nice to work in?
Laura: Yes, it's great.

OVER TO YOU

Think of eight questions you can ask people when you meet them for the first time. Use the topics below or your own ideas.

Subject
1 name   _____ ?
2 nationality   _____ ?
3 place of residence   _____ ?
4 job   _____ ?
5 company name   _____ ?
6 phone number   _____ ?
7 email address   _____ ?
8 finish work – what time? _____ ?

Present continuous (1)
I am doing

ⓐ Form

We make the present continuous by using the verb *to be* and the *-ing* form of the verb:

	be	*-ing*		*be*	*-ing*
I	*am*	*working*	*We*	*are*	*working*
You	*are*	*working*	*They*	*are*	*working*
He/She/It	*is*	*working*			

We often use the short forms (*I'm, you're, he's, she's, it's, we're, they're*) when we are speaking:
   A: *Where's Anna?*   B: *She's **taking** Ms Sanchez to the airport.*

ⓑ Talking about now

We often use the present continuous when we are talking about something that is happening at the moment of speaking:

  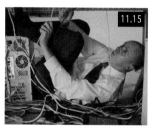

It is 11.15. Juanita **is talking** on the phone.

Martin and Ingrid **are leaving** the office.

George **is trying** to fix the Internet connection.

ⓒ Permanent and temporary situations

For permanent or long-term situations we use the present simple (see Unit 4). We use the present continuous to talk about something that is temporary or short-term (e.g. a conference), and things that have a definite beginning and end (e.g. a project).

   Grace works for OUP in Nairobi. (permanent, long-term)
   *At the moment she **is working** on a new dictionary.* (temporary, short-term)

① Form

Complete the dialogue with *am*, *is*, or *are* and the *-ing* form of the verbs in brackets.

Andy: Hi, Jemal. Andy here. I ¹ᵃᵐ ᶜᵃˡˡⁱⁿᵍ (call) because we need some help down here.
Jemal: OK. What's the problem?
Andy: We ² _____ (try) to set up the exhibition, but there's only me and Bill here. Can Selma or Fatih come down?
Jemal: I'm sorry, but Selma's busy. She ³ _____ (help) Sedat today, and Fatih ⁴ _____ (work) from home.
Andy: What about the two new people from Sales?
Jemal: No, they ⁵ _____ (meet) the Istanbul team at the moment. Look, I know. I can come and help. I ⁶ _____ (finish) a report at the moment, but I can be there in twenty minutes. Is that OK?
Andy: Great – thanks a lot. See you soon.

② Talking about now

Look at the CCTV pictures and the notes. Say what is happening at the office.

1 Mr Peters/lock/store room.   Mr Peters is locking the store room.
2 Anna/leave/manager's office.   _____ .
3 Someone/take away/a computer.   _____ .
4 David/turn off/lights.   _____ .
5 Klaus/drive/out of the car park. _____ .
6 Two men/wait/at the back door. _____ .

③ Permanent and temporary situations

Look at the notes. Write sentences about the people's jobs and say what they are doing this week.

1 (Lukas, pilot) – This week/have/a holiday in Greece.
2 (Markus and Ingrid, newsreaders) – This week/make/commercial in New York.
3 (Sue, nurse) – This week/attend/conference in Paris.
4 (Johannes, lorry driver) – This week/do/language course in Seville.
5 (Franz, chef) – This week/play/golf with friends in La Manga.
6 (Bob, builder) – This week/sail/in the South of France.

1 Lukas is a pilot. This week he is having a holiday in Greece.
2 _____ .
3 _____ .
4 _____ .
5 _____ .
6 _____ .

OVER TO YOU

Say what you are doing. Answer the questions.

Right now

1 What room are you working in? _____ .
2 What are you wearing? _____ .
3 Are you listening to music or the radio? _____ .
4 Are you working at a desk? _____ .
5 What are you writing with? _____ .

Current projects

6 What courses are you doing at work? _____ .
7 What languages are you learning? _____ .
8 What are you doing at work this month? _____ .
9 What are your other colleagues doing this month? _____ .
10 What is your company doing this year? _____ .

Present continuous (2)
questions and negatives

ⓐ *Yes/No* **questions and short answers**

We make *Yes/No* questions by changing the word order. The verb *to be* comes first. We make short answers with the verb *to be*:

Questions	Short answers	
Am I working?	*Yes, I am.*	*No, I'm not.*
Are you working?	*Yes, you are.*	*No, you aren't.*
Is he/she/it working?	*Yes, he/she/it is.*	*No, he/she/it isn't.*
Are we working?	*Yes, we are.*	*No, we aren't.*
Are they working?	*Yes, they are.*	*No, they aren't.*

A: *Are you driving at the moment?*   B: *Yes, I'll call you back later.*

ⓑ Question words

We can also make questions by using question words before the verb:
A: *Where is Andy working today?*   B: *He's working in London.*
A: *Who is he working with?*   B: *He's working with Bob.*
A: *How is the project going?*   B: *It's going well, thanks.*

ⓒ Negatives

Look at the table:

Long form	Short form
I am not working.	*I'm not working.*
You are not working.	*You aren't working.*
He/She/It is not working.	*He/She/It isn't working.*
We are not working.	*We aren't working.*
They are not working.	*They aren't working.*

We often use short forms when we are speaking:
A: *Is Joan in the office?*   B: *No, she isn't working today.*

❶ *Yes/No* **questions and short answers**

Make *Yes/No* questions and short answers from the notes.

1 Hans/work today?   A: Is Hans working today?
                       B: No, he isn't. He is sick.

2 you/look for something?   A: ....?
                              B: .... I can't find my keys.

3 photocopier/work/yet?   A: ....?
                            B: .... We're waiting for the repair man.

4 they/have a meeting?   A: ....?
                           B: .... Please don't disturb them.

5 Gina/work with you?   A: ....?
                          B: .... , and she's a great help.

② **Question words**

Make questions from the notes in the box using the *-ing* form of the verb. Match them with the answers.

~~How/you/feel~~   What/you/eat?   What/Herr Braun/do?   Who/you/phone?
Where/Olga/give/the presentation?   Who/Hans/have lunch with?

1 How are you feeling?   Fine, thanks.
2 _____ ?   With Klaus.
3 _____ ?   Pasta.
4 _____ ?   In Room 23.
5 _____ ?   Mr Lee in Beijing.
6 _____ ?   He's having an English lesson.

③ **Negatives**

In this picture there are three men (Pierre, Alain, Michel) and four women (Anna, Marie, Gina, Laure). Make sentences from the notes. Say who is who.

1 Anna/not talk/to Pierre. Anna is not talking to Pierre.
2 Pierre/not talk/to Alain or Michel. _____
3 Alain/not hold/a glass of wine. _____
4 Anna/not wear/a red dress. _____
5 Marie/not leave/the party. _____
6 Pierre/not talk/to Laure or Marie. _____

OVER TO YOU

Read these situations. For each one, think of a question using the present continuous form of the verbs in brackets.

1 You meet someone at a conference. You want to know about their hotel.
   (stay) What hotel are you staying at?
2 You meet someone at the airport. You want to know about their destination.
   (go) Where _____ ?
3 You want to buy a colleague another drink. His glass is 80% empty.
   (drink) What _____ ?
4 A colleague is on the phone. You want to know who the other person is.
   (talk to) Who _____ ?
5 A colleague calls you at home. You want to know why.
   (call) Why _____ ?
6 A colleague was sick last week. You want to ask her how she is now.
   (feel) How _____ ?

9 Present simple or present continuous (1)

PRESENTATION **ⓐ Routine or moment of speaking?**

We use the present simple for things that happen every day or regularly:

We use the present continuous for things that a[re] happening **now**, at the moment of speaking:

Normally I **take** the train to work.

Today, there's a train strike so I'**m taking** the bus.

ⓑ Long-term or short-term situations

We use the present simple to talk about permanent or long-term situations:

> I **work** for Costar Construction. We **build** houses, hotels, and roads.
> (I work for them all the time. We do this all the time.)

We use the present continuous to talk about situations that are temporary or short-term. We often use it with words like *today, this week, this month*:

> This month I **am working** on a housing project near Oxford.
> (I am only doing this for four weeks.)

PRACTICE **① Routine or moment of speaking?**

Complete the dialogues with the present simple or the present continuous form of the verbs in brackets.

1 A: Is Jack here? I need to speak to him.
   B: No, sorry, he isn't here. Oh, look, he's there in the car park. He is leaving (leave).

2 A: Do you always travel by train?
   B: No. Usually I _____ (take) my car.

3 A: Are you busy at the moment?
   B: I _____ (have) lunch. Call me in an hour.

4 A: Can we have a meeting tomorrow?
   B: Sorry, I _____ (not/work) on Wednesdays.

5 A: Could I speak to Ken Olsen?
   B: I'm sorry, he _____ (have) a meeting at the moment.

6 A: Maria is here early!
   B: No, she always _____ (get) here at eight.

7 A: Are you at the office?
   B: No, I _____ (call) from the train.

8 A: Are 4x4s cheap to run?
   B: No, they _____ (use) a lot of petrol.

2 Long-term or short-term situations

Complete the sentences from the notes. Say what the companies do and what projects they are doing at the moment.

1	**COMPANY**	work/T&R	I work for T&R.
	MAIN BUSINESS	operate/cruise ships and ferries.	We operate cruise ships and ferries.
	CURRENT ACTIVITY	run/Christmas cruises in the Caribbean.	At the moment we are running Christmas cruises in the Caribbean.
2	**COMPANY**	work/Honda	I _____ .
	MAIN BUSINESS	manufacture/cars	We _____ .
	CURRENT ACTIVITY	develop/a new hydrogen car	At the moment _____ .
3	**COMPANY**	work/Danzig Telecom	I _____ .
	MAIN BUSINESS	install/mobile phone systems	We _____ .
	CURRENT ACTIVITY	build/a new telecoms system in India.	At the moment _____ .
4	**COMPANY**	work/Gravis Books	I _____ .
	MAIN BUSINESS	publish/books and magazines	We _____ .
	CURRENT ACTIVITY	produce/a new encyclopedia	At the moment _____ .

3 Long-term or short-term situations

Complete the text with the present simple or present continuous form of the verbs in brackets.

Come to the Harrison's Sale – on NOW!
Massive sale! Hundreds of bargains!

Afghan Bokharas from $299
These beautiful carpets ¹ **COME** (come) from Afghanistan. In our amazing Summer Sale we ² _____ (sell) them for only $299.

Men's Fashion
Armani suits ³ _____ (look) great for every occasion. This week we ⁴ _____ (give away) a FREE silk tie with every order.

Health and Beauty
Allure by Chanel ⁵ _____ (be) one of the world's most beautiful perfumes. In the sale we ⁶ _____ (offer) 50ml bottles for only $22.

Food and Wine
Chateau La Lagune ⁷ _____ (be) a Bordeaux classic. It ⁸ _____ (taste) fantastic and it usually ⁹ _____ (cost) $60. This week we ¹⁰ _____ (cut) the price by 50% – down to only $30!

ONE WEEK ONLY — ONE WEEK ONLY — ONE WEEK ONLY — ONE WEEK ONLY — ONE WEEK ONLY — ONE WEEK

OVER TO YOU
Write about your company and a current project.

I work for Testra Trading.
We import things from all over the
world and sell them to stores
in Europe and the USA.

At the moment we are working
in China. We are looking for
new suppliers and we are
trying to find an office in Beijing.

Your company:
_____
_____
_____
_____

A current project:
_____
_____
_____
_____

Present simple or present continuous (2)
actions and states

ⓐ Actions and states

They are building a new skyscraper.

There are many verbs that refer to actions. Here are some examples:
She is driving to work.
He is selling flowers.
We can use verbs like this in the present continuous.

She doesn't like lifts.

There are other verbs that refer to states (stative verbs). Here are some examples:
I enjoy my job.
Sara knows Xavier.

❗ We do not use verbs like this in the continuous form.
wrong: *I ~~am knowing~~ Paris well.*
right: *I know Paris well.*

ⓑ Common stative verbs

Here are some verbs that we normally use in the simple form, not the continuous form.

Verbs of thinking, knowing: *know, want, understand, believe, think* (have an opinion), *feel* (have an opinion).
   A: *I want to start my own company.*
   B: *I know, but I don't understand why. I don't think it's a good idea.*

Verbs of liking and disliking: *love, like, don't mind, don't like, dislike, hate.*
   A: *I love the new design. What do you think?*
   B: *I'm not sure. I like the design, but I hate the colour.*

Verbs of possession, verbs of appearance: *have, own, belong to, appear, look like, seem.*
   A: *Who does that car belong to?*
   B: *It looks like Mr Danzig's.*

① Actions and states

Are the sentences about actions or states? Write *action* or *state*.

1 a Natasha owns a large yacht.   *state*
  b She is sailing round the Bahamas. ....
2 a Jason is talking to a new supplier. ....
  b He doesn't know him very well. ....
3 a Clara is a vegetarian. ....
  b She doesn't like meat. ....

❷ Common stative verbs
Complete the text with the words in the boxes.

TERENCE CONRAN is the founder of
Habitat and one of Europe's top designers.

| ~~has~~ | belongs | likes | look | know | believe |

He ¹ **has** over 40 years' experience of being a shop-
keeper, designer, and restaurateur.
He sells furniture and household goods in his Conran
Shops, with branches in London, Paris, New York, and
Tokyo. (Habitat was sold in 1990 and now
² _____ to Ikea.) His designs always ³ _____
clean and modern, and have simple lines. He
⁴ _____ to remind people of William Morris's
famous saying: 'Have nothing in your house that you
do not ⁵ _____ to be useful or ⁶ _____ to be
beautiful'.

| hate | look like | loves | thinks |

Terence Conran also owns a range of huge restaurants
of 300 or more seats which ⁷ _____ old Parisian
brasseries. They serve mainly French food, which
Conran ⁸ _____ , and they are good value for
money. Conran is not a fan of fast food, and
⁹ _____ hamburgers are terrible. 'I ¹⁰ _____
McDonalds', he says, 'and everything it stands for.'

| know | seems | want |

Terence Conran changes with the times and takes on
new ideas. But he ¹¹ _____ to ¹² _____ what
people ¹³ _____ – and he gives it to them. Maybe
that is the secret of his success.

❸ Review
Say if the sentences are right or wrong and correct the mistakes.

1 I ~~am not understanding~~ you.   wrong   don't understand
2 I love seafood.   right   _____
3 At the moment Mr Lund is attending a conference in Oslo. _____ _____
4 Klaus is wanting a new job.   _____ _____
5 You aren't seeming very happy with this proposal. _____ _____
6 Are you liking classical music?   _____ _____
7 I think that's a good idea.   _____ _____
8 I am feeling it's a good offer.   _____ _____
9 Their new people carrier looks like a bus.   _____ _____
10 Do you own your house?   _____ _____

OVER TO YOU   Write sentences about yourself using the verbs in this unit.
Possessions Write about things you have and things you want.

_____   .

_____   .

Likes and dislikes Write about things you like or don't like.

_____   .

_____   .

Opinions Write about what you or other people think of your company or business.

_____   .

_____   .

Appearance Write about how you look and the clothes you wear at work/home.

_____   .

11 Past simple (1)
regular verbs: *I worked*

PRESENTATION **a** **Form**

The past simple tense of all regular verbs ends in *-ed*:

Present	*work(s)*	*live(s)*	*stay(s)*
Past	*worked*	*lived*	*stayed*

Now Mr Leary works in the City.
In 1967 he worked in Carnaby Street.

For irregular verbs see Unit 13.
For spelling rules see page 150.

b **Use**

We use the past simple tense to talk about actions in the past. We often use time expressions to say when something happened:

In 1995 *I worked for Goldman Sachs.*
From 1992 to 1998 *Peter lived in Madrid.*
Last August *my boss stayed at the Oriental.*

c **Time expressions**

Look at the prepositions and other words we use with time expressions:

exact time	*at*	*I started work **at 9.30/at midday/at 5 o'clock**.*
days of the week	*on*	*Joanna travelled to Brazil **on Monday/on Friday**.*
months	*in*	*They arrived **in May/in June/in July**.*
years	*in*	*The problems started **in 1967/in 1998/in 2004**.*

With some expressions there is no preposition:
- *(Ø) yesterday*
- *(Ø) the day before yesterday*
- *(Ø) last week*
- *(Ø) last year*
- *(Ø) five years ago*
- *(Ø) two weeks ago*

PRACTICE **1** **Form**

Read the sentences. Are they about the present or the past?

1 Jane and Stephen Felton work in a village near Birmingham.   present
2 They opened their pottery business in 1990.   past
3 They started by selling to local people.
4 Later on they opened their own showroom.
5 Now they supply customers in Europe and the USA.
6 They started exporting in 1996.
7 They enjoy their business.
8 They work hard and are very successful.

2 Use

Complete the text with the past simple of the verbs in the boxes.

HEWLETT-PACKARD — *The early years 1938–1960*

The 1930s

Income (1939): $5,369. Employees: 2

| graduate | decide | ~~study~~ |

Bill Hewlett and Dave Packard ¹studied at Stanford University. When they ² _____ , they ³ _____ to start a business.

| rent | work | move |

In 1938, Dave ⁴ _____ into a flat in Palo Alto, California, and Bill ⁵ _____ a small house at the back. They ⁶ _____ in a small garage in the garden.

| call | design | use |

They ⁷ _____ their first product, which they ⁸ _____ the HP200A. Walt Disney engineers ⁹ _____ the HP200A to test sound equipment in cinemas showing Fantasia.

The 1940s

Income (1949): $2.2 million. Employees: 166

| add | order | start |

Hewlett-Packard ¹⁰ _____ many new products to their range, and when the Second World War ¹¹ _____ , the US government ¹² _____ large quantities of electronic equipment.

The 1950s

Income (1959): $48 million. Employees: 2,378

| manufacture | expand | enter |

In the 1950s, Hewlett-Packard ¹³ _____ rapidly in the USA and Europe. In 1958, they first ¹⁴ _____ the printers market after taking over FL Moseley, a company that ¹⁵ _____ graphic plotters.

3 Time expressions

Complete the sentences with *in*, *on*, *at*, or Ø (no preposition).

1 Did you visit the exhibition Ø yesterday?
2 I stayed in Bolivia in May.
3 I had a meeting _____ 10.30.
4 Did you call back _____ Monday?
5 She left the company _____ two months ago.
6 He joined the company _____ 1996.
7 The letter arrived _____ the day before yesterday.
8 We moved to new premises _____ 2002.
9 The plane arrived _____ five o'clock.
10 There was a sales meeting _____ July.

VER TO YOU

Answer the questions about your school, college, or university.

1 Where did you attend school or university? I attended Leipzig University.
2 What did you study? _____ .
3 What subjects did you like? _____ .
4 What subjects did you dislike? _____ .
5 Did you learn about anything useful for your current job? _____ .
6 Did you work in the holidays? _____ .
7 When did you graduate? _____ .
8 When did you start your first job? _____ .

12 Past simple (2)
regular verbs: questions and negatives: *Did I ...?, I didn't ...*

ⓐ Making questions

With regular verbs, we make questions in the past simple with *did* + bare infinitive:

Did	*I/you/he/she/it/we/they*	*like ... ?*

Did you like the presentation?
Did they attend the conference?

! We can't use the past tense form of the main verb to make a question.
wrong: ~~*Liked you the hotel?*~~
right: *Did you like the hotel?*

ⓑ *Wh-* questions

We use the same pattern with question words *when, where, why, who, how,* etc.:
  A: *When did you arrive?*   B: *I arrived last night.*
  A: *Where did you stay?*   B: *I stayed at the Hilton.*

ⓒ Negatives

We make negatives in the past simple with *did not/didn't*:

I/You/He/She/It/We/They	*didn't like ...*

*They **didn't like** the restaurant last night.*
*She **didn't finish** the report.*

! In questions and negatives, we use *did/didn't* + bare infinitive.
wrong: *Herr Luebbe ~~didn't stayed~~ at the Marriott Hotel last week.*
right: *Herr Luebbe **didn't stay** at the Marriott Hotel last week.*

① Making questions

Read the questions and correct the mistakes.
1 ~~Do you finish~~ the report last night?   Did you finish
2 Wanted you to see me yesterday?   ....
3 Did you attended the conference last year?   ....
4 Did the payment arrived yesterday?   ....
5 Do you stay at the Hilton last time?   ....
6 Posted you the letter on Friday?   ....
7 Did they changed the time of yesterday's meeting?   ....
8 Does she travel to Spain last week?   ....

2 Wh- questions

Blanche is a buyer for a Brazilian fashion company. Make questions about her last business trip from the notes.

1 What country/she/travel to?   What country did she travel to?
2 Why/she/travel/to Venice?   _____ ?
3 When/she/arrive?   _____ ?
4 Where/she/stay?   _____ ?
5 What tourist sights/she/visit?   _____ ?
6 When/she/return/to Brazil?   _____ ?

Write the answers to questions 1–6. Use the notes and pictures to help you.

7 (Italy)   She travelled to Italy.
8 (to attend the IWT conference)   _____ .
9 (18 June)   _____ .
10 (Palazzo Hotel)   _____ .
11 (Doge's palace, Campanile)   _____ .
12 (21 June)   _____ .

3 Negatives

Complete the sentences with the negative form of the verbs in the box.

order	look at	visit	~~answer~~	stay	use

1 I was very busy, so I didn't answer the phone.
2 The presentation was very boring, so Peter _____ to the end.
3 They _____ the instructions, so they had problems.
4 Their products were not reliable, so we _____ them again.
5 Our guests _____ the factory because it was closed.
6 Sally had a lot of stock, so she _____ any more.

OVER TO YOU

Answer these questions about the first job that you had.

1 Did you work for a big or a small organization? _____ .
2 What department did you work in? _____ .
3 When did your working day start? _____ .
4 When did your working day finish? _____ .
5 Did you enjoy the work? _____ .
6 Did you like the people? _____ .
7 What didn't you like about the job? _____ .
8 Did you earn a lot of money? _____ .
9 How long did you stay? _____ .

13 Past simple (3)
irregular verbs

ⓐ ***be*** **and** ***have***

These are both irregular verbs:

	Positive	Question	Negative
be	*I/He/She/It was …*	*Was I/he/she/it …?*	*I/He/She/It wasn't …*
	We/You/They were …	*Were we/you/they …?*	*We/You/They weren't …*
have	*I//He/She/It had …*	*Did I//he/she/it have …?*	*I/He/She/It didn't have …*
	We/You/They had …	*Did we/you/they have …?*	*We/You/They didn't have …*

A: ***Did you have** a good meeting?*   B: *Yes thanks – it **was** very successful.*

ⓑ Other irregular verbs

Many common verbs are irregular. They do not add *-ed* in the past simple tense. They change their form in other ways:

> *do – did   come – came   run – ran   go – went   buy – bought   make – made*

*Heinrich Boll **went** to America in 2004 and **did** an MBA. When he **came** back, he **bought** a small engineering company, and he **ran** it with a partner. He **made** a lot of money.*

❗ See the list of common irregular verbs on page 151.

ⓒ Questions and negatives

In questions and negatives, irregular verbs are like regular verbs. They use ***did/didn't*** + bare infinitive.

Questions	Negatives
Did I/you/he/she/it/we/they go …	*I/you/he/she/it/we/they didn't go …*

A: ***Did you go** to the meeting yesterday?*   B: *No, I **didn't have** time.*

❗ Do not use the past simple form of the main verb in questions or negatives.
wrong: *Did you ~~saw~~ Petra yesterday?*
right: *Did you see Petra yesterday?*

❶ ***be*** **and** ***have***

Complete the dialogue with the correct form of *be* or *have*.

A: Jane, it's nice to see you back. How ¹**was** (be) your trip to Amman?

B: It ² _____ (be) fine thanks.

A: ³ _____ (you/have) a lot of meetings?

B: Yes, I ⁴ _____ (have) some every day, and my meetings with Mohammed ⁵ _____ (be) very successful.

A: Oh, good – the last time he ⁶ _____ (be) in England, he seemed interested in the dealership. But what about Amir? ⁷ _____ (you/have) any meetings with him?

B: No, I ⁸ _____ (not/have) the chance to see him or his manager – they ⁹ _____ (not/be) in the office when I called. They ¹⁰ _____ (be) in Dubai.

2 Other irregular verbs

Complete the text with the past simple of the verbs in brackets.

MONEY, MONEY, MONEY

One evening in 1949, Frank McNamara ¹ **had** (have) an important dinner meeting with two business colleagues. Before leaving the house, he ² _____ (get) changed into a new suit. Unfortunately he ³ _____ (forget) that his wallet was in the old jacket pocket. So he ⁴ _____ (leave) home with no money.

● He ⁵ _____ (meet) the two businessmen at a New York restaurant, and they had an expensive meal. After dinner, the waiter ⁶ _____ (bring) Frank the bill. When he ⁷ _____ (put) his hand in his jacket pocket, he ⁸ _____ (find) that his wallet ⁹ _____ (not/be) there.

What ¹⁰ _____ (make) the problem worse was that he ¹¹ _____ (not/know) the manager of the restaurant, and his two colleagues ¹² _____ (not/have) any cash with them. In the end, he ¹³ _____ (ring) his wife at home. She ¹⁴ _____ (drive) over to the restaurant with his wallet and ¹⁵ _____ (pay) the bill. After that incident, Frank ¹⁶ _____ (think) of a new way of paying for meals in restaurants – by using a card. He ¹⁷ _____ (set) up a new company called Diners Club. In 1950, people all over New York ¹⁸ _____ (begin) to use these credit cards to pay for meals. At first, about twenty restaurants

in the city ¹⁹ _____ (take) the cards, but Diners Club cards quickly ²⁰ _____ (become) very well known across the country.

● Diners Club cards were very popular with travelling salesmen who ²¹ _____ (go) from city to city. If you had a card, it ²² _____ (mean) that you ²³ _____ (not/have) to travel with lots of cash, and people ²⁴ _____ (feel) safer. The company ²⁵ _____ (grow) quickly, and soon other banks ²⁶ _____ (see) that it was a good idea. In 1958, American Express and Bank Americard (VISA) ²⁷ _____ (come) out. The age of plastic money had arrived.

3 Questions and negatives

Make sentences about the text in 2 with the negative form of the verbs in the box.

feel	have	know	pay	~~take~~

1 When Frank McNamara left his house, he **didn't take** his wallet with him.
2 He _____ the manager of the restaurant.
3 His colleagues _____ any cash with them.
4 Until Diners Club started, people used cash – they _____ by cheque or credit card.
5 People _____ safe travelling with lots of cash.

Complete the questions with the verbs in the box.

bring	have	set	~~eat~~	ring

6 A: Where **did** the three men **eat**?   B: They ate at an expensive restaurant.
7 A: _____ Frank's colleagues _____ any cash?   B: No, they didn't have any money.
8 A: Who _____ Frank _____?   B: He rang his wife.
9 A: What _____ Frank's wife _____?   B: She brought his wallet.
10 A: _____ Frank _____ up Diners Club in 1958?   B: No, he set it up in 1950.

OVER TO YOU

Write true sentences about yourself and these times.

1 In 2000, I _____ .
2 Five years ago, I _____ .
3 Last year _____ .
4 Last summer _____ .
5 Last week _____ .

14 Past continuous
I was doing

ⓐ Form

We make the past continuous by using *was/were* and the *-ing* form of the verb:

Positive	Question	Negative
I was working.	*Was I working?*	*I was not working.*
You were working.	*Were you working?*	*You were not working.*
He/She/It was working.	*Was he/she/it working?*	*He/She/It was not working.*
We were working.	*Were we working?*	*We were not working.*
They were working.	*Were they working?*	*They were not working.*

In the negative, we often use the short forms *wasn't* or *weren't*:
*My mobile **wasn't working**, so I bought a new one.*

ⓑ Uses

The past continuous can tell us about something that was already happening at a point of time in the past. Look at these examples:
*At 2.30 yesterday afternoon, Lena **was listening** to a presentation.*
(The presentation started at 2.00 and finished at 3.00.)

*At 2.30 yesterday afternoon, Alexander **was writing** a report.*
(He started at 1.30 and finished at 5.30.)

*At 2.30 yesterday afternoon, Katia **was visiting** a supplier.*
(She left in the morning and came back in the evening.)

It is not always necessary to use a time expression, especially if we are explaining why something happened.
*They sold the company because it **wasn't making** money.*

ⓒ *When* and *while*

Sometimes a short action interrupts a longer action. We can use the time words *while* or *when* with the past continuous when we want to compare a long action with a short action in the past:

***While/When** I was writing my report, the computer suddenly crashed.*

You can also change the order:

*The computer suddenly crashed **while/when** I was writing my report.*

Writing a report is a long action. A computer crashing is a short action.

❗ We don't usually use while with a short action in the past simple.
wrong: *I was writing my report ~~while~~ the computer suddenly crashed.*
right: *I was writing my report **when** the computer suddenly crashed.*

PRACTICE

① Form

Complete the sentences with the past continuous form of the verbs in brackets.
1 What **were you doing** (you/do) on 11 September?
2 My wife and I first met when _____ (we/work) for the BBC.
3 They were surprised to see you because _____ (they/not expect) you.
4 When I looked out of the window, I saw that _____ (it/rain).
5 _____ (the train/wait) when you got to the station?
6 While _____ (he/travel) round Asia, Mr Lee made some important contacts.

② Uses

Complete the text with the past continuous form of the verbs in brackets.

NEW YORK CITY BLACKOUT | Last month, 21 US cities had no electricity. New York stopped. Here, three employees from our New York office tell their stories.

Annie Saunders
Human Rescources Manager
I ¹_____ (come) back to the office by cab when it happened. In about five minutes, the streets were full of people, and we couldn't move. only real problem was how to pay the cab ver. I couldn't get any money because the h machines ²_____ (not/work).

Ken Lo
Vice-President
I ³_____ (go) down in the elevator when the power went off. I was there in the dark for maybe two hours. Then, while I ⁴_____ (think) of what to do, I heard someone calling to me. It was a fire fighter, and he got me out.

Uma Jensen
Senior Account Executive
Jackie Landers and I ⁵_____ (have) a meeting with a big new client at the time. Of course we had to stop, but it was OK because the meeting ⁶_____ (not/go) very well.

③ When and while

Complete the sentences with the past simple or past continuous form of the verbs in brackets.
1 Gunnar hurt his back while he **was carrying** (carry) a heavy box.
2 When Jeanne was walking down the stairs, she _____ (fall).
3 Vlad got an electric shock while he _____ (fix) the lights.
4 Olga cut her hand while she _____ (mend) the broken window.
5 Len _____ (break) his arm when he was cleaning the machine.
6 Raj was making coffee when he _____ (burn) his hand.

OVER TO YOU

Write down something that happened to you when you were doing these things.
What happened when …

1 you were attending a conference?
When I was attending a conference in Beirut last year, I met an old friend of mine.
2 you were having a meeting?

3 you were looking for a job?

4 you were having a holiday abroad?

5 you were going home from work?

6 you were flying or travelling somewhere?

15 Used to
I used to do

ⓐ Form

We can talk about past habits with *used to* + bare infinitive:

Positive:	*I/You/He/She/It/We/They*	***used to work.***
Questions:	*Did I/you/he/she/it/we/they*	***use to work?***
Negative:	*I/You/He/She/It/We/They*	***didn't use to work.***

*I **used to work** in London, but I work in Berlin now.*

ⓑ Past habits and activities

We use ***used to*** to talk about past habits and activities that have stopped or finished.
Ten years ago Leon Dubarry was the CEO of a large company. Now he is retired. Look at the
changes in his life.

Ten years ago

*He **used to travel** abroad every week.*
*He **used to go** to lots of meetings.*
*He **used to smoke.***

Now

He stays in the South of France.
He doesn't go to meetings.
He is a non-smoker.

ⓒ Past states

We can also talk about past states with ***used to***:
Twenty years ago, there was a cinema in the town centre. It is not there now.
*There **used to be** a cinema in the town centre.*

Twenty years ago, the town had a lot of small businesses. They are not there now.
*The town **used to have** a lot of small businesses.*

PRACTICE **① Form**

Rewrite the sentences with *used to* + bare infinitive.

1 I am a non-smoker now.   I used to smoke.
2 Did you once work for Nabisco?   Did you use to work for Nabisco?
3 The factory was originally in Charentes.
4 The unions aren't powerful any more.
5 In the past I lived in Kuwait too.
6 Did you once work with Alain?
7 In the past, I didn't have a long journey to work.
8 In the past, factories were very dangerous.
9 Ninety years ago, it took a long time to travel to
   the USA.
10 In the past, we didn't need IT specialists.

② Past habits and activities

Read about the changes at Emperor Mines in Fiji.

EMPEROR GOLD MINE

When the current team took over the management of the Emperor Gold Mine in 1992, the mine was in a bad state.

The miners worked with very old equipment, so the mine was not efficient. There were a lot of accidents, and the workers often went on strike.

Relationships between the management and workers were bad. The management did not run training courses, and they did not communicate well.

The new management of Emperor Mines Limited changed everything. It is now profitable, and makes up 7% of Fiji's national income. It is the country's second largest employer, and has a good relationship with the Fiji government.

Look at the notes. Write sentences about the mine with *used to* or *didn't use to*.

1 old equipment	The miners used to work with very old equipment.
2 efficient	The mine didn't use to be efficient.
3 accidents	_____ .
4 strike	_____ .
5 relationships	_____ .
6 training courses	_____ .
7 communicate	_____ .
8 profitable	_____ .

③ Past states

Read the text about London's Docklands.

Docklands is an area by the river near the centre of London where ships used to come. It started to decline in the 1960s and closed in 1981. In 1982, redevelopment began, and it is now an important commercial centre.

Docklands in the 70s	Docklands now
was an area of high unemployment	has lots of job opportunities
was difficult to travel to	has good transport links
had social problems	is a popular area
had poor housing	has skyscrapers and luxury flats
had no facilities	has a university, an airport, an exhibition centre

Write sentences about the changes in Docklands with *used to be* or *used to have*.

1 It used to be an area of high unemployment, but now it has lots of job opportunities.
2 It _____ .
3 _____ .
4 _____ .
5 _____ .

OVER TO YOU

Think about changes in your life and work. Write sentences using *used to*.

	Past	Now		
Home:	Hannover	Stuttgart	(live)	I used to live in Hannover, but now I live in Stuttgart.
Job:			(be)	_____ .
Employer:			(work for)	_____ .
Salary:			(earn)	_____ .
Ambitions:			(want)	_____ .

16 Future (1)
I will

a **Form**

We can use *will* + bare infinitive to talk about the future:

Positive	Question	Negative
I will work.	*Will I work?*	*I will not work.*
You will work.	*Will you work?*	*You will not work.*
He/She/It will work.	*Will he/she/it work?*	*He/She/It will not work.*
We will work.	*Will we work?*	*We will not work.*
They will work.	*Will they work?*	*They will not work.*

! The short form of *will not* is *won't*.

b **Use**

We can use *will* to make predictons about the future:
> *In the year 2050, many workers in Europe will be over 65.*
> *Sophia won't be happy when she sees this!*

We often use *will* after *I think …* or *I don't think …* :
> *I think the stock market will rise for two or three years.*
> *I don't think shares will fall.*

For appointments or arrangements, use the present continuous (see Unit 17):
> *I am seeing Mr Tanaka tomorrow afternoon at 3.30. (not will see)*
For plans or intentions, use *going to* (see Unit 18):
> *I am going to emigrate to Australia in October. (not will emigrate)*

c **Quick decisions**

We often use the short form of *will* when we make a quick decision:
> A: *Do you want a lift to the station?*
> B: *No, thanks – I think I'll walk.*

> A: *I'm afraid the flight on the 19th is full.*
> B: *Is it? OK then, I'll go on the 20th.*

1 **Form**

Complete the sentences with *will/won't* and the words in brackets.

1 What will the weather be (the weather/be) like tomorrow?
2 .... (I/not be able) to come to the meeting.
3 Don't worry. .... (Everything/be) OK.
4 When .... (the economy/start) to improve?
5 Our costs are higher, so .... (our prices/rise).
6 Do you think that .... (interest rates/go up) next month?

② Use

Complete the text with *will/won't* and the verbs in the boxes.

become	~~change~~	grow

We all know the pictures of Chinese city streets full of bicycles, but in the future, all of that [1] **will change**. The car market in China is booming, and next year experts think that it [2] _____ by 30%. Volkswagen Chairman Bernd Pischetsrieder says that China [3] _____ VW's main market very soon.

cost	export	not/be	not/continue	start

At the moment, the trade is one-way, but that [4] _____ for long. In the future, VW and Honda [5] _____ cars from China to Australia and Europe. There are local companies too – next year Chinese company Geely [6] _____ selling the Uliou saloon in the USA. It [7] _____ easy for American car makers to compete because the Uliou [8] _____ around $7,000.

have	increase	become	lead

But not everyone is happy. In about 2020, China [9] _____ the world's largest car market, and green groups are worried that this [10] _____ a bad effect on the environment. Oil consumption [11] _____ every year, and this [12] _____ to very serious pollution.

③ Quick decisions

Complete the replies with the ideas in the box.

~~call back later~~	come next week	send it today
use another one	have a word with her	take another route

1 A: I'm sorry, the line is busy.
   B: OK, I'll call back later.
2 A: I'm afraid Meeting Room 23 is booked.
   B: OK, _____ .
3 A: Andersens wants that report immediately.
   B: OK, _____ .
4 A: I'm afraid I can't see you this week.
   B: That's OK – _____ .
5 A: Amelie seems very upset.
   B: Does she? _____ .
6 A: The motorway is blocked.
   B: Is it? OK, _____ .

Answer the questions. Give your ideas about the future using *I think* or *I don't think*.

1 What will happen to the price of oil?
   I think it will go up.
2 What will happen to interest rates?
   _____ .
3 Who will win the next election in the USA?
   _____ .
4 Who will win the next election in your country?
   _____ .
5 What will happen to the climate of the world?
   _____ .
6 What will happen to sea levels?
   _____ .
7 What important things will happen in your home life?
   _____ .
8 Do you think you will move to another town or city?
   _____ .

Future (2)
I am doing

PRESENTATION   **ⓐ Form**

We can use the present continuous to talk about the future:

Positive	Questions	Negative
I am working.	*Am I working ...?*	*I'm not working.*
We/You/They are working.	*Are we/you/they working ...?*	*We/You/They aren't working.*
He/She/It is working.	*Is he/she/it working ...?*	*He/She/It isn't working.*

A: *Are you seeing Anja tomorrow?*
B: *No, I'm not seeing her tomorrow – I'm seeing her on Friday.*

ⓑ Use

We use the present continuous to talk about appointments and arrangements. We often use a future time word (*tomorrow, next week,* etc.):
I'm coming to London next Friday.
I'm seeing Bob Simpson in the afternoon.
I'm not going back until Saturday.
Are you doing anything on Friday evening?

❗ Do not use *will* to talk about things you have arranged to do with someone else.
wrong: *I will have dinner with Mr Mori tonight.*
right: *I am having dinner with Mr Mori tonight.*

ⓒ Timetables

We can use the present simple (*I do, I come,* etc.) to talk about timetables:
A: *Do you know the train times to Munich this afternoon?*
B: *Yes, there's a train that leaves at 2.35, and it gets in at 4.10. And there's a later one that goes at 3.20 and arrives at 5.05.*

PRACTICE   **❶ Form**

Say if the sentences are right or wrong and correct the mistakes.

1 Are you staying for the presentation?   right
2 They ~~aren't come~~ to the conference next week.   wrong   aren´t coming
3 You've seeing Raoul tomorrow, aren't you?
4 What do you do this evening?
5 Juanita isn't coming to the meeting tomorrow.
6 Tanya seeing Mrs Davis tomorrow.
7 I don't doing anything tonight.
8 What time are you leave tomorrow?
9 Are you doing anything on Friday?
10 Jan's going to New York next week.

2 Use

Max Black is in Switzerland to give some talks. Read his schedule for the visit. Max is in Tina's car, leaving the airport. Complete the dialogue with the present continuous form of the verbs in brackets.

Publicity tour: 23–26 May

Schedule for Max Black

Tuesday 23 May.	MB arrives at Bern Airport 19.30. Tina Brown to meet. To Allegro Hotel with Tina.
Wednesday 24 May.	10.00 Tina to meet MB at Allegro Hotel
	11.00–12.30 Exhibition & Presentation at BEA Conference Centre Title: Managing Success
	13.30 lunch with Henri Daoud (Chairman SCI Bank)
	16.00 meet Pauline Freyer, Allegro Hotel
	To Zurich. Hotel Schweizerhof

Tina: As I said, we have made a few changes to your schedule for the next few days.

Max: That's OK, can you tell me what [1] *is happening* (happen)?

Tina: Sure – well, tonight [2]_____ (you/stay) at the Allegro Hotel, and [3]_____ (I/meet) you there tomorrow morning at 10.00.

Max: OK, and where [4]_____ (we/do) the exhibition?

Tina: [5]_____ (We/do) it at the BEA Conference Centre – it's very close – and [6]_____ (you/give) your talk at 11.00. After that, [7]_____ (you/have) lunch with Henri Daoud – he's the Chairman of the SCI Bank. Now, I spoke to him today, and [8]_____ (he/take) you back to the hotel after lunch.

Max: OK, so how [9]_____ (I/get) to Zurich?

Tina: [10]_____ (Pauline Freyer/come) to the hotel at 4 p.m., and [11]_____ (she/drive) you to Zurich.

Max: [12]_____ (Where/we/stay) in Zurich?

Tina: [13]_____ (You/stay) at the Hotel Schweizerhof – it's very nice.

3 Timetables

Complete the dialogue with the present simple form of the verbs in brackets.

LONDON WATERLOO	06.29	07.43	08.39	10.42	12.39	14.42	16.39	
Ashford	07.20	–	09.30	–	13.30	–	17.30	
Bruxelles Midi/Zuid arr		10.01	11.03	12.10	14.05	16.10	18.02	20.10
Bruxelles Midi/Zuid dep		10.37	11.25	12.37	14.37	16.37	18.25	20.37
The Hague HS	12.57	13.27	14.57	16.57	18.57	20.27	22.57	
AMSTERDAM CS	13.38	14.06	15.38	17.38	19.38	21.06	23.38	

A: Can you tell me about trains to Amsterdam from about 08.00?

B: Sure. There's a train that [1] *leaves* (leave) at 08.39.

A: Is it a direct train?

B: Yes, it [2]_____ (go) via Brussels, but you [3]_____ (not/change) trains.

A: OK, so what time [4]_____ (it/get) to Brussels?

B: It [5]_____ (arrive) at 11.03 and it [6]_____ (depart) at 11.25.

A: And when [7]_____ (it/arrive) in Amsterdam?

B: It [8]_____ (get) there at 15.38.

OVER TO YOU

Write down four things that you or your colleagues have arranged to do this week or this month.

1 *I am having a meeting with Kira on Tuesday 18th.*

2 _____ .

3 _____ .

4 _____ .

5 _____ .

Write down four things that you or your family have arranged to do socially this weekend or this month.

6 *We are having some people to dinner on Saturday.*

7 _____ .

8 _____ .

9 _____ .

10 _____ .

18 Future (3)
I am going to do

PRESENTATION **ⓐ Form**

We can use *am/is/are going to* + bare infinitive to talk about the future:

Positive	Negative	Question
I am going to work.	*I'm not going to work.*	*Am I going to work?*
You are going to work.	*You aren't going to work.*	*Are you going to work?*
He/She/It is going to work.	*He/She/It isn't going to work.*	*Is he/she/it going to work?*
We are going to work.	*We aren't going to work.*	*Are we going to work?*
They are going to work.	*They aren't going to work.*	*Are they going to work?*

A: *Are you going to work late tonight?*
B: *No, I'm not going to work late tonight. I'm going to work at the weekend.*

ⓑ Talking about decisions

I *am going to* often means the same as *I have decided to*. We use *going to* to talk about things we intend to do or have decided to do:
I am going to look for a new job. (= I have decided to look for a new job.)
Jackie is going to study engineering. (= Jackie has decided to study engineering.)

ⓒ Talking about plans

We can use *going to* to talk about definite plans:
We are going to start production in China in May.
We are going to manufacture the new model, the NV 300, there.
We are going to produce 2,000 units a week.

ⓓ Making predictions

We can also use *going to* to make predictions. We often use this when we can see that something is going to happen:
Look at the time. We're going to be late.

PRACTICE **❶ Form**

Complete the dialogue with *going to* and the words in brackets.

A: I hear that Andrew is ill and he ¹ is not going to come (not/come) in next week.
   What ² _____ (we/do)?
B: Don't worry, everything is organized. Anna ³ _____ (look after) the
   trainees, and Bob and Sue ⁴ _____ (help) with the exhibition.
A: He's got a meeting in London too, hasn't he?
B: Yes. I spoke to his secretary, and she ⁵ _____ (ring) them up and
   cancel it. I ⁶ _____ (not/send) anyone else, because Andrew needs to
   be there.
A: ⁷ _____ (Who/look after) his visitors from Frankfurt?
B: I've asked Harry to do that. He ⁸ _____ (collect) them from the
   airport, and then take them out in the evening.

40   Future (3): *I am going to do*

❷ Talking about decisions

Match the beginnings of sentences 1–7 with endings a–g.

1 Helene's very busy, so   a we are going to meet them at their office.
2 Maria isn't happy at work, so   b we are going to close the factory.
3 They can't meet us here, so   c she is going to look for a new job.
4 We are very pleased with your work, so   d it is going to raise taxes.
5 We need to cut costs, so   e we are going to give you a bonus.
6 Anna's car keeps breaking down, so   f she isn't going to come to the meeting.
7 The government needs more money, so   g she is going to sell it.

❸ Talking about plans

A manager from Kerzner International is talking about the company's plans for a new hotel. Complete the text with *going to* and the verbs in brackets.

INTERNATIONAL HOTELIER

Sol Kerzner [1] *is going to open* (open) his next luxury resort on the man-made Palm Island in Dubai.

'There [2] _____ (be) two hotels – the first hotel [3] _____ (have) 1,200 beds, and we [4] _____ (build) a second hotel with 800 beds for the middle market.'

The funds for the project [5] _____ (come) from Kerzner International and Istithmar (owned by the government of Dubai). Both Kerzner and Istithmar [6] _____ (buy) $100 million of Class A common stock, and commercial banks [7] _____ (provide) the rest of the funding.

❹ Making predictions

Look at the pictures. Say what the people are going to do with the words in the box.

write/cheque	order/lunch	answer/phone	change/tyre	~~go/home~~	paint/office

2 _____ .

3 _____ .

4 _____ .

...he is going to go home.

5 _____ .

6 _____ .

VER TO YOU

Write about some of the plans that you have over the next few months:

1 I'm going to do a training course.
2 _____ .
3 _____ .
4 _____ .

Write about some of the plans your company has for the coming year:

5 We are going to open a new factory.
6 _____ .
7 _____ .
8 _____ .

19 Future (4)
I am going to do, I will do, or *I am doing*

ⓐ *going to*

We use *going to* when we talk about plans, decisions, and intentions:

She is going to fly to Madrid this afternoon.
She is going to give a presentation.

We can also use *going to* for predictions:
*The new model is **going to be** a big success. There is a lot of interest in it.*

ⓑ *will*

We use *will* to make predictions about the future:
*In a few years, this investment **will be** worth a lot of money.*
We often use *will* after *I think* and *maybe* and when we are making a decision as we speak:
A: *Do you want to see the report now?*
B: *No, thanks. I think **I'll look** at it tomorrow.*

ⓒ **Present continuous**

We use *is doing*, *am doing*, *are doing*, etc. to talk about arrangements and appointments with other people:
A: *Can you come to the meeting on Friday afternoon?*
B: *No, I'm sorry, but I can't. **I am seeing** Jorgen at 3.15.*

❗ Remember that we do not use the present continuous with stative verbs (see Unit 10).
wrong: *I ~~am being~~ there tomorrow afternoon.*
right: *I **will be** there tomorrow afternoon.*

❶ *going to* **or** *will*?

Complete the sentences with *will*, *'ll*, or *going to*.

1 A: I can't get this computer to write in two columns.
   B: It's not difficult. Move over and I´ll show you what to do.
2 A: Have you chosen the factory for the new model?
   B: Yes, we ⎯⎯⎯⎯⎯ produce it in Shanghai.
3 A: Hello, I'm Mr Danvers. I have an appointment with George Drake.
   B: Please take a seat and I ⎯⎯⎯⎯⎯ tell Mr Drake you're here.
4 A: How can you produce an extra 1,000 units per week?
   B: We ⎯⎯⎯⎯⎯ take on 180 new employees.
5 A: Is your son planning to look for a job?
   B: No, he ⎯⎯⎯⎯⎯ go to university first.
6 A: Are you planning to have the conference in France again?
   B: No, we ⎯⎯⎯⎯⎯ hold it in Greece this year.
7 A: I'm sorry, I'm very busy right now.
   B: That's OK. I ⎯⎯⎯⎯⎯ come back later if you like.
8 A: What's the big meeting about?
   B: I don't know, but the CEO wants everyone there. She ⎯⎯⎯⎯⎯ make an announcem

2 *will* or present continuous?

Complete the dialogue with *will* or the present continuous form of the verbs in brackets.

Alan: I know it's a promotion, but I'm a bit worried about moving to Paris for a year.
Lucy: Oh, don't worry. It's a great city. You ¹**will have** (have) a lovely time.
Alan: I hope so, but I don't speak French.
Lucy: You can learn some. ²**Are you having** (you/have) any lessons before you go?
Alan: Yes, I ³_____ (have) lessons from Mme Marechal. We ⁴_____ (start) next week.
Lucy: That ⁵_____ (be) fine, then. She's a great teacher and I'm sure you ⁶_____ (learn) a lot. Have you got a place to stay?
Alan: Yes, I ⁷_____ (stay) in a company flat in the Boulevard St Michel.
Lucy: That's great, so you ⁸_____ (not/have to) spend time looking for an apartment. Have you got the phone number?
Alan: Yes, it's on my mobile. I ⁹_____ (see) what it is. Here we are – it's 22 44 36 78.
Lucy: OK, I ¹⁰_____ (make) a note of that. I ¹¹_____ (come) to Paris in May for some meetings. I ¹²_____ (give) you a ring when I arrive.
Alan: That'd be great.

3 Review

Will, present continuous, or *going to*? Choose the correct option from the words in *italics*.

1 The weather *will be/is being* nice tomorrow.
2 I can't see you at 3.30 tomorrow. I *am having/will have* a meeting with Peter all afternoon.
3 I think the new IT system *will be/is being* very expensive.
4 It is probable that the economy *is recovering/will recover* next year.
5 Don't take the bus. I'*ll give/am giving* you a lift if you want.
6 A: Are sales going well?
   B: Yes, we're definitely *reaching/going to reach* our targets this year.
7 A: Shall we meet at 10.30 tomorrow?
   B: Yes, that's fine. I'*m not doing/won't do* anything tomorrow.
8 A: I think Xavier needs to know about these changes.
   B: OK, I *am sending him/'ll send* him an email.

OVER TO YOU

Plans

Give details of two plans or decisions you or your company have made. Say what the plan is and when it is going to happen.

1 (you) I'm going to start an accountancy training course in September.
2 (you) _____ .
3 (your company) _____ .

Predictions

Make two predictions about politics or the economy. Say what will happen and when.

4 (politics) I think the government will lose the election next year.
5 (economy) I think _____ .
6 (politics) I think _____ .

Arrangements

Give details of two meetings you are having in the next few days. Say who you are meeting, where, when, and why.

7 I am seeing Sally in London on Tuesday to talk about the new catalogue.
8 _____ .
9 _____ .

20 Present perfect (1)
I have done

ⓐ Form

We make the present perfect with *have* and the past participle*:

I have worked.	*He/She/It has worked.*	*We have worked.*
You have worked.		*They have worked.*

In New York, the Dow Jones has fallen by 830 points.

We often use the short form (*I've, you've, he's,* etc.) when we are speaking:
  A: *Don't forget that invoice for Johnson's.*   B: *That's OK – I've posted it.*

* The past participle is a form of the verb. With regular verbs, the past participle ends in -*ed* and has the same form as the past simple. With irregular verbs, the past participle does not usually end in -*ed*. For a list of irregular verbs, see page 151.

ⓑ Recent actions with *just*

We often use *just* with the present perfect to talk about very recent actions. *Just* means *a short time ago*. It goes after *have/has*.

I am going to email you the document.

Thanks. Your email has just arrived.

ⓒ Unfinished and finished times

We often use the present perfect with words that refer to unfinished periods of time, like *(so far) today, (so far) this week/month/year, up to now,* etc.:
  *You have been late three times **this week**, and it's only Wednesday.*

We often use the present perfect when we mean 'in my life up to now':
  I have had three different careers.

We do not use the present perfect with time words like *yesterday, last week, on Monday, at 5.3 in July, in 1994,* etc. With these past times we use the past simple tense:

Present perfect	**Past simple**
We have sold 18,000 DVDs so far this year.	*We sold 58,000 DVDs last year.*
(It is now April.)	

❶ Form

Complete the dialogues with the present perfect form of the verbs in brackets.

1 A: Is Dave here?
   B: Sorry – he **has gone** (go) to lunch.
2 A: Where are the Adams files?
   B: I don't know. Someone
      _____ (take) them.
3 A: Are your offices still in Paris?
   B: No, we _____ (relocate) to Lille.

4 A: Can I see the figures?
   B: Yes, I _____ (make) you a co
5 A: We need some more air-conditioning
      units.
   B: I know. I _____ (order) some
6 A: I'm not sure where the Black report is
   B: Are you telling me that you
      _____ (lose) it?

② Recent actions with *just*

For each set of pictures write two sentences. Say what each person:

a is going to do b has done

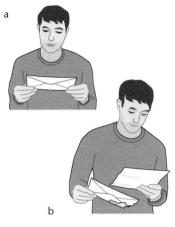
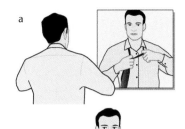

1 open/letter	2 take off/tie	3 plane/land
a He is going to open the letter.	a	a ....
b He has just opened the letter.	b	b ....

③ Recent actions with *just*

Complete the sentences with *just* and the verbs in the box.

> announce   explode   fall   finish   ~~rise~~   resign

1 The price of oil **has just risen** to $50 a barrel.
2 The government crisis is getting worse. The Prime Minister and his deputy

     ....
3 The crisis meeting at the UN .... , but there is no agreement.
4 The unions .... that they are going to hold a three-day strike.
5 According to reports in the last few minutes, a bomb .... at a bank in Istanbul.
6 Shares in Intech .... to a new low of $0.23.

④ Unfinished and finished times

Say if the sentences are right or wrong and correct the mistakes.

1 I ~~have met~~ Amanda last week.   wrong   I met
2 I saw Joanna last Friday.   right   ....
3 We've had two industrial disputes this year.   ....
4 I have been to a lot of meetings this week.   ....
5 Peter rang yesterday.   ....
6 We have arrived at 6.30 last night.   ....

OVER TO YOU

You meet an old colleague. You have not seen him/her for six months. Tell him/her about the things you have done between six months ago and now. Talk about:

1 any trips abroad you have made   I've been to Poland and Hungary.
2 any changes at work   ....
3 any changes at home   ....
4 anything you have started learning   ....
5 any good news about your colleagues   ....

Remember, do not use past time words with the present perfect.

21 Present perfect (2)
questions and negatives

ⓐ Questions

Look at the way we make questions in the present perfect:

Have I worked?	*Has he/she/it worked?*	*Have we worked?*
Have you worked?		*Have they worked?*

A: *Have you lived here for a long time?*   B: *Yes, I've lived here for nearly ten years.*

We can use the following short answers:

Yes, I have.	*Yes, we have.*	*No, I haven't.*	*No, we haven't.*
Yes, you have.	*Yes, they have.*	*No, you haven't.*	*No, they haven't.*
Yes, he/she/it has.		*No, he/she/it hasn't.*	

A: *Have you seen the new design?*   B: *No, I haven't.*

ⓑ Negatives

Look at the way we make negatives:

I have not worked.	*He/she/it has not worked.*	*We have not worked.*
You have not worked.		*They have not worked.*

We often use short forms (*I haven't worked*, *she hasn't worked*, etc.) when we are speaking:
A: *What does John think of the proposals?*   B: *We haven't talked about them.*

ⓒ *ever* and *never*

We often use *ever* and *never* to ask and talk about experiences. *Ever* and *never* go before the past participle (*been, worked,* etc.).
A: *Have you ever been to New York?*   B: *No, I've never been to America.*

ⓓ Details

When we ask about or give details of a specific experience, we often use the past simple tense, with a time word.

A: *Have you ever worked abroad?*	(Present perfect – asking about general experience)
B: *Yes, I have.*	(Present perfect)
A: *Where did you work?*	(Past simple – asking about details)
B: *In 2002, I spent nine months in Egypt.*	(Past simple – talking about details)

① Questions

Match questions 1–8 with answers a–h.

1 Have you and Vlad talked about this?
2 Have you heard the news?
3 Has Amelia sent the invoices?
4 Have you had a bad day?
5 Have the tickets arrived?
6 Has Jacob phoned?
7 Has the shop shut?
8 Have they fixed your car?

a Yes, he has. He's left a message for you.
b No, it hasn't. It stays open late on Fridays.
c Yes, we have. And he agrees with me.
d No, I haven't. What has happened?
e Yes, they have. It's working fine now.
f Yes, she has. They're in the post.
g Yes, I have. Everything has gone wrong.
h Yes, they have. They're on your desk.

2 Negatives

Tiziana is talking to her boss. Put the dialogue in the right order 1–9.

a _____ Tiziana: I don't know – I'm expecting a call today, but he hasn't phoned.

b _____ Tiziana: No, we haven't. It's nearly ready, but Paolo hasn't done the cover.

c _____ Serge: Why hasn't he done it? What's the problem?

d _____ Tiziana: He is ill at the moment. He hasn't been in all week.

e _____ Serge: What's the problem? Are you saying that you haven't finished it?

f _____ Serge: We can't wait around for him to phone. Get a freelancer to do the cover.

g _____ Serge: When is he coming back?

h _____ Tiziana: OK, I'll get a freelancer to do it.

i   *1*   Tiziana: Serge – have you got a moment? We've got a problem with the catalogue.

3 *ever* and *never*

Make questions and answers with *ever* and *never*.

1 A: you/work abroad?
  A: Have you ever worked abroad?
  B: never/work abroad.
  B: No, I've never worked abroad.

2 A: you/use Linux?
  A: _____ ?
  B: never/use Linux.
  B: _____ .

3 A: you/fire anyone?
  A: _____ ?
  B: never/fire anyone.
  B: _____ .

4 A: your boss/be to London?
  A: _____ ?
  B: never/be to London.
  B: _____ .

4 Details

Complete the dialogues with the present perfect and the past simple.

1 A: you/ever/meet the Prime Minister?
  A: Have you ever met the Prime Minister?
  B: yes/have.
  B: Yes, I have.
  A: when/you/meet him?
  A: When did you meet him?
  B: I/meet/him/last year.
  B: I met him last year.

2 A: you/be to China?
  A: _____ ?
  B: yes/have.
  B: _____ .
  A: when/you/go there?
  A: _____ ?
  B: I/go there/last July.
  B: _____ .

3 A: you/ever/work in South America?
  A: _____ ?
  B: yes/have.
  B: _____ .
  A: where/you/work?
  A: _____ ?
  B: I/work/in Brazil in the 1990s.
  B: _____ .

VER TO YOU

Make questions from the notes and write true answers with *Yes, I have* or *No, I haven't*.

1 you/have sushi?
  A: Have you ever had sushi? B: Yes, I have.

2 you/be/to England?
  A: _____ ? B: _____ .

3 you/work abroad?
  A: _____ ? B: _____ .

4 you/give a presentation in English?
  A: _____ ? B: _____ .

5 you/meet the head of your company?
  A: _____ ? B: _____ .

6 you/fly First Class?
  A: _____ ? B: _____ .

7 you/miss a plane?
  A: _____ ? B: _____ .

8 you/run a large department?
  A: _____ ? B: _____ .

22 Present perfect (3)
already, yet

ⓐ *already*

We use *already* and the present perfect to talk about tasks that we complete early. Look at Jane's list. It is 10 a.m. She has done jobs 1, 2, and 3. She finished them early. She can say:

I have already answered my emails.
I have already made an appointment with Mrs Stevenson.
I have already had a meeting with Viktor.

> Morning:
> 1 answer my emails ✓
> 2 make an appointment with Mrs Stevenson ✓
> 3 meeting with Viktor ✓
> 4 book hotel for Mr Li ✗
> 5 arrange taxi for Mr Li ✗
> 6 write report for Sales Department ✗

ⓑ *not ... yet*

We use *not ... yet* and the present perfect to talk about tasks that are not completed. *Yet* usually goes at the end of the sentence. Look at Jane's list. It is 10 a.m. She has not done jobs 4, 5, or 6. She is going to do them later today. She can say:

I haven't booked the Hotel for Mr Li yet.
I haven't arranged the taxi for Mr Li yet.
I haven't written the report for the Sales Department yet.

ⓒ **Asking questions**

We can ask questions about the progress of a task, project, or event using *yet* with the present perfect:

Dan: *Have you written that report yet?*
Jane: *No, I haven't. I'm going to write it this afternoon.*
Dan: *Have you made that appointment with Mrs Stevenson yet?*
Jane: *Yes, I have. I did it at 9.30.*

PRACTICE

① *already*

A managing director arrives at a meeting late. Look at the agenda and complete the dialogue with the words in brackets.

1 Staff annual leave

2 Procedures for absence and sick leave

3 DX 9 marketing campaign

4 Productivity

5 Sales figures (3rd quarter)

6 Christmas party

A: Sorry I'm so late, but I'm glad you've started the meeting. Jason, can you tell me what stage we are at?

B: Yes, of course. We ¹ *have already talked* (already/talk) about the first two items on the agenda, and we ² _____ (already/agree) that Ben can deal with them.

A: That sounds fine. Now, what about the marketing campaign?

B: We ³ _____ (already/discuss) that too, and it's going very well. The advertising agency ⁴ _____ (already/make) the TV commercial, and Leonora from Publicity ⁵ _____ (already/write) some very good copy for the magazine campaign.

A: Fine – now, there's just one thing. We must make sure the Legal Department have a look the TV commercial.

B: That's all OK – they ⁶ _____ (already/see) it and they ⁷ _____ (already/say) that it's fine.

48 Present perfect (3): *already, yet*

② *not ... yet*

The organizers of the Olympic Games are having problems. Look at the pictures and the notes and make sentences with *not ... yet*.

...ot complete/
...wimming pool

not finish/
main stadium

not build/
Olympic Village

not construct/
new railway

not plant/
Olympic Park

1 They haven't completed the swimming pool yet.
2 _____ . 4 _____ .
3 _____ . 5 _____ .

③ Asking questions

Make questions with the present perfect of the verbs in brackets and *yet*.

1 (Bob/send) Has Bob sent them the new brochures yet?
2 (you/receive) _____ the invoice _____ ?
3 (you/see) _____ the sample design _____ ?
4 (they/sign) _____ the contract _____ ?
5 (you/move) _____ to your new offices _____ ?

④ Review

Complete the dialogues with the present perfect and *already*, *not ... yet*, or *yet*.

1 Klaus: Mathias, this is Hanna Rikardsdottir.
   Mathias: Yes, I know – we have already met (meet).
2 Krystyna: (you/speak) _____ to Marek _____ ?
   Jan: Yes, I talked to him this morning.
3 Katie: What are the sales figures like this year?
   Sophie: Really good – we _____ (reach) our targets.
4 Bob: What are we waiting for?
   Dave: The Chairman _____ (not arrive).
5 Oliver: Do you want to get something to eat?
   Caroline: No, thanks, I _____ (have lunch).
6 Lukas: Could I have your report, Niklas?
   Niklas: I'm sorry, I _____ (not finish).

OVER TO YOU

Write about your career and your achievements in your job. Think of four things that you have already done.

1 I have already run a department in the company.
2 _____ .
3 _____ .
4 _____ .
5 _____ .

Write about your career and your achievements in your job. Think of four things that you have not done yet, but which you will do in the future.

6 I haven't won any company prizes yet.
7 _____ .
8 _____ .
9 _____ .
10 _____ .

23 Present perfect (4)
for, since

PRESENTATION **ⓐ Time periods**

We can talk about a period of time with *for*. If the period began and ended in the past, we use the past simple tense:

We moved to London in 1996. We left London in 1999.
*We **lived** in London **for three years**.*

If the period began in the past and continued up to the present, and is true now, we use the present perfect:

We moved to London in 1996. We live in London now.
*We **have lived** in London **for many years**.*

With the present perfect simple and *for* and *since,* we often use the verbs *be* and *have* and other verbs that describe states:

*I **have been** with the company for five years.*
*We **have had** an office in Tokyo for 50 years.*
*I **have known** Bill Andrews for ages.*

For action verbs with *for* and *since*, see Unit 25.

ⓑ *for*

When we use *for* and the present perfect, we are talking about periods of time that are not finished. We need to say how many hours, days, weeks, etc.:

*I have worked here **for five days/for three weeks/for six months/for a long time**.*

ⓒ *since*

We can also use *since* to talk about periods of time that are not finished. We use the present perfect and say when the action started:

*I have been here **since 3.30/since Monday/since November/since 2004**.*

There are other ways to say when the period of time started.

*I have been interested in engineering **since I was at university**.*

ⓓ *How long ...?*

We can ask questions about periods of time with *How long ...?*:

A: *How long have you been with the company?*
B: *I have been here for nine months.* or *I have been here since January.*

PRACTICE **① Time periods**

Complete the sentences with the past simple or present perfect of the verbs in brackets.

1 Luis had a job in Milan from 2001 to 2004. He doesn't have a job there now.
    He **worked** (work) in Milan for three years.
2 Antonia moved to Rome three years ago. She is in Rome now.
    She _____ (be) in Rome for three years.
3 I went to the Chicago office in May. I came back to the London office in June.
    I _____ (be) in the Chicago office for two months.
4 The meeting started at 1 p.m. It finished at 7 p.m.
    The meeting _____ (go on) for six hours.

❷ *for*

Read the newspaper article.

JACK STEELE is the owner of the Durban Aviation School, and he teaches company executives to fly aeroplanes and helicopters. He opened the school seven years ago with a partner, and then five years ago he bought his partner's share and became the sole owner. At first, the school was in Pretoria, but it moved to Durban four years ago. He still has the ten Cessna light aircraft that he bought seven years ago, and he now also has four R22 Robinson helicopters, which he bought a year ago. 'The Cessnas are great to fly,' he explains, 'but the Robinsons are an extra challenge.' The students agree, and Chris Marsh, who started lessons two years ago, says that the helicopters are great fun to fly.

Answer the questions with *for* and the present perfect.

1 How long has the school been open?   It has been open for seven years.
2 How long has Jack owned the school? ....
3 How long has the school been in Durban? ....
4 How long has he had the Cessnas? ....
5 How long has he had the helicopters? ....
6 How long has Chris been at the school? ....

❸ *since*

Rewrite the sentences using *since* and the present perfect.

1 I learned about the problem in January. I know about the problem now.
   (know about the problem) I have known about the problem since January.
2 We moved to our new offices on the 19th. We are in them now.
   (be in our new offices) ....
3 Laura bought a Powerbook in May. She has it now.
   (have a Powerbook) ....
4 I met Mr Ng in 2001. I know him now.
   (know Mr Ng) ....
5 We got broadband in July. We have it now.
   (have broadband) ....

❹ *How long ...?*

Make questions from the notes.

1 How long/you/know Anna?   How long have you known Anna?
2 How long/he/have that Mercedes? .... ?
3 How long/Peter/have an assistant? .... ?
4 How long/you/be unemployed? .... ?
5 How long/you/know about their plans? .... ?
6 How long/Maria/be ill? .... ?

◗VER TO YOU **Use the notes to write sentences about yourself. Then write a second sentence with *for* or *since*.**

1 banker, accountant, engineer?   I am an accountant.
   How long?   I have been an accountant for three years.
2 assistant, manager, director?   I am ....
   How long?   I ....
3 Fiat, Mercedes, Renault   I have ....
   How long?   I have had ....
4 single, married, divorced   ....
   How long?   ....

24 Present perfect (5)
present perfect or past simple

PRESENTATION

ⓐ Use of the present perfect

with *just* to talk about very recent actions:
> *I've just sent you an email.*

with *ever* and *never* to ask and talk about experiences:
> *Have you ever been to the USA?*
> *No, I have never been to the USA.*

with *yet* and *already* to check and talk about progress:
> A: *How are they getting on with the new website?*
> B: *They've already put up the home page, but they haven't done any of the product pages yet.*

with *for* and *since* to talk about duration:
> *I have been with the company for three years.*
> *I haven't spoken to Jack since last Monday.*

with unfinished times (for example *today, this week, this month, this year*, etc.):
> *We have spent $300,000 on advertising this year.* (It is only September; the year is not finished.)

ⓑ Use of the simple past

to say when a recent action happened:
> *I sent you an email two minutes ago.*
> *I visited their website this morning.*

to say when we had an experience:
> *I didn't go to the USA last year, but I went to Brazil and Uruguay.*

to say when some progress on a project happened:
> *They put up the home page last week.*

to say how long a finished action lasted:
> *I worked for the company for three years, and in 2002 I left to start my own business.*

to talk about finished times:
> *We spent $300,000 on advertising last year.* (from January to December)

PRACTICE

① Recent actions

Complete the newspaper article from the financial pages. Use the present perfect or the past simple form of the verbs in brackets.

Buy, sell, or hold? Share news from Investor online

TCN holdings ¹**has just announced** (just/announce) profits of $233m, mainly from gas and oil projects in Eastern Europe, and the company ² _____ (just/buy) two oil refineries in Romania. CEO Nicholas Leicester, who ³ _____ (take) control last year, is keen to increase profits. He ⁴ _____ (appoint) a new Finance Director in July, and in December the company ⁵ _____ (sell) its loss-making South African gold mines. The marke[t] clearly likes the changes, and share[s] ⁶ _____ (just/rise) to an all[-]time high of $3.22.

RECOMMENDATION: BUY or HOLD

② Experience and progress

Complete the interview with the present perfect or the past simple of the verbs in brackets.

Experience

Jonas: Could you tell us a little about your work experience?
¹**Have you ever worked** (you/ever/work) in Poland or the Czech Republic?

Laura: Yes, I ² _____ . I ³ _____ (work) in Poland from 2002 to 2004, and I speak the language well. I ⁴ _____ (never/be) to the Czech Republic, but I would like to visit it.

Progress

Jonas: Thank you. Now could you tell me … are you applying for jobs in other companies?

Laura: Yes, there is one other company I am interested in.

Jonas: 5_____ (you/have) an interview there yet?

Laura: Yes, I 6_____ (go) to see them last week. In fact, they 7_____ (already/offer) me a job.

Jonas: Do you think you will take it?

Laura: I 8_____ (not make) a decision yet.

Jonas: OK, thank you for letting me know.

for and *since*

Jonas: Before you go, can I check that we have references for you?

Laura: Yes, they're on my CV – the first one is Janis Godfrey, my current boss.

Jonas: 9_____ (how long/she/know) you?

Laura: She 10_____ (be) my boss for two years. I've been with the company for longer than that, as you know, but she 11_____ (take) over my department two years ago. And the other referee is an old colleague, Ken Smith. I 12_____ (know) him for long time – in fact we 13_____ (work) together at ICC Korea for two years from 1996 to 1998.

3 **Unfinished and finished time**

Complete the sentences with the past simple or present perfect of the verbs in brackets.

1 Sales **have fallen** (fall) this year, but we hope they will recover before December.

2 You _____ (be) late three times this month, and it's only the 15th.

3 The company _____ (get) into financial trouble last year.

4 Jenna needs to talk to you – she _____ (already/phone) twice this week.

5 The new computers _____ (arrive) last week.

6 I _____ (not/see) Harry today, but I may see him this afternoon.

7 I _____ (not/see) Harry this morning, so I phoned him after lunch.

8 I'm calling about the units we _____ (order) last month.

VER TO YOU

You meet an old colleague in the street. Tell him/her three pieces of recent news about your office or workplace.

1 Dave has just moved to the London office.

2 _____ .

3 _____ .

4 _____ .

You have a meeting with your boss to check on your progress. Tell him/her about three things you have done or haven't done yet this month.

5 I've ordered the new equipment, but it hasn't arrived yet.

6 _____ .

7 _____ .

8 _____ .

You are at an interview. Write down three things you could say to tell them about your experience.

9 I have run a medium-sized department for three years.

10 _____ .

11 _____ .

12 _____ .

25 Present perfect continuous
I have been doing

ⓐ Form

We make the present perfect continuous with *have/has been* + *-ing* form:

Positive	Negative	Question
I have been working.	*I have not been working.*	*Have I been working?*
You have been working.	*You have not been working.*	*Have you been working?*
He/She/It has been working.	*He/She/It has not been working.*	*Has he/she/it been working?*
We have been working.	*We have not been working.*	*Have we been working?*
They have been working.	*They have not been working.*	*Have they been working?*

When we are speaking, we often use the short forms (*I've, you've, haven't, hasn't*, etc.):
  A: *How long have you been working for Lazards?*   B: *I've been working for them since May.*

ⓑ Use

We use *have been doing/has been doing* to talk about activities that started in the past and a
still happening now. We often use the present perfect continuous to talk about the duration
an activity:

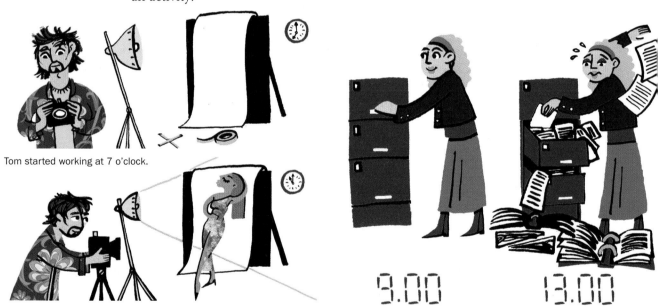

Tom started working at 7 o'clock.

It is 11 o'clock. Tom is working now.

Tom has been working for four hours.

I've been looking for my report since 9 o'clock.

❗ Do not use the present continuous with *since*.
wrong: *I am living here since 2003.*
right: *I have been living here since 2003.*

❗ We do not use the present perfect continuous with stative verbs like *be, like, own, belong,*
know, etc. With these verbs, we use the present perfect simple (see Unit 23).

I met Ms Fonseca a long time ago. I know Ms Fonseca now.
wrong: *I have been knowing Ms Fonseca for a long time.*
right: *I have known Ms Fonseca for a long time.*

1 **Form and use**

Robert Lord started working in Chinese medicine twenty years ago, and five years ago he started running his own biotech company. He and his colleagues began looking for new drugs, based on Chinese medicines, for use in the West.

Three years ago they found a Chinese medicine for hepatitis, and they began to test it in the laboratory. Two months ago they applied for a licence to produce the new drug, and now they are waiting to hear the result.

Make questions and answers about Robert and his company from the notes.

1 How long/he work/in Chinese medicine?
   How long has he been working in Chinese medicine?   (twenty years)
   He has been working in Chinese medicine for twenty years.

2 How long/he run/his own company?
   _____ ? (five years)
   _____ .

3 How long/they look/for new drugs?
   _____ ? (five years)
   _____ .

4 How long/they test/the drug for hepatitis?
   _____ ? (three years)
   _____ .

5 How long/they wait/for a licence?
   _____ ? (two months)
   _____ .

2 **Review**

All these sentences have one or two mistakes. Correct the mistakes and rewrite the sentences.

1 I ~~am working~~ here since three months. I have been working here for three months.
2 How long have you been knowing Xavier? _____ ?
3 My boss has been being away for two weeks. _____ .
4 I am learning English since three years. _____ .
5 How long have you been lived in the States? _____ ?
6 *The Times* newspaper has been belonging to Mr Murdoch since 1976.

   _____ .

7 We are working on this project since last July. _____ .
8 Interest rates have been fallen since last year. _____ .

OVER TO YOU **Imagine an old friend or colleague says these things to you. You last met five years ago. What questions can you ask, beginning with *How long* ...?**

1 I live in Glasgow now. How long have you been living there?
2 I am working for Jensen Pharmaceuticals now. _____ ?
3 I am married. _____ ?
4 I am working with an old friend of yours, Olga Petersen.

   _____ ?

5 We are doing a lot of business in Eastern Europe.

   _____ ?

Say how long you have been doing these things:

6 learning English   I have been learning English for two months.
7 living where you live now   _____ .
8 working for your company   _____ .
9 working in your department   _____ .

26 Passive (1)
is done, are done

a **Form**

Look at this sentence:
Nissan employs 130,000 people.

We can say this in another way:
130,000 people are employed by Nissan.

We make passive sentences like this by using the verb *to be* and the past participle (e.g. *broke, chosen, done, forgotten*). This is the present simple passive:

Positive	Negative	Questions
I am employed.	*I am not employed.*	*Am I employed?*
You are employed.	*You are not employed.*	*Are you employed?*
He/She/It is employed.	*He/She/It is not employed.*	*Is he/she/it employed?*
We are employed.	*We are not employed.*	*Are we employed?*
They are employed.	*They are not employed.*	*Are they employed?*

b **Regular and irregular verbs**

The past participle of regular verbs is the same as the past tense. Past participles end in *-ed*:

Verb	Past simple	Past participle
print	*printed*	*printed*
export	*exported*	*exported*
service	*serviced*	*serviced*

Our books are printed in Singapore.
Most of our best fruit is exported.
How often are the machines serviced?

Irregular verbs have different patterns:

take	*took*	*taken*
make	*made*	*made*
forbid	*forbade*	*forbidden*

All our visitors are taken to the factory first.
This model is not made of aluminium.
Is smoking forbidden in your office?

You need to learn the past participles of irregular verbs. See the list on page 151.

c **Use**

We often use the present simple passive to talk about processes. This is because the action is more important than the person who is doing the action:

Millions of items are sold on the Internet auction site eBay. Each item is shown on the website, and buyers are asked to send in bids. At the end of the auction, the item is sold to the buyer with the highest bid. Usually the seller is paid by Paypal, and when the money is received, the item is sent to the buyer.

① Form

Complete the dialogues with *am*, *is*, or *are*.

1 A: Excuse me, are you allowed to smoke here?
   B: No, it _____ forbidden all over the airport.
2 A: These models _____ not manufactured in the USA, are they?
   B: No, they _____ made in China.
3 A: When is payday in your company?
   B: I _____ paid monthly, but some people _____ paid every week.
4 A: What happens after the interview?
   B: Your application _____ discussed and your references _____ checked.
5 A: Do you produce the books here?
   B: No, they _____ printed in Singapore and then they _____ shipped to Germany.

② Regular and irregular verbs

Complete the sentences with the past participle of the regular verbs in the box.

| appoint   check   ~~invite~~   manufacture   receive |

1 Every year our important clients are invited to a party.
2 Different components for the Airbus are _____ in France, Germany, and the UK.
3 We will send the goods as soon as payment is _____ .
4 We have a main staff meeting every time a new manager is _____ .
5 Our computers are _____ for viruses every 24 hours.

Complete the sentences with the past participle of the irregular verbs in the box.

| give   grow   send   spend   meet |

6 A lot of the world's coffee is _____ in South America.
7 Details of our latest prices are _____ on page 11.
8 As an international consultant, I am _____ all over the world.
9 As a manager, a lot of my time is _____ dealing with people's problems.
10 Most of our visitors are _____ at the airport by a member of staff.

③ Use

Complete the text with the passive form of the verbs in brackets.

Roses are one of Kenya's most important crops, and Kenyan flowers [1]are exported (export) all over the world.

Some of the roses [2]_____ (produce) in glasshouses, and others [3]_____ (grow) in the open air.

When the flowers [4]_____ (pick), they [5]_____ (take) to cold storage rooms. Here they [6]_____ (cool) to 1°C so that they will last longer.

The flowers [7]_____ (pack) into flat boxes, and then they [8]_____ (transport) to the airport in refrigerated lorries. They [9]_____ (fly) to Germany, the UK, and other European countries, where they [10]_____ (sell) to supermarkets and other outlets.

Holland also has a large floriculture industry. Many of the roses that [11]_____ (import) into Holland [12]_____ (repackage) . Then they [13]_____ (export) to countries like Japan and the USA.

VER TO YOU

Write sentences about yourself. Say:

1 what you are allowed to do at work.   We are allowed to wear what we want.
2 what you are not allowed to do at work.   _____ .
3 what you are expected to do at work.   _____ .
4 how often you are paid.   _____ .
5 how often you are asked to work at weekends.   _____ .
6 how often you are sent emails you don't want.   _____ .

PRESENTATION **ⓐ Form**

To make the past tense in the passive, we use *was/were* + the past participle:

Positive	Negative	Question
I was employed.	*I was not employed.*	*Was I employed?*
You were employed.	*You were not employed.*	*Were you employed?*
He/She/It was employed.	*He/She/It was not employed.*	*Was he/she/it employed?*
We were employed.	*We were not employed.*	*Were we employed?*
They were employed.	*They were not employed.*	*Were they employed?*

A: *Were you promoted last year?*
B: *No, I wasn't promoted. I was transferred to a different department.*

ⓑ Use

The past simple passive is often used to talk about inventions, company histories, and other events in the past:

*Cadburys **was founded** in 1824, when John Cadbury opened a shop in Birmingham selling tea, coffee, cocoa, and drinking chocolate. In those days cocoa beans **were imported** from South America, and John Cadbury produced a range of chocolate drinks.*

! Remember that we often use the past simple passive with the verb *be born*.
wrong: *I am born in 1975.*
right: *I was born in 1975.*

ⓒ *by*

In any passive tense, we can use *by* if it is important to say who does an action:
*Our first Internet banking division **was run by** Maxine Arnauld.*

If it is not important, we can leave out this information.
*The components **were sent** to you last month.*

(We do not need to say that they were sent *by someone at the factory*.)

PRACTICE **① Form**

Complete the sentences with the past simple passive of the verbs in the box.

be born	direct	not/make	add	write	establish

Picture A tells you that Sigmund Freud ¹**was born** in 1856.

Picture B tells you that this film ² _____ by Alfred Hitchcock.

Picture C tells you that the book ³ _____ by Max Hope.

Picture D tells you that the conference centre ⁴ _____ in 1911.

Picture E tells you that the product ⁵ _____ from concentrate, and that no preservatives or other chemicals ⁶ _____ to the juice.

2 Use

Read about the history of Airbus. Complete the text with the past simple passive of the verbs in brackets.

Airbus ¹**was formed** (form) in 1970 when the French company Aerospatiale and the German company Daimler-Benz Aerospace agreed to work together to manufacture large passenger planes. The two companies ² _____ (join) by the Spanish company Casa in 1971, and British Aerospace became part of the consortium in 1979. The first aircraft, the A300, ³ _____ (produce) in 1972. The first planes were very successful, and 55 planes ⁴ _____ (order) by different airlines, mostly European. However, in 1975, the company had serious problems, and no orders ⁵ _____ (receive) for sixteen months. The problems ⁶ _____ (solve) when the American company Eastern Airlines leased four A300B4s in 1977. The planes were very popular. The following year, 23 A300s ⁷ _____ (sell) to Eastern Airlines, and 46 more planes ⁸ _____ (buy) by other US Airlines. This let Airbus into the American market, which at the time ⁹ _____ (dominate) completely by Boeing.

In 2000, Airbus began work on the A380, the biggest passenger plane in the world. It ¹⁰ _____ (design) to have 555 seats, two decks, shops, bars, and even a gymnasium. When the A380 ¹¹ _____ (launch) in January 2005, 45 of the new planes ¹² _____ (order) by Emirates of Dubai at a cost of $19 billion, making this the biggest deal in aviation history.

3 by

Rewrite the sentences with the passive. Use *by* if you need to.

1 Bill Gates founded Microsoft. **Microsoft was founded by Bill Gates.**

2 Where did you hold your last conference? _____ ?

3 Something delayed the project for three months. _____ .

4 In 2004, Banco Santander took over Abbey National. _____ .

5 People introduced rubber to Malaysia after 1900. _____ .

6 They built the London Eye in 1999. _____ .

OVER TO YOU **Write true sentences about yourself and your company using the words below.**

1 I/be born _____ .

2 My company/found _____ .

3 My department/set up _____ .

4 My boss/appoint _____ .

5 I/promote _____ .

28 Ability and permission
can, could

PRESENTATION **ⓐ Talking about ability**

We use *can* or *can't* + bare infinitive to talk about ability:
*Jacqueline is a bilingual secretary. She **can** speak English and French.*
*Mr Watson needs an interpreter. He **can't** speak Japanese.*
*I don't understand. **Can** you speak English?*

❗ Remember to use the bare infinitive. Do not use *to*.
wrong: *I ~~can to speak~~ Spanish.*
right: *I **can** speak Spanish.*

ⓑ Past ability

The past of *can* is *could*. We use *could* or *couldn't* to talk about general ability in the past:
*Jacqueline's mother was French but she lived in England. She **could** speak English and French when she was four years old.*
*Mr Watson went to Japan last year. He needed an interpreter because he **couldn't** speak Japanese.*
*I **couldn't** hear the speaker very well. **Could** you hear what he was saying?*

ⓒ Talking about permission

We use *can* or *can't* to talk about things that are allowed or not allowed:
A: *I need a cigarette. **Can** I smoke in here?*
B: *No, I'm sorry, you **can't** smoke in here – it's a non-smoking office. But there is a smoking area in the canteen – you **can** smoke there.*

PRACTICE **① Talking about ability**

> ### Wanted:
> **bilingual** secretary.
> Must be **numerate** and
> **computer literate**. Minimum 4
> years' experience in banking or
> financial services. For further
> details, write to:

> *Fundraiser for special
> needs children's centre.*
> Charity working with **blind**
> and **deaf** children requires a
> fundraising coordinator to
> oversee

> *Independently-minded, the
> ideal candidate will have good
> time-management skills;
> excellent interpersonal and
> communication skills, and also
> requires 3 years' experience*

Complete the sentences with *can* or *can't* and the words in the box.

~~speak two languages~~	see	hear	explain things well
use a PC	deal with figures	deal with people	organize your work well

1 If you are bilingual, you can speak two languages.
2 If you are numerate, you ....
3 If you are computer literate, you ....
4 If you are blind, you ....
5 If you are deaf, you ....
6 If you have good time-management skills, you ....
7 If you have good interpersonal skills, you ....
8 If you have good communication skills, you ....

2 Past ability

Complete the sentences with *can*, *can't*, *could*, or *couldn't*.

1 The presentation was OK, but you spoke too quietly and lots of people couldn´t hear you.
2 I loved the hotel – the views were great and from my room I _____ see the sea.
3 We wanted to run some TV ads, but we _____ afford it, so we advertised on the radio.
4 I can use Microsoft Word and Excel, but I _____ use Powerpoint.
5 Ask Jamil to translate this letter – I think he _____ read Arabic.
6 The negotiations went wrong because we _____ agree on a price.
7 I grew up in Madrid, so when I was three or four, I _____ speak Spanish and English.
8 I speak a little French, but I _____ understand people when they speak too fast.

3 Talking about permission

Look at these signs. Say what each one means. Use *can* or *can't* and the words in the box.

> use your mobile   park   leave the building   smoke   turn right   ~~pay by credit card~~
> take photos   drink the water

1 You can pay by credit card.
2 _____
3 _____
4 _____

5 _____
6 _____
7 _____
8 _____

OVER TO YOU

For each topic, write about one thing you can do and one thing you can't do.

1 languages   I can speak English, but I can't speak Arabic.
2 music   _____ .
3 computers   _____ .
4 sport   _____ .
5 work skills   _____ .
6 clothes at work   _____ .

29 Requests and offers
Could you ...?, Shall I ...?, Would you like me to ...?

PRESENTATION **ⓐ Requests**

We can use *can* or *could* to make requests:
A: *Can I use your phone?*   B: *Yes, of course.*
A: *Could you do me a favour?*   B: *Yes, of course.*
In this example, *could* does not refer to the past. When making requests, *Could I ...?* is more common and more polite than *Can I ...?*

! In everyday situations, such as shopping, going to a restaurant, or talking to colleagues, do not use direct commands. Instead, use *Could I ..., please?* or *Could you ..., please?*
wrong: ~~Give me~~ Mr Cohen's email address.
right: *Could I have Mr Cohen's email address, please?*

ⓑ Offers

We can use *Shall I ...?* or *I'll ...* to offer help:
A: *It's very hot in here.*   B: *Shall I open the window?*
A: *I need to order a taxi to the station.*   B: *Don't worry. I'll give you a lift if you like.*

ⓒ Would you like ...?

Look at the way we use *Would you like ...?* and *Would you like me to ...?*:
Would you like = Do you want ...?
Would you like a coffee? (= Do you want a coffee?)
Would you like to have a drink? (= Do you want to have a drink?)

Would you like me to ...? = Shall I ...?
Would you like me to send you a price list? (= Shall I send you a price list?)

PRACTICE **① Requests**

Complete the telephone conversation with the requests in the box.

> Could you ask her to ring Mr Baxter urgently?   Could I have your number?
>
> Could you hold on a minute, please?   ~~Could I have the Finance Department, please?~~
>
> Could you take a message for me?   Could I speak to Jane Grace, please?

A: Good morning, Pearson Enterprises.
B: Good morning. ¹Could I have the Finance Department, please?
C: Good morning. Finance.
B: Good morning. ² _____
C: I'm sorry, but she's not at her desk. I'll go and see if she's here.
  ³ _____

B: Yes, I'll hold.
C: I'm afraid I don't know where she is.
B: ⁴ _____
C: Yes, sure.
B: ⁵ _____
C: OK – ring Mr Baxter urgently. ⁶ _____
B: Yes, it's 3452 2422.
C: That's fine. I'll make sure she gets the message.

2 Polite requests

Rewrite the sentences with *Could I ..., please?*, or *Could you ..., please?* More than one answer is possible.

1 Open the window.   Could you open the window, please?
2 I want a coffee. _____ ?
3 Take this report to Hans. _____ ?
4 Let me use your phone. _____ ?
5 Give me a mineral water. _____ ?

3 Offers

Complete the dialogues with *I'll ...* or *Shall I ...?* and the notes in the box.

send an email   give someone a lift   come another day   send a new one   ~~give someone a hand~~   give someone a message

1 A: I don't think I can move this printer by myself.
   B: I'll give you a hand. or Shall I give you a hand?
2 A: I need to get to the bank but I haven't got a car.
   B: _____ ?
3 A: I think the brochure I have is out of date.
   B: _____ ?
4 A: I'm terribly busy – I'm afraid I can't see you now.
   B: _____ ?
5 A: I need to see those sales figures today. The post will take too long.
   B: _____ ?
6 A: I can't get through to Bill on the phone, but I have to talk to him.
   B: _____ ?

4 *Would you like ...?*

Rewrite the sentences beginning *Would you like ...?* or *Would you like me to ...?*.

1 Shall I call back later?   Would you like me to call back later?
2 Do you want a receipt? _____ ?
3 Shall I send you the details? _____ ?
4 Do you want to come to dinner? _____ ?
5 Do you want to think about it? _____ ?
6 Shall I send them a reminder? _____ ?

OVER TO YOU

Write two polite requests you might make in these situations.

1 in a restaurant   Could I have the wine list, please?
_____ ?
2 at the office _____ ?
_____ ?
3 on the phone _____ ?
_____ ?
4 at the airport check-in desk _____ ?
_____ ?

Write one offer you might make in each of the situations above.

5 _____ ?
6 _____ ?
7 _____ ?
8 _____ ?

30 Suggestions
Why don't you ...?, Let's ..., What about ...?

ⓐ Suggesting action

When we want to advise someone to take action, we can use *Why don't you* + bare infinitive:

> *Why don't you complain to the manager?*
> (= I think you should complain to the manager.)
> *Why don't you give Mme Dubois a ring?*
> (= I think you should call Mme Dubois.)

ⓑ Making suggestions

We can use these words to make suggestions about what we and other people can do:

Let's go out tonight. (use the bare infinitive: *go*)
Why don't we go out tonight?
What about going out tonight? (use the *-ing* form: *going*)
How about going out tonight?

> *Let's have lunch tomorrow.*
> *What about giving them a 5% discount?*

ⓒ *I suggest ...*

In more formal English, we can use *I suggest that you* + bare infinitive:

> *I suggest that you try again next year.*
> (= I think you should try again next year.)

① Suggesting action

Rewrite the sentences with *Why don't you* ...

1 I think you should give M Andrieux a ring. Why don't you give M Andrieux a ring?
2 I think you ought to get a new Mac. _____
3 I think you should send them a reminder. _____
4 I think you ought to ask Bill to come to the meeting. _____
5 I think you should leave now. _____
6 I think you ought to take the train tomorrow. _____
7 I think you should come to the conference. _____
8 I think you ought to write to the CEO. _____

❷ Making suggestions

Amélie and Jean are discussing their next sales conference. Write their suggestions from the notes.

1 what/have/jazz band?
 What about having a jazz band?
2 how/invite/some important clients?
 _____?

3 why/have it/a nice hotel?
 _____?

4 let/hire/a good after-dinner speaker.
 _____.

5 what/have/the conference in Paris?
 _____?

6 how/get/different caterers this year?
 _____?

7 why/try/save money this year?
 _____?

8 let/ask the staff/their ideas.
 _____.

❸ *I suggest …*

A consultant has looked at a furniture company that is losing money. Write his advice and suggestions with *I suggest that …* and the ideas in the box .

| give them new incentives   ~~increase your prices~~   advertise more |
| find new suppliers   move to new premises   design some new ones |

1 Your profit margins are too low, so *I suggest that you increase your prices.*
2 Your products are not well known, so _____ .
3 Your products are old-fashioned, so _____ .
4 Your raw materials are expensive, so _____ .
5 Your staff are not motivated, so _____ .
6 Your workshops are too small, so _____ .

OVER TO YOU

You are in a meeting about promoting a new car. Suggest ways of selling the new model to customers. Use the ideas in the box or your own ideas.

~~give a year's free insurance~~	pay the road tax
give free CD player	offer interest-free credit
organize a competition	let the showrooms have big discounts
offer free servicing for a year	include air conditioning

1 Why *don't we give them a year's free insurance?*
2 What _____?
3 How _____?
4 Let's _____.
5 What _____?
6 How _____?
7 Let's _____.
8 Why _____?

31 Advice
if I were you, should, ought to

ⓐ Giving advice

We often use the structure *If I were you ...* to give advice to friends and colleagues:
If I were you, I'd start looking for another job.
I'd is the short form of *I would*. It is followed by the bare infinitive.

To form the negative, we change *would* to ***wouldn't***:
*If I were you, I **wouldn't** argue with the boss.*

ⓑ *should* and *ought to*

We can use the modal verb ***should*** + bare infinitive for advice. We often use *I think* or *I don't think*:
*I think you **should** get a new car.*
*I don't think you **should** accept the offer.*

We can also use ***ought to*** + bare infinitive:
*I think you **ought to** get a new car.*
*I don't think you **ought to** accept the offer.*

ⓒ Criticizing

We can use the following expressions to criticize the things people do:
shouldn't* + *so much
***shouldn't* + *so* + adverb**
should* + *more
*You shout too much. You **shouldn't** shout **so much**.*
*You leave the office too early. You **shouldn't** leave the office **so early**.*
*In meetings, you don't talk enough. In meetings, you **should** talk **more**.*

❶ Giving advice

A friend is coming to an interview at your company. Give them advice using *If I were you, I'd ...* or *If I were you, I wouldn't ...*

1 Wearing a suit is a good idea.
   If I were you, I'd wear a suit.
2 Finding out about the company is a good idea.
   _____ .
3 Preparing some questions is a good idea.
   _____ .
4 Asking about holidays is a bad idea.
   _____ .
5 Arguing about the salary is a bad idea.
   _____ .
6 Arriving on time is a good idea.
   _____ .
7 Complaining about your last boss is a bad idea.
   _____ .
8 Explaining why you want the job is a good idea.
   _____ .

② should and ought to

Look at the pictures. Give advice using the phrases in the box and *I think he should* or *I think he ought to.*

A   B

> ~~get out of the field~~   get a better ladder   come down immediately   take off his T-shirt

Picture A

1 I think he ought to get out of the field.

2 _____ .

Picture B

1 _____ .

2 _____ .

③ Criticizing

Read the notes on Mr Jensen's appraisal form. Write what his boss says using *You should ... more* or *You shouldn't ... so ... .*

APPRAISAL PAGE 3

Name: George Jensen

Date: 14/8

NEGATIVE COMMENTS by other members of the department:

1 He shouts too much.
2 He doesn't help the staff enough.
3 He goes home too early.
4 He doesn't communicate enough.
5 He criticizes too much.
6 He doesn't praise the staff enough.

---

1 You shouldn't shout so much.
2 You should help the staff more.
3 _____ .
4 _____ .
5 _____ .
6 _____ .

OVER TO YOU

Give advice and make suggestions. Use your own ideas.

1 Jane looks very tired.   I think she ought to have a break.

2 Bill spends two hours driving to work. _____ .

3 These new fax machines don't work. _____ .

4 Their offer is too low. _____ .

5 The meeting isn't important for David. _____ .

6 Jan wants to go to that busy restaurant. _____ .

7 Our boss has made some big mistakes. _____ .

8 It wasn't your fault. _____ .

Uncertainty
may, might

ⓐ Form

We can use the modal verbs *may* and *might* when we are not sure about something. They are followed by the bare infinitive:

*Johannes **may be** in Mr Braun's office.*
*I **might not come** to the meeting tomorrow.*

May is sometimes a little more certain than *might*, but the difference is very small.

ⓑ Talking about now

We can use *may* or *might* to talk about a present situation:

A: *Where's Clara? I need to speak to her.*
B: *I'm not sure. She **might not be** here today.*
C: *I don't know. She **might be** at home.*
D: *I've no idea. She **may be** out to lunch.*
E: *Ask Larry – he **might know** where she is.*

ⓒ Talking about the future

We can use *may* or *might* to talk about the future:

At the moment, the economy is fine, but next year …

 *… unemployment might go up.*

 … interest rates may rise.

 … the stock market may fall.

 … production might go down.

ⓓ Talking about possibilities

When we are sure about something in the future, we can use *will* or *won't*. When we are not so sure, we can use *will probably*, *may/might*, or *probably won't*:

100% chance	*will*	*We will make a profit this year.*
75% chance	*will probably*	*We will probably make $1.5 million.*
50% chance	*may*	*We may make more than $2 million.*
50% chance	*might*	*We might make more than $2 million.*
25% chance	*probably won't*	*We probably won't make less that $1 million.*
0% chance	*won't*	*We won't make a loss this year.*

❗ Note the position of *probably*. In a positive sentence it comes after *will* and in a negative sentence, before *won't*.

① Form

Say if the sentences are right or wrong and correct the mistakes.

1 I might not come to the conference.　　　　right
2 Mr Ang ~~may ringing~~ you this afternoon.　　wrong　may ring
3 He might not to pass his accountancy exams.　　......　......
4 The printer might need some more ink.　　......　......
5 We may hold our next conference in Istanbul.　　......　......
6 I might will have to go to Greece next week.　　......　......

② Talking about now

A car company has developed a new car. The design is top secret. Complete the sentences with *might* or *may* and the verbs in the box to guess what the car is like.

~~be~~   be able   cost   have   look   run

1 It **might be** environmentally friendly.
2 It _____ on hydrogen fuel.
3 It _____ to drive across water.
4 It _____ automatic parking.
5 It _____ like a sports car.
6 It _____ less than $50,000.

③ Talking about the future

Datalogic is a small software company based in central London. It is thinking about relocating to offices 200 km away. Write about the advantages and disadvantages of relocating to the new site. Use *may* or *might*.

~~lose customers~~   get cheaper premises   lose some of their staff   save money on rent   ~~make some useful new contacts~~   waste a lot of time moving   find bigger offices   have problems recruiting

Disadvantages of moving to the new site:
1 They may lose some of their customers.
2 _____ .
3 _____ .
4 _____ .

Advantages of moving to the new site:
5 They might make some useful new contacts.
6 _____ .
7 _____ .
8 _____ .

④ Talking about possibilities

Rewrite the predictions to show how likely they are.
1 The price of oil will fall next year. (25%) The price of oil probably won't fall next year.
2 Our market share will increase next year. (75%) _____ .
3 Inflation will go down next year. (50%) _____ .
4 The dollar will go up next year. (50%) _____ .
5 The cost of living will fall next year. (25%) _____ .
6 There will be tax rises next year. (50%) _____ .

OVER TO YOU

Write sentences about what you might or might not do, or what might or might not happen ...

1 to you tonight — I might get home late.
2 to you this weekend _____ .
3 to you this year at work _____ .
4 to you in the next five years at work _____ .
5 after the next general election _____ .
6 to your company next year _____ .
7 to one of your products next year _____ .
8 to one of your colleagues next year _____ .

33 Obligation (1)
must, mustn't, needn't

PRESENTATION **ⓐ Form**

We can use *must* + bare infinitive to talk about obligation and necessity. *Must* is a modal verb and it does not change at all:

Positive	Questions	Negative
I must work.	*Must I work?*	*I mustn't work.*
You must work.	*Must you work?*	*You mustn't work.*
He/She/It must work.	*Must he/she/it work?*	*He/She/It mustn't work.*
We must work.	*Must we work?*	*We mustn't work.*
They must work.	*Must they work?*	*They mustn't work.*

❗ Remember that *must*, like all modals, takes an infinitive without *to*.
wrong: *You must* ~~to reply~~ *immediately.*
right: *You must reply immediately.*

ⓑ Use

We use *must* to say what we feel is necessary:
   You must be here by 5.30 tomorrow afternoon. (= I strongly advise that you are here then.)
   My plane leaves in half an hour – I must go now. (= It is necessary for me to go now.)

We often use *must* in written English and in notices:

DECLARATION
You, or someone on your behalf, must sign below.

I _____

declare that the information given above is true and complete.

> **Passengers MUST keep their baggage with them at all times.**

ⓒ Negatives

We use *mustn't* to give strong advice or an instruction not to do something. We use *needn't* to say something is not necessary:
   You mustn't tell John about the party – it's a secret. (= I am telling you not to do this.)
   You needn't make a reservation. We have a few tables free. (= It is not necessary.)

ⓓ Past tense

The past tense of *must* is *had to*:
   When I arrived at the airport, I had to buy a visa.

1 Form

Say if the sentences are right or wrong and correct the mistakes.

1 You must reply to that letter. *right*
2 You ~~must to ring~~ Janine today. *wrong must ring*
3 You don't must drop this box – it is fragile.
4 Tell Berndt he musts give me the report today.
5 You must leave before 4.30.
6 What time do we must be there?
7 You must remember to call Frau Prosser.
8 Patrizia, you must to check these invoices more carefully.

2 must and mustn't

An accountant is talking to a new client. Complete the dialogue with must or mustn't.

A: OK, let's go over the most important points again. First of all, when you buy something or order something, you ¹*must* keep the receipts.

B: Sometimes you don't get a receipt – parking the car, for example.

A: Well, then you ² _____ write the details down in a book and you can claim the money later. But you ³ _____ remember that the money for the business and your own money are different. You ⁴ _____ use money from the business to buy cigarettes, for example.

B: And what about these VAT* forms? When ⁵ _____ I fill them in?

A: You ⁶ _____ send them in every three months – I will remind you and help you with the figures, but they ⁷ _____ be late or you will cause a lot of trouble.

* VAT = Value Added Tax

3 mustn't and needn't

Complete the sentences with mustn't or needn't.

1 You *mustn't* use the company phone line to make personal calls.
2 You _____ go to the bank for money – you can use the cash machine at the supermarket.
3 There will be plenty of seats, so you _____ book one in advance.
4 Tell Bill the meeting is very important. It starts at 8.15 and he _____ be late.
5 You _____ make a decision now – you can have a few days to think about it.
6 Next time you give a presentation, you _____ move around so much. Try to stand still.
7 By the way, you _____ worry about that invoice. Ahmed paid it last week.

OVER TO YOU

Think of some things these people might say to you. Use must, mustn't, or needn't.

1 your boss   _____
2 a colleague at work   _____
3 a friend   _____
4 your husband/wife/partner   _____
5 your doctor   _____
6 a policeman   _____
7 your accountant   _____
8 a tax inspector   _____

34 Obligation (2)
have to, don't have to, can't

PRESENTATION **ⓐ Form**

We use *have to* + bare infinitive when we are talking about obligation:

Positive	Question
I have to work.	*Do I have to work?*
You have to work.	*Do you have to work?*
He/She/It has to work.	*Does he/she/it have to work?*
We have to work.	*Do we have to work?*
They have to work.	*Do they have to work?*

A: *When do we have to leave?*
B: *We have to leave at 4.15.*

We can also use *have got to* instead of *have to*. The meaning is the same:

A: *When have we got to leave?*
B: *We have got to leave at 4.15.*

ⓑ Talking about obligations

We use *have to* when we talk about obligations, rules, and duties:

Hussein's doing his final accountancy exam next week. He has to do a lot of revision.
(Nobody is giving an instruction. It is just a fact that his revision is necessary.)
When the MD is away, I have to look after his clients.
(Again, this is not an instruction. It is just a routine necessity.)
A: *What time do we have to go to the meeting?*   B: *About 6.30.*
(This is a question about what is necessary for them to do.)

ⓒ Negatives

There are two kinds of negative for *have to*. One is the negative form *don't have to/doesn't have to*. The other is *can't*. They mean different things:

I work flexitime, so I don't have to be in the office from 9.00 to 5.00.
(= There is no obligation to be in the office from 9.00 to 5.00.)
You can't smoke on aeroplanes.
(= It is not permitted.)

PRACTICE **① Form**

Say if the sentences are right or wrong and correct the mistakes.

1 Favel ~~has to working~~ late this evening.   *wrong   has to work*
2 Do you have to wear a tie?   *right*
3 Do we have to come in tomorrow?
4 I am have to discuss the problem with the manager.
5 Do you have to work at weekends?
6 Why do you have to drive to work?

❷ Talking about obligations

Look at the two job descriptions. Natasha got job A. Write five sentences about what she has to do at work.

<table>
<tr><td>Temporary secretary – to assist the MD.
Duties involve typing letters, doing the filing, going to meetings, and making appointments. Good salary and transport allowance.</td></tr>
</table>

1 (MD)   She has to assist the MD.
2 (letters)   .
3 (filing)   .
4 (meetings)   .
5 (appointments)   .

Varda got job B. Ask her five questions about what she has to do at work.

Conference coordinator to assist the Conference Director.
Duties include making bookings, arranging accommodation, preparing timetables, organizing speakers, and giving presentations.

6 (bookings)   Do you have to make bookings?
7 (accommodation)   ?
8 (timetables)   ?
9 (speakers)   ?
10 (presentations)   ?

❸ Negatives

Complete the text with *have to/has to* or *don't have to/doesn't have to*.

***Working Mother* magazine recently voted Abbot Laboratories one of the top ten employers in America.**

Luisa Sanchez, mother of three-year-old Ella, says Abbot is a great place to work. 'We have work flexibility here, and that means that I [1]don't have to work a full five-day week. I only come in three days a week and I spend Thursdays, Fridays, and weekends at home. When I am at work I [2]_____ do eight hours a day, but I [3]_____ work 9 to 5. I can choose when I come in and leave – 7 to 3 or 10 to 6 – it's up to me.'

Like other employees, Luisa makes use of the childcare centre, which is the biggest in the country, so she [4]_____ find a childminder when she comes to work. Employees can also use the on-site fitness centre, so they [5]_____ pay to join another gym. There are also excellent on-site medical facilities for any employees who [6]_____ get treatment for minor illnesses or injuries. ■

Complete the text with *have to/has to* or *can't*.

Aaron Jacobsen, a work-life balance expert, says that Abbot's employee-friendly ideas are still unusual. 'Sadly, there are many, many companies in this country that are not like Abbot. There are plenty of companies where you [7]_____ work part-time because they only have full-time jobs. There are companies where you [8]_____ take a child to the workplace because there is no place for them to stay. That's not fair on the mothers. They [9]_____ make sure that someone is there to look after their children – they [10]_____ just leave them home alone all day. And sadly, that means that many mothers [11]_____ give up their careers to stay at home and look after their children.' ■

OVER TO YOU

Write sentences on each topic. Say what you *have to* do, *don't have to* do, or *can't* do.

1 Taking part in a meeting   You don't have to take notes. You can't smoke. You have to pay attention.

2 Travelling by plane

3 Driving in England

4 Advertising your product

35 Imperative
instructions and directions

PRESENTATION **ⓐ Giving instructions and directions**

When we give instructions and directions, we often use the imperative. This has the same form as the bare infinitive:

*Slow down. OK, **let** it down a bit. Steady, steady. **Go** right a bit. **Come** back a bit. That's fine. **Let** it down slowly ... you're nearly there. **Stop!** That's it.*

The imperative is often used in manuals and written technical instructions:

Switch the power OFF.   **Insert** the card into slot G.
Unscrew the back panel.   **Turn** the power back ON.
Insert the disc and **follow** the instructions on screen.

We often use the imperative to give directions:

A: *Can you tell me the way to the Said Business School?.*
B: *Yes, **carry on** down this road until you come to the library, then **go** straight on to the traffic lights. When you get there, **turn** right, then **take** the first on the left, and you'll see it on your right.*

ⓑ Negative instructions

For negative instructions, we use *Do not* or *Don't* + bare infinitive:

In spoken English, we use *don't*:

A: *I'm sorry – I forgot to bring the figures for March.*
B: **Don't** *worry, I can get them from Amanda.*

> Care of your MP3 Player
>
> **IMPORTANT**
>
> DO NOT allow the player to get wet
> DO NOT expose to extreme heat or cold
> DO NOT drop

ⓒ Explaining

When we are explaining how to do something, we often use the *you* form of the present simple:

*It's very easy to fit – **you take** the old ink cartridge out. Then **you remove** the plastic film, and **you push** the new cartridge into the slot until it clicks. That's all.*

PRACTICE **❶ Giving instructions and directions**

Look at the plan of the offices of WorldMedia. Write down the directions to the places from reception.

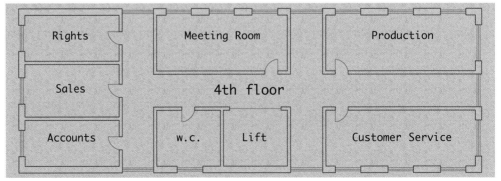

1 A: Can you tell me the way to the Accounts Department?
  B: Yes, of course. Take the lift to the fourth floor. When you get there, turn left, and go down the corridor. Take the first turning on your left, and it's on the right hand side.

2 A: Can you tell me the way to the Production Department?
  B: _____ .

3 A: Can you tell me the way to the Rights Department?
  B: _____ .

2 Instructions

Read the advice on what to do at a job interview. Complete the text with the positive and negative instructions in the box.

don't arrive
don't ask
don't forget
don't cross
prepare
listen
give
~~talk~~
finish

Most interviewers form their opinion of you in the first few minutes of a meeting. Here's how to make a good impression.

In the days before your interview, ¹**talk** to people who have worked at the company. Learn the name and title of the person you're going to meet. Check the time of the interview and ² _____ late. ³ _____ to greet the secretary or administrative assistant; it's polite, and this person may have a lot of influence. Smile and look the interviewer in the eye. ⁴ _____ your arms or legs. ⁵ _____ a few questions and ⁶ _____ carefully. ⁷ _____ the impression that you're part of the team by using 'we'. For example, say, 'How do we deal with the press?' ⁸ _____ with a positive statement and a firm handshake. Finally, ⁹ _____ about money at the start of the interview.

3 Explaining

Alan is telling a colleague how to book an online ticket. Complete the dialogue with the words in the box.

you choose   you click   you confirm   you fill   you give   ~~you go~~   you tell

Alan: First of all, ¹you go to the airline's website, so for BA it's britishairways.com, and you'll see the main menu.

Lars: OK, so what do I choose?

Alan: The link that says 'Booking my trip'. A new page comes up, and ² _____ them which airport you want to go from and where you want to go to. Then ³ _____ in the details of how many passengers there are, and so on.

Lars: What about the dates?

Alan: For the dates, ⁴ _____ on the calendar and choose the days you want to travel on. Then it gives you details of times and prices, and ⁵ _____ the flights you want.

Lars: What about paying?

Alan: When you're sure all the details are OK, ⁶ _____ that you want to buy the ticket. Then ⁷ _____ them your credit card details, and that's it.

OVER TO YOU

Imagine a business person from another country is coming to your country. Think of some useful advice to give them about your country and the way you do business.

Do	Don't
1 Make sure you arrive at meetings on time.	6 Don't kiss business colleagues on the cheek.
2 _____ .	7 _____ .
3 _____ .	8 _____ .
4 _____ .	9 _____ .
5 _____ .	10 _____ .

36 Zero conditional
if you work ..., you get

a **Form**

We use the zero conditional to talk about things that are generally true, or that always happen.

In sentences like this, both verbs are in the present simple:

If + present simple	present simple
If you heat water to 100°C,	*it boils.*

We can change the order of the sentence:

present simple	*if* + present simple
Water boils	*if you heat it to 100°C.*

If you heat water to 100°C, it boils. We all know that. But alcohol boils if you heat it to 78.5°C. So remember, if you cook a wine sauce for a few minutes, all the alcohol goes away.

In sentences like this, you can replace *if* with **when** or **every time**:
When you heat water to 100°C, it boils.
Every time you heat water to 100°C, it boils.

b **Talking about facts**

We often use *if* sentences like this to talk about scientific facts:
If you burn coal and other fossil fuels, this creates smoke.
If the smoke mixes with water, it turns to acid rain.
If the acid rain falls on trees, they die.

c **Routines, systems, and processes**

We can also use *if* sentences like this to talk about routines, systems, and processes:
In general, the tax system is quite simple. If you earn less than $5,000, you do not pay any tax.
If you earn between $5,000 and $38,000, you pay tax at 25%.
If you earn more than $38,000, you pay tax at 45%.

PRACTICE **1** **Form**

Complete the sentences with the verbs in brackets.

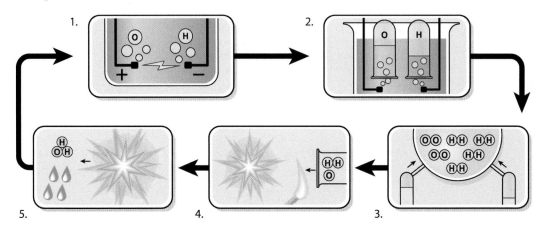

1 If you pass electricity through water, the water changes into two gases. (pass, change)
2 If you _____ the bubbles, you _____ hydrogen and oxygen. (collect, get)
3 If you _____ two parts of hydrogen and one part of oxygen, you _____ an explosive mixture. (mix, get)
4 If you _____ the gas, it _____. (light, explode)
5 When the gas _____, it _____ back into water. (explode, turn)

❷ Routines, systems, and processes
Complete the text with the correct form of the verbs in brackets.

I would like to tell you a little about the website design and maintenance services we offer. We normally work with smaller companies because if companies ¹are (be) fairly small, they very often ²don't have (not/have) their own computer specialists. So if a small company ³_____ (want) to create a website, it ⁴_____ (be) much easier to hire people like us to do it for them. And, of course, you ⁵_____ (get) a better product if you ⁶_____ (use) professional designers.

SITE MAINTENANCE DIVISION

After-sales is an important area. We have another department to look after our existing clients, and we have two website maintenance contracts. If a customer ⁷_____ (have) a small to medium-sized website, we ⁸_____ (suggest) the quarterly contract. If a client ⁹_____ (choose) one of these, we ¹⁰_____ (check) their website every twelve weeks and make sure that everything is working properly. We recommend this option because we have found that people ¹¹_____ (not/have) so many problems if we ¹²_____ (carry) out regular checks, update the software, and so on. We also ¹³_____ (offer) an emergency-only contract if a client ¹⁴_____ (not/want) to pay for the quarterly contract. With an emergency contract, we only ¹⁵_____ (visit) the company if their website suddenly ¹⁶_____ (stop) working. These problems can be difficult to sort out because if a website ¹⁷_____ (crash) completely, it often ¹⁸_____ (mean) that there is a virus in the system.

OVER TO YOU **Complete the sentences with your own ideas. Write about what generally, always, often, or sometimes happens.**
1 If I have a lot of extra work, I often take it home.
2 If I am not very busy at work, I sometimes _____ .
3 If we have a good weekend, I generally _____ .
4 When the company has a good year, _____ .
5 If I work overtime, _____ .
6 When I have to give a presentation, _____ .
7 If my boss is not around, _____ .
8 If I go on a long-distance flight, _____ .

Conditional 1
if you work ..., you will get

a) Form

We can use *if* sentences to talk about the future. We use the present simple in the *if* part of the sentence and *will* + bare infinitive in the other part:

If + present simple	*will* + infinitive
If we sell these items at $3.65,	*we will make a good profit.*

We can change the order of the sentence:

will + infinitive	*if* + present simple
We will make a good profit	*if we sell these items at $3.65.*

! Remember that we do not use *will* in the *if* part of the sentence.
wrong: *If Enrico ~~will come~~ tomorrow, I will give him the contract.*
right: *If Enrico comes tomorrow, I will give him the contract.*

b) Use

In the *if* part of the sentence, we talk about real possibilities in the future. In the other part of the sentence, we talk about the result:

Jack's business colleague, Mr Suzuki, is coming tomorrow. At the moment Jack is ill at home.
If Jack comes in tomorrow, he will look after Mr Suzuki.
If Jack doesn't come in tomorrow, I will take Mr Suzuki to the factory.

We use *if* + the present simple to talk about Jack. Maybe he will come in tomorrow. Maybe he will not come in tomorrow. We do not know. Both are possible.

c) *If* + imperative

We can also use *if* sentences with imperatives to give instructions:

If + present simple	imperative
If Hans Larsen rings this afternoon,	*ask him to call me.*
	give him a message.
	tell him I want to see him.

d) *If* and *when*

There is an important difference between *if* and *when*:
I will call you if the train is late. (Maybe the train will be late. Maybe it will not be late.)
I will call you when the train gets in. (I know the train will arrive. I am 100% sure.)

1) Form

Say if the sentences are right or wrong and correct the mistakes.

1 If you order before 12.00, the goods will arrive the next day.   right ....
2 You won't pay for delivery if your order will be worth over $50.   ....
3 If you return any goods, we will give you a full refund.   ....
4 We will replace any goods if they are faulty.   ....
5 If you find us a new customer, we will send you a free gift.   ....
6 If you will order online, we will give you a 5% discount.   ....

② Use

Complete the dialogue with the correct form of the verbs in brackets.

Elsa: I'm giving a presentation at the Conference Centre in Stockholm. Do you know anything about the rooms there?

Björn: Yes, they've got two types – they call them Meeting Rooms or Conference Rooms. They [1] **will give** (give) you a Conference Room if you [2] **have** (have) 200 or 250 people. If you only [3] _____ (get) a small audience, they [4] _____ (put) you in a Meeting Room.

Elsa: And they have projectors, do they?

Björn: Yes, if you [5] _____ (have) a Conference Room, they [6] _____ (supply) everything. But take a radio microphone. They have fixed microphones, but they aren't very good.

Elsa: That's for the big room, is it?

Björn: Yes, you [7] _____ (not/need) a microphone if you [8] _____ (be) in one of the small rooms.

Elsa: OK, so if I [9] _____ (call) the centre, [10] _____ (they/be) able to give me a radio microphone?

Björn: No, they haven't got any – but I know we have some here. If you [11] _____ (give) Janet a ring, she [12] _____ (tell) you where they are.

③ *If* + imperative

Complete the sentences with the correct form of the verbs in the box.

(work, be)   ~~(come, give)~~   (phone, order)   (see, tell)   (let, need)   (be, not/disturb)

1 If Hussein **comes** in this afternoon, **give** him the report.
2 Please _____ me know if you _____ any help.
3 If Herr Braun _____ in a meeting, please _____ him.
4 If you _____ Georg, _____ him I want to see him.
5 If you _____ Petersens, _____ some more paper.
6 _____ from home if the weather _____ bad tomorrow.

④ *If* and *when*

Complete the sentences with *if* or *when*.

1 My train is getting in now. I'll call you back **when** I get to the office.
2 I don't know when I will arrive – _____ I am late, start the meeting without me.
3 I am still doing an evening course every Monday. I'll have more free time _____ it is over.
4 I'd like to talk to you, but _____ you're busy, I will come back later.
5 I hope that is all clear. _____ there is anything you don't understand, please ask me.
6 The next meeting isn't very important. _____ you want to miss it, that's OK.

OVER TO YOU

Write true sentences about yourself.

What will you do if ...
1 you have some free time tonight?   If I have some free time tonight, I'll watch TV.
2 you have some free time at the weekend? _____ .
3 you need some cash this week? _____ .
4 you don't feel well next week? _____ .
5 you go abroad next year? _____ .
6 you buy a new car? _____ .

38 Conditional 2

if you worked ..., you would get

PRESENTATION **ⓐ Form**

We can use *if* sentences to talk about imaginary situations. We use the past simple in the *if* part of the sentence and *would* + bare infinitive in the other part:

If + past simple	*would* + infinitive
If I had $1,000,000,	*I would buy a boat.*

We can change the order of the sentence:

would + infinitive	*if* + past simple
I would buy a boat	*if I had $1,000,000.*

When we are speaking, we often use the short form *'d* in the place of *would*.
> *If I spoke French, I'd apply for that Paris job. (= I would apply.)*

❗ Do not use *would* in the *if* part of the sentence.
wrong: *If I ~~would have~~ the money, I would buy a new car next year.*
right: *If I had the money, I would buy a new car next year.*

ⓑ Use

We use sentences like this for imagined conditions and results:

> **condition**   **result**
> *If I had a year off work,   I would start my own business.*
> (But I do not think I am going to have a year off work. It is not a real possibility.)

Here are some more examples:
> *If I owned Microsoft, I would give free software to schools.*
> (But I do not own Microsoft, so I will not do this.)
> *If you ordered 20,000 units, we would give you a 40% discount.*
> (But you only want about 10 units, so you will not get this discount.)

We often use the expression *If I were you* to give advice (see Unit 31):
> *If I were you, I would look for another job.*

ⓒ First or second conditional?

Look at the difference between these sentences:

> *I'll buy it if you give me credit.*
> (This is real a possibility, so we use the first conditional, *if* + present simple.)

> *I would buy it if you gave me 70% discount.*
> (This is not a real possibility, so we use the second conditional, *if* + past simple.)

PRACTICE **❶ Form**

Say if the sentences are right or wrong and correct the mistakes.

1 If I ~~would work~~ in London, I would speak English every day.   wrong   worked
2 Our costs would be lower if we didn't have offices in Tokyo.   right
3 What would you do if you would lose your job?
4 I would use a Mac if the software wasn't so expensive.
5 If we don't have our own lorries, our costs would be higher.
6 If you needed technical advice, who would you ask?
7 If we would have a fire here, the insurance company would pay.
8 She will be very useful to us if she joined the company.

② Use

A manager of a low-cost airline is talking about his company. Rewrite his notes with *If ...* .

> - We don't use big airports – our landing costs are not high.
> - We don't serve meals – we don't need a lot of cabin crew.
> - We use the Internet – we don't need a lot of offices.
> - We are reliable – people come back to us.
> - We don't issue tickets – we don't need a lot of office staff.
> - Our flights are cheap – they are popular.
> - We have a great safety record – people feel safe with us.

1 If we used big airports, our landing costs would be high.
2 _____ .
3 _____ .
4 _____ .
5 _____ .
6 _____ .
7 _____ .

③ First or second conditional?

Make sentences using one part from A, one part from B, and one part from C.
Use the correct form of the verbs in brackets.

A	B	C
I (apply) for that job	the hotel (be) full,	but it's too expensive for us.
If Amy (be/not) better tomorrow,	if I (have) three months' holiday,	but I have no qualifications.
We (buy) the house	if I (have) an MBA,	He will ring and tell us when he knows.
I (travel) to Australia	if he (have) time.	but I only have three weeks.
Peter (come) to the party	she (take) the day off	and she will stay at home.
If we (not book) quickly,	if we (have) the money,	so we should book a room today.

1 I would apply for that job if I had an MBA, but I have no qualifications.
2 _____ .
3 _____ .
4 _____ .
5 _____ .
6 _____ .

OVER TO YOU

Complete the sentences with your own ideas.
1 If I took a year off, I would learn another language.
2 If I got promoted, _____ .
3 I would be very surprised if _____ .
4 I would be very angry if _____ .
5 If people at my company went on strike, _____ .
6 I would look for another job if _____ .
7 If my boss was away for six months, _____ .
8 I would take the day off if _____ .

39 *-ing* or infinitive (1)

PRESENTATION

ⓐ *-ing* **form**

The following common verbs and expressions are usually followed by the *-ing* form:

avoid	delay	look forward to	stop	there's no point
carry on	finish	mind	suggest	
consider	like (= enjoy)	put off	It's (not) worth	

You can't **avoid paying** taxes.
I'm **looking forward to going** away.
We have **stopped doing** business with them.
Have you **considered looking** for another job?
I don't **mind taking** the train to work.
There's no point complaining – he won't change his mind.

ⓑ **Infinitive**

The following common verbs are usually followed by the infinitive with *to*:

can afford	decide	fail	plan	refuse
agree	deserve	manage	prepare	want
arrange	expect	offer	promise	would like

I **can't afford to get** a new car this year.
Unfortunately, we **failed to win** the contract.
I think you **deserve to get** a bonus.
Do you **want to take** out insurance?
We are **expecting to finish** the order soon.
I **would like to see** you tomorrow.

! Remember that with *look forward to*, we use an *-ing* form, not the infinitive.
wrong: *I ~~look forward to hear~~ from you.*
right: *I **look forward to hearing** from you.*

PRACTICE

❶ *-ing* **form**

Complete the email with the *-ing* form of the verbs in the box.

~~change~~ get hear install return start work

Barry

This is just a quick note to ask if you would mind ¹changing the date of our meeting.

At the moment I am still in Bahrain working on the telecom project, but we are behind

schedule. We haven't finished ² .... the new software, so I have had to put off ³ ....

to London for two weeks. Bob Simpson suggested ⁴ .... a new contractor, but I don't

agree. There's no point ⁵ .... again, and so I am going to carry on ⁶ .... here.

Anyway, could we meet on 18 July? Please let me know.

I look forward to ⁷ .... from you.

Danny

❷ Infinitive

Complete the reply with the infinitive of the verbs in the box.

do	have	lower	pay	~~sort out~~	use

Danny

The 18ᵗʰ is fine – in fact it is better because I want ¹to sort out a problem this end.

The problem is that we were expecting ² .... our usual contractor, but his price was very high. I talked to him about it a few days ago. I said we couldn't afford ³ .... that much money, but he refused ⁴ .... the price.

I am planning ⁵ .... a meeting with a new contractor, and I hope that he will offer ⁶ .... the job for less.

See you on the 18ᵗʰ.

Best wishes

Barry

❸ -ing or infinitive?

Complete the text with the -ing form or the infinitive of the verbs in brackets.

Dixons, the UK's largest electrical chain, said that it is going to stop ¹stocking (stock) video cassette recorders. The company expects ² .... (sell) its remaining VCRs by Christmas, and it does not plan ³ .... (buy) any more.

The main cause of the death of the VCR is competition from DVDs. These are cheaper and faster, and customers like ⁴ .... (use) them. Manufacturers have also managed ⁵ .... (cut) the price of DVD recorders, and many customers can now afford ⁶ .... (buy) them.

However, Curry's, Dixon's sister company, will carry on ⁷ .... (sell) the machines for the moment. 'We have decided ⁸ .... (keep) VCRs on the shelves,' a spokesperson said. 'There are still lots of customers who want ⁹ .... (buy) them, and we expect ¹⁰ .... (have) them in the shops for a few more years.'

The first video recorder went on sale in Dixons in 1978 for £798.75, the equivalent of about €5,000 in today's money.

(VCR = video cassette recorder)

OVER TO YOU

Complete the sentences with information about yourself and your work.

you

1 I like going for walks.
2 I don't like ....
3 I want ....
4 I am looking forward ....
5 I can't afford ....

your work

6 I like ....
7 I don't mind ....
8 I would like ....
9 I deserve ....
10 I am planning ....

40 -ing or infinitive (2)

ⓐ Purpose

We can use the infinitive (*to do, to talk*, etc.) to explain things:

A: *Why did you go to Bologna last week?*   B: *I went **to attend** the Book Fair.*
*I am calling **to ask** for some advice.*
*I am writing **to tell** you about our latest offer.*
*The CEO has gone **to talk** to the shareholders.*

❗ We use the infinitive (not *-ing* or *for*) to talk about purpose.
A: *Why did Juan move to the USA?*
wrong: B: *Juan moved to the USA ~~for to get~~ a job.*
wrong: B: *Juan moved to the USA ~~for to getting~~ a job.*
right: B: *Juan moved to the USA **to get** a job.*

ⓑ Prepositions + -ing

After prepositions we use verbs in the *-ing* form:

Time prepositions	*before*	*Before joining IBM, I worked for Dell.*
	after	*After working for Dell, I joined IBM.*

Adjectives + prepositions	*responsible for*	*I'm responsible for meeting visitors.*
	good at	*He is good at dealing with people.*
	interested in	*They're interested in buying the business.*
	capable of	*We're capable of producing 200 units a day.*

① Purpose

Say if the sentences are right or wrong and correct the mistakes.

1 Pierre's just gone to the bank ~~for getting~~ some money.   wrong   to get
2 Sylvie is coming to talk about the project.   right
3 I need a taxi for to take me to the airport.
4 We often change the password to make the system safer.
5 Giancarlo rang for to invite you to the party.
6 They are hiring extra sales reps for selling the new product.
7 I am writing to complain about the service I have received.
8 Do you need a passport for to travel round the EU?

② Purpose

Complete the sentences with the infinitive of the verbs in the box.

~~arrange~~   collect   cut   manufacture   promote   store

1 I'm calling **to arrange** a meeting.
2 We're building a bigger warehouse .... the new stock.
3 We are running TV advertisements .... our latest products.
4 I think Pauline's gone to the airport .... Mr Jensen.
5 The company fired 500 workers .... costs.
6 Motorola has opened a new factory .... computer chips.

❸ Prepositions + -ing

Complete the sentences with one word from each box.

before	~~after~~	at
in	for	of

doing	dealing	leaving
~~having~~	speaking	watching

1 I get up at 6.30. Then, *after having* breakfast at 7.00, I catch the train at 7.40.
2 You need to speak to Mrs Davies about this problem. She is responsible _____ _____ with complaints.
3 You'll need to help Joe with this project. He is not capable _____ _____ it by himself.
4 I like playing golf, but I'm not interested _____ _____ it on TV.
5 This job involves a lot of international travel, so we need someone who is good _____ _____ English.
6 I usually check my emails again in the evening _____ _____ the office and going home.

❹ Review

Complete the CV with the infinitive or the *-ing* form of the verbs in brackets.

Education and courses

Malston High School	When I left school, I went to Bristol [1] *to study* (study) economics, as I
Ecole Stanislas, Paris	wanted a degree [2] _____ (get) a good job. Last Easter I went to Paris [3] _____ (do) a short course in Business French, and I am thinking about [4] _____ (start) a new language next year – maybe Spanish or German.

Work experience

Marks and Spencer	When I was a student, I worked at Marks and Spencer (Summer 2003, 2004)
HSBC Bank	in the holidays [5] _____ (earn) extra money and also [6] _____ (get)
(Summer 2005)	experience of [7] _____ (work) in retailing. In my second year there, I was responsible for [8] _____ (organize) special promotions. Last year I got a job in a bank because I was interested in [9] _____ (find out) more about finance.

Interests

Football	I am keen on [10] _____ (play) football and other team games.
Tennis	At university I was the captain of the tennis team and was in charge of
Guitar	[11] _____ (organize) matches against other teams.
	I am quite good at [12] _____ (play) the classical guitar. At the moment I am preparing to take Grade 5.

OVER TO YOU

Imagine you are at an interview. Answer these questions about yourself.

1 A: Are you the sort of person who lives to work, or someone who works to live?
   B: I am the sort of person who lives to work.
2 A: Tell me about your qualities and skills. What are you good at?
   B: _____
3 A: And now be honest. What are you bad at?
   B: _____
4 A: Tell me about some of the responsibilities you have in your current job.
   B: _____
5 A: And away from work, what are your hobbies and interests?
   B: _____

41 Verbs + infinitive

a **Verb + object + infinitive**

These common verbs can be followed by an object (*him, it, the man,* etc.) and the infinitive:

advise	*ask*	*tell*	*would like*
allow	*persuade*	*want*	

*I **want** you to send that letter today.*
*They **allow** us to use their database.*
*She **has advised** him to move to another department.*
*The boss **told** me to come back later.*
*We **would like** you to reduce your prices.*

❗ Do not use *that* after *want* and *would like.*
wrong: *Mrs Quintana wants ~~that you contact~~ her today.*
right: *Mrs Quintana wants **you to contact** her today.*

b ***make* and *let***

After *make* and *let* we use an object (*him, it, the man,* etc.) + bare infinitive. We use *make* for things that people do not want to do. We use *let* for things that people want to do.
*Jo's boss **made** her write the report again.* (not ~~to write~~)
(She didn't want to do it again, but he told her to.)
*My boss **let** me have the day off.* (not ~~to have~~)
(I wanted the day off, and she said it was OK.)

1 **Verb + object + infinitive**

Read the instructions and write what the manager said to her staff.

1 Julia, could you get hold of Herr Maier?
2 Hans, check the contracts.
3 Paula, write the report again.
4 OK Georg, you can leave early.
5 Tim, you should apply for a promotion.
6 Frieda, I think you should do a course on presentations.

1 She asked Julia to get hold of Herr Maier.
2 She wanted Hans _____ .
3 She told _____ .
4 She allowed _____ .
5 She persuaded _____ .
6 She advised _____ .

2 Verb + object + infinitive

Say if the sentences are right or wrong and correct the mistakes.

1 Would you like ~~for~~ us to send you an estimate?   wrong   Would you like us
2 I would like to ask you something.
3 Jan wants that you go up to her office.
4 I told to you to be more careful.
5 Would you like for me to give you a hand?
6 There's someone I want you to meet.
7 Do they allow to you to smoke at work?
8 I want to ask you to do me a favour.

3 make and let

A manager of a new health resort is giving an interview to a local magazine about his clients. Look at the pictures. What does he *make* them do? What does he *let* them do?

1 go for long runs   He makes them go for long runs.
2 watch TV in the evenings
3 relax in the swimming pool
4 eat very small meals
5 work out in the gym
6 have cold showers

OVER TO YOU

Complete the sentences about you and your boss.

1 My boss allows me to organize my own time.
2 My boss doesn't allow me _____ .
3 My boss sometimes asks me _____ .
4 My boss never asks me _____ .
5 My boss would like me _____ .
6 My boss sometimes lets me _____ .
7 My boss never lets me _____ .
8 My boss makes me _____ .

42 Adjectives
-ing and -ed

ⓐ Adjectives ending in -ed

Adjectives ending in *-ed* tell you how someone feels:

> *Mr Kennedy is **interested in** photography.*
>
> (= Mr Kennedy likes photography. He wants to learn more about it.)

Here are some pairs of adjectives with similar meanings. The second adjective in each pair is stronger:

annoyed – infuriated	*excited – thrilled*	*surprised – amazed*
confused – bewildered	*frightened – terrified*	*tired – exhausted*
disappointed – depressed	*interested – fascinated*	*uninterested – bored*

ⓑ Adjectives ending in -ing

Adjectives ending in *-ing* tell you how something makes you feel. They tell you about the effect something has on people:

> *Laura arrived home after a **tiring** journey.*
>
> (= It was a long journey. It made her feel tired.)

annoying – infuriating	*exciting – thrilling*	*surprising – amazing*
confusing – bewildering	*frightening – terrifying*	*tiring – exhausting*
disappointing – depressing	*interesting – fascinating*	*uninteresting – boring*

ⓒ -ed or -ing?

Adjectives ending in *-ing* tell us what something is like.
Adjectives ending in *-ed* describe the result or effect:

> *Friedrich's presentation was **boring**. Everyone was **bored**.*

① Adjectives ending in -ed

Complete the puzzle with the missing words. Find the key word which is a capital city.

1 He did the same job every day for twenty years, so he was ....

2 I was .... to see Hans in London. I thought he was in Geneva.

3 After her long day's work, Amy was very ....

4 I was .... because he cancelled the meeting and didn't tell me.

5 I was .... that we didn't meet our sales target last month. Maybe this month will be better.

6 I am .... in the news, so I buy a paper every day.

7 Peter says it costs $12. David says it costs $22. Ken says it costs $9. I am .... !

8 The sales team is very .... about the new car – it will sell really well.

The key word is: ....

② Adjectives ending in -ing

Put the letters in brackets in the right order and complete the sentences.

1 I enjoy travelling, but long flights are tiring (giinrt).
2 It is very _ o _ _ _ _ (bginor) to do the same job day after day after day.
3 That is very _ n _ _ _ _ _ _ _ _ (geeiinnrstt) news – tell me more.
4 The Paris Metro is easy to understand, but the London Underground is very
  _ _ _ f _ _ _ _ _ (cfginnosu).
5 It is _ _ _ _ p _ _ _ _ _ _ _ _ (gadiioinnppst) that we didn't get the contract, but we can try
  again next year.
6 'RobotKill' is an _ _ c _ _ _ _ _ (cegiintx) computer game that teenagers will love.
7 The new program is OK, but it has a few _ _ _ o _ _ _ _ (gainnnoy) little problems.
8 I never watch horror movies. I don't like _ _ _ g _ _ _ _ _ _ _ (efgghiinnrt) films.

③ -ed or -ing?

Complete the true story about Bruce Dickinson with the -ed or -ing form of the words in brackets.

If you travelled on the airline Astraeus, you might be [1] amazed (amaze) to hear that your pilot was the famous rock star Bruce Dickinson of Iron Maiden. Most people would be [2] _____ (thrill) to be a successful rock star, but Bruce wanted to do something different.

A few years ago, he began to find the lifestyle [3] _____ (exhaust). He was always [4] _____ (fascinate) by planes, and so he started training as a pilot.

Now he does both jobs, and flies Boeing 747s as a second career. If he ever begins to find airports [5] _____ (bore), he can always change clothes, pick up a guitar, and give an [6] _____ (excite) concert.

OVER TO YOU

Write sentences about yourself or your colleagues with the words below.

1 annoyed   I was annoyed when I didn't get a bonus last year.
2 surprised   ....
3 tired   ....
4 confused   ....
5 excited   ....
6 interesting   ....

Write sentences about how these things make you feel.

7 your work   ....
8 your journey to work   ....
9 learning English   ....
10 travelling on business   ....

43 Adjectives and adverbs (1)

ⓐ Adjectives

An adjective tells us more about a noun. Adjectives come before the noun or after the verb *to be*:

A: *What did they order?*
B: *They ordered the **new** software and a **hard** drive.*

A: *What are your colleagues like?*
B: *They are **nice**.*

❗ Remember that adjectives do not change with plural nouns.
wrong: *I'm looking for two ~~olds~~ files.*
right: *I'm looking for two **old files**.*

ⓑ Adverbs – form

Many adverbs are made by adding *-ly* to the adjective:

	Adjective		Adverb
My new PA is	slow.	She works	slowly.
	careful.		carefully.
	neat.		neatly.
	quick.		quickly.
	efficient.		efficiently.

ⓒ Adverbs – use

An adverb tells us more about a verb. Many adverbs that describe actions end in *-ly*. These usually come after the verb or verb + noun:

*My boss drives **slowly**.*   (verb + adverb)
*My boss drives his company car **slowly**.*   (verb + noun + adverb)

① Adjectives

This is a report about a new MP3 player. Put the words in the right order. Write the sentences in the 'Good' column or the 'Bad' column.

1 attractive/The/is/design
2 instructions/are/The/simple
3 is/high/price/The
4 It/is/reliable/not

5 has/a/It/small/hard/disk
6 expensive/uses/It/batteries
7 The/is/bright/screen
8 support/There/excellent/is/customer

Good	Bad
The design is attractive.	The _____
The _____ .	It _____
The _____ .	It _____
There _____ .	It _____

2 Adverbs – form

Change the adjectives in the box to adverbs and complete the sentences.

> bad   careful   immediate   silent   slow   sudden   ~~urgent~~

1 We need more IT specialists *urgently*.
2 In October 1987, the stock market crashed _____ .
3 This is urgent! Reply _____ by phone or email.
4 Please listen _____ to the instructions.
5 The company did _____ last year and lost money.
6 The new printer is great. It works almost _____ .
7 We are going to be late. The traffic is moving very _____ .

3 Adjective or adverb?

Choose the correct option from the words in *italics*.

A: Are you OK?
B: Yes, I'm ¹*fine/finely,* thanks.
A: I don't like driving ²*slow/slowly*.
B: No, I noticed.
A: But I drive ³*careful/carefully*.
B: I'm ⁴*glad/gladly* to hear it!

A: Johnson, I want to ask you a
⁵*simple/simply* question.
B: OK, boss.
A: Did you check the figures
⁶*careful/carefully*?
B: Um … I looked at them
⁷*quick/quickly*.
A: I see. Well, we have a
⁸*serious/seriously* problem.

OVER TO YOU

Write true sentences about you and your work. Use one word from each set or use your own ideas.

> (big, small, old)   (amusing, nice, helpful)   (interesting, tiring, boring)
> (casually, smartly, fashionably)   (slowly, badly, accurately)   (confidently, badly, fluently)

1 What is your company like?   It's a very big organization.
2 What are your colleagues like?   _____ .
3 What is your job like?   _____ .
4 How do you dress at work?   _____ .
5 How do you type?   _____ .
6 How well do you speak English?   _____ .

44 Adjectives and adverbs (2)

PRESENTATION **ⓐ Adjectives and irregular adverbs**

Some adverbs and adjectives are the same:

Adjective	Adverb
It's a **hard** decision.	Anna works **hard**.
I would like a **fast** car.	Don't drive so **fast**.
It's a **straight** road.	I went **straight** to the office.
I'm on the **early** flight.	I need to get up **early**.
You can catch a **late** train.	I arrived at work **late**.

Some words that end in *-ly* are adjectives, not adverbs:

friendly **lonely** **lovely** **daily** **monthly** **quarterly** **hourly**

*My boss is a **friendly** guy.*

ⓑ *good* and *well*

Take extra care with *good* and *well*.
good is an adjective:
*2004 was a very **good** year for the company.*
well is the adverb from *good*:
*In 2004, the company did **well**.* (not ~~goodly~~)

But *well* can also be an adjective:
A: *How are you?*   B: *I'm very **well**, thank you.*

ⓒ Verbs of the senses + adjectives

We use adjectives, not adverbs, after the following verbs:
look, sound, smell, taste, feel.
*The new design **looks good**.*
*I like that idea – it **sounds interesting**.*
*I don't like this plan – it **doesn't feel right**.*

PRACTICE **① Adjectives and irregular adverbs**
Put the word in brackets in the right place.

1 (hard) Thank you all for your work.   Thank you all for your hard work.
2 (early) My boss never goes home. ....
3 (fast) Our company is growing. ....
4 (fast) Peter is a learner. ....
5 (hard) You work, so you will get a rise. ....
6 (early) The train leaves at 6.13 a.m. ....

2 Adjectives with -ly

Make adjectives from the words in the box and complete the sentences.

| quarter   friend   day   month |

1 Someone delivers the _____ newspapers every morning.
2 She seems very _____ and I like her a lot.
3 The Bank publishes its _____ report in May, August, November, and February.
4 I am going to miss the _____ meetings in May and June.

3 good and well

Complete the sentences with good or well.

1 He is a very good customer of ours.
2 I felt that the day went very _____ .
3 The cars left the factory in _____ condition.
4 I hope things are going _____ .
5 He has left hospital and will be _____ again soon.
6 She gave me some _____ advice.
7 The program has worked _____ .
8 I think this is a _____ investment.

4 Verbs of the senses + adjectives

Jane, Adam, and Ivan work for a coffee company, Wilson's. They are talking about a new product. Complete the dialogue with the correct form of the words in brackets.

Jane: So, Adam, what do you think of the new coffee?
Adam: I like it a lot – [1]it tastes good (it/taste/good). I think people will like it.
Ivan: Yes, I agree – and [2]_____ (it/smell/really nice) too – just like filter coffee.
Jane: OK, so the coffee is fine. Now, what do you think of the name? They want to call it 'Wilson's Brown'.
Ivan: I'm sorry, but I don't like the name 'Wilson's Brown' at all. I think [3]_____ (it/sound/terrible).
Adam: You're right – maybe we can call it 'Wilson's Gold' or 'Extra' or 'Classic' – [4]_____ (they/sound/OK), but 'brown' is not a good idea.
Jane: OK, so we'll think about the name again. What about the label? [5]_____ (it/look/all right)?
Adam: Yes, I think (it/look/fine) [6]_____ .
Jane: Ivan, [7]_____ (you/not look/very happy) about it. Is there a problem?
Ivan: I don't like the black and white. I think [8]_____ (it/look/boring). It needs a warm colour – red or gold perhaps.
Jane: OK, I'll tell design – and thanks for your help.

OVER TO YOU

Write true sentences, using an adjective or adverb, about:

1 your journey to work

I get to work fast.
I usually have a good journey.

2 your boss _____ .
3 when you get to work _____ .
4 how often you have meetings _____ .
5 what your office looks like _____ .
6 how well you speak English _____ .

PRESENTATION

ⓐ Adverbs of frequency

Look at the information about five parcel delivery companies:

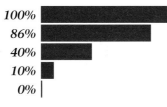

100%	PDQ *always* delivers on time.
86%	Inter Post *usually/often* delivers on time.
40%	Mail Inc. *sometimes* delivers on time
10%	Parcel Express *hardly ever/rarely* delivers on time.
0%	Track Box *never* delivers on time.

ⓑ Word order

Look at the word order of *always, usually, sometimes, hardly ever, never*:

Before the main verb:	PDQ *always comes* on time.
After *to be* (am, is, are, was, were):	PDQ *is usually* very polite.
Between verbs with two parts:	PDQ *has never made* a mistake.

ⓒ Expressions of frequency

We can also talk about frequency like this:

once a day, twice a week, three times a month, four times a year, etc.

These expressions come at the end of the sentence:
*Jason goes to London **once a week**. (every Tuesday)*
*I check my emails **twice a day**. (at 10.00 and 3.30)*
*We publish a report **four times a year**. (in March, June, September, December)*

PRACTICE

① Adverbs of frequency

Read Jill's answers to this questionnaire. Then write sentences about Jill.

Are you a workaholic?

	Always	Often	Sometimes	Hardly ever	Never
1 I talk about work at home.		■			
2 I contact the office during the holidays.				■	
3 I forget birthdays and other family occasions.			■		
4 I spend time on my hobbies at weekends.		■			
5 I work from home at weekends.					■
6 I arrive early for work.			■		
7 I eat and work at the same time.	■				
8 I have time to relax in the evening.				■	

(How to score: for questions 1,2,3,5,6,7; always = 5 often = 4 sometimes = 3 hardly ever = 2 never = 1
for questions 4 and 8: always = 1 often = 2 sometimes = 3 hardly ever = 4 never = 5
Your score: 30 – 40 You work much too hard. Take a break. 11 – 29 You have a good balance of work and home.
0 – 10 You need to work much harder or you'll get fired.)

1 She often talks about work at home.
2 _____ .
3 _____ .
4 _____ .
5 _____ .
6 _____ .
7 _____ .
8 _____ .

Now answer the questionnaire yourself.

❷ Word order

Put the words in brackets in the right place.

1	(never)	I smoke in the office.	I never smoke in the office.
2	(always)	Our meetings are useful.	_____ .
3	(hardly ever)	José takes time off.	_____ .
4	(always)	Mr Jackson has worked for us.	_____ .
5	(usually)	Do you drive to work?	_____ .
6	(hardly ever)	Pierre is late for meetings.	_____ .
7	(sometimes)	I fly Business Class.	_____ .
8	(always)	Anna gets to work a little early.	_____ .
9	(usually)	My boss doesn't check my work.	_____ .
10	(hardly ever)	The CEO is here.	_____ .

❸ Expressions of frequency

Look at the dates and times, and complete the sentences.

1	10 April, 30 April	We meet for lunch twice a month.
2	Monday, Wednesday, Friday	I use the company gym _____ .
3	9.30, 3.30	The post comes _____ .
4	June 2005, December 2005, June 2006	We have a big sales conference _____ .
5	2003, 2004, 2005, 2006	The company report comes out _____ .
6	5 May, 5 June, 5 July	I pay my credit card bill _____ .
7	Monday 6 a.m., Tuesday 6 a.m.	We run anti-virus software _____ .

OVER TO YOU

Answer these questions about yourself. Use *always, sometimes, once a week, three times a year*, etc.

1 How often do you give presentations? I give presentations once a month.
2 How often do you get angry with people? I never get angry with people.
3 How often do you come to work by car? _____ .
4 How often do you fly Business Class? _____ .
5 How often do you have meetings? _____ .
6 How often are you early for work? _____ .
7 How often are you late for work? _____ .
8 How often do you go out with friends? _____ .
9 How often do you take exercise? _____ .
10 How often do you go on holiday? _____ .

46

Comparing adjectives (1)
older than

ⓐ Short adjectives

We compare one-syllable adjectives like **old** and **young** by adding **-er** and using the word **than**:
  Krista is 28 years old.   *Lars is 43 years old.*
  *Krista is **younger than** Lars. Lars is **older than** Krista.*
We compare some two-syllable words in the same way:

narrow – narrower	clear – clearer	quiet – quieter

  *This part of the city is **quieter than** the centre.*

ⓑ Spelling

If the adjective ends with a short vowel and one consonant,
we repeat the last letter and add **-er**.

hot – hotter	big – bigger	fit – fitter

  *New York is **bigger than** Washington DC.*

If the adjective has two syllables and ends in **-y**, we add **-ier**.

easy – easier	sunny – sunnier	funny – funnier

  *Corsica is **sunnier than** Ireland.*

Corsica   Ireland

ⓒ *good* and *bad*

The adjectives **good** and **bad** are irregular:

good – better
bad – worse

  *This year's results are **better than** last year's.*
  *Last year's results were **worse than** this year's.*

① Short adjectives

Write sentences from the notes about two Personal Digital Assitants.

The **Filebox** seems very big and heavy, but it is very fast and has a great screen. The **DX9** is quite fast, comes at a really good price, and has a nice design.		DX9	FILEBOX
	Size:	*****	**
	Weight:	****	**
	Speed:	***	****
	Screen brightness:	****	*****
	Price:	*****	**
	Design:	*****	***

1 DX9/small/Filebox   The DX9 is smaller than the Filebox.
2 DX9/light/Filebox
3 Filebox/fast/DX9
4 Filebox/bright/DX9
5 DX9/cheap/Filebox
6 DX9/nice/Filebox

❷ Spelling

Complete the dialogue with the comparative form of the adjectives in brackets.

John: Hi, Sara, how is the new job?

Sara: Hi, John. It's fine thanks, and I'm much ¹**happier** (happy) now.

John: That's great. By the way, where's your office? Are you still in town?

Sara: No, we're in Wales now, right in the countryside. It's ² _____ (quiet) than London, of course, but it's much ³ _____ (pretty), and my office is a lot ⁴ _____ (big) than the old one.

John: What's the journey like?

Sara: It's great – I go in by bike every day. It means I'm a lot ⁵ _____ (fit) than I was.

John: Do you ever take the train to work?

Sara: No. The journey's a bit ⁶ _____ (long), but it's much ⁷ _____ (easy) than going into the middle of London.

❸ *good* and *bad*

Say if the sentences are right or wrong and correct the mistakes.

1 I need to move to ~~a more better room~~, please.   wrong   a better room

2 I hope our sales figures next month are better.   _____ _____

3 The new model is gooder than the last one.   _____ _____

4 The problems were more bad than I thought.   _____ _____

5 The economic situation is getting worse.   _____ _____

6 My new PC is more better than the old one.   _____ _____

OVER TO YOU ## Comparing countries

Look at the pictures. Write sentences comparing the UK with your country. Use one of the words in brackets to help you.

1 the weather in the UK (*cold, hot,* or *good*?)

4 Public transport (*cheap, good,* or *slow*?)

2 British food (*nice, cheap,* or *good*?)

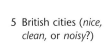

3 The cost of living (*high* or *low*?)

5 British cities (*nice, clean,* or *noisy*?)

1 The weather in Spain is better than the weather in the UK.

2 _____ .

3 _____ .

4 _____ .

5 _____ .

47

Comparing adjectives (2)
more modern than

a Long adjectives (two or more syllables)

For long adjectives, we use *more than*. The adjective does not change:

modern – *more modern than*	elementary – *more elementary than*
difficult – *more difficult than*	cosmopolitan – *more cosmopolitan than*

Gold is *more expensive than* silver.
Calculus is *more difficult than* arithmetic.
Email is *more modern than* telegraphs.

! Remember that after the adjective, we use *than*. We do not use *as* or *that*.
wrong: *The Lexus is more expensive as a Fiat.*
wrong: *The Lexus is more expensive that a Fiat.*
right: *The Lexus is more expensive than a Fiat.*

! Remember that we do not use *more … than* with short adjectives.
wrong: *Is London more big than Paris?*
right: *Is London bigger than Paris?*

! Short adjectives which end in *-ed* (pleased, tired, etc.) use *more … than*.
wrong: *I think I'm pleaseder than him to be here.*
right: *I think I'm more pleased than him to be here.*

b *not as … as*

To make a negative comparison, we can use *not as … as* with short or long adjectives. The adjectives do not change:
Economy class seats are *not as wide as* business class seats.
Economy class is *not as comfortable as* business class.

1 Long adjectives

Read the sentences and correct the mistakes.

1 Champagne is more expensiver than table wine.   *is more expensive than*
2 My boss is more younger than me.
3 My current job is interesting more than my last one.
4 Supermarkets are more convenient small shops.
5 My new laptop is moderner than my old one.
6 Planes are more faster than trains.
7 Do you think Japanese is difficulter than English?
8 Moscow is more colder than London.

② *Long adjectives*

Look at the pictures. Write sentences about the two places with the words in the box.

crowded
peaceful
exciting
developed
traditional
popular
tranquil
old-fashioned

Paxos

Ibiza

1 Paxos is more peaceful than Ibiza.   5 Ibiza is more crowded than Paxos.
2 _____ .   6 _____ .
3 _____ .   7 _____ .
4 _____ .   8 _____ .

③ *not as ... as*

Rewrite the sentences with *not as ... as* and the words in the box.

hot   dangerous   fast   expensive   ~~big~~   tall

1 Lauda Air is smaller than British Airways.
  Lauda Air is not as big as British Airways.
2 Gold is cheaper than platinum.
  Gold _____ .
3 The Empire State Building is shorter than the Petronas Towers.
  The Empire State Building _____ .
4 Italian food is milder than Thai food.
  Italian food _____ .
5 Cars are safer than motorbikes.
  Cars _____ .
6 Our Internet connection at home is slower than the one at work.
  Our Internet connection at home _____ .

④ **Review**

Complete the text with the comparative form of the words in brackets.

If you're unhappy in your work, that's great, according to new research from Canada.

The researchers say that unhappy people are ¹ **better** (good) at their work than happy employees. Sad workers seem to be ² _____ (careful) than happy ones, and they concentrate on what they are doing.

Happy workers, on the other hand, are ³ _____ (not/productive) as unhappy ones. They talk too much, waste a lot of time and are ⁴ _____ (not/reliable) as their sad co-workers. If bosses start to think that happy workers are ⁵ _____ (lazy) than unhappy ones, they will have to try and make everyone as miserable as possible.

OVER TO YOU

Write true sentences about yourself from the notes.

1 I/old/my boss   I am not as old as my boss.
2 My current job/interesting/my last job   _____ .
3 I/young/my boss   _____ .
4 The company I work for/famous/Microsoft   _____ .
5 We/good/our main competitors   _____ .
6 I/experienced/some of my colleagues   _____ .
7 I/happy/some of my colleagues   _____ .
8 I/rich now/when I was a student   _____ .

48 Superlatives
oldest, most expensive

PRESENTATION **ⓐ Short adjectives**

When we compare three or more things with a short adjective, we can add *-est* to the adjective. We usually put *the* before the adjective:

> *The Plaza 66 is tall.*
> *The Jin Mao Tower is taller than the Plaza 66.*
> *The World Financial Centre is **the tallest** building in Shanghai.*

For spelling rules, see page 150.

We also compare two-syllable adjectives ending in *-y* (*easy, sunny, funny*) in this way:

> *Majorca is sunny.*
> *Tunisia is sunnier than Majorca.*
> *Cyprus is **the sunniest** winter destination.*

⚠ Short adjectives which end in *-ed* (pleased, tired, etc.) use *the most*.
wrong: *Johann is ~~the tiredest~~ of all of us.*
right: *Johann is **the most tired** of all of us.*

Top Winter Sun Tourist Destinations
HOURS OF SUNSHINE (February average)

Majorca	6
Tunisia	6.5
Cyprus	7

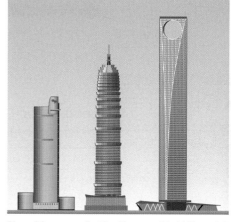

Plaza 66 (288m) Jin Mao Tower (421m) World Financial Centre (492m)

ⓑ Longer adjectives

When we compare three or more things with a long adjective, we use *the most*:

ZEN €60   JUDE €70   ASPIRE €75

> *Zen is expensive.*
> *Jude is more expensive than Zen.*
> *Aspire is **the most expensive**.*

ⓒ Irregular forms

The superlative forms of *good* and *bad* are irregular:

> *The results in May were good.*   *Sales in January were bad.*
> *The results in June were better.*   *Sales in February were worse.*
> *The results in October were **the best**.* *Sales in April were **the worst**.*

① Short adjectives

Complete the text with the superlative form of the adjectives in brackets.

At the Geneva Motor Show, the big car makers showed us a picture of the future.

¹The **newest** (new) cars from car-making alliance TPCA (Toyota, Peugeot, Citroen, Alliance) are special because they are some of ²_____ (cheap) cars they have ever made. The Citroen C1, Peugeot 107, and Toyota Aygo, which will cost about €8,500, all have the same basic design. Toyota, now one of ³_____ (big) car makers in the world, provides the engines, and the cars are all made in the same factory in Kolin, where labour costs are among ⁴_____ (low) in Europe. Cheap does not mean bad quality. The new range has one of ⁵_____ (clean) engines of any modern car, and meets ⁶_____ (late) standards for CO_2 emissions.

② Longer adjectives

Complete the text with the superlative form of the adjectives in brackets.

One of the stars of the show was the new Aston Martin V8 Vantage. According to Aston boss Ullrich Bez, it is ¹the **most compact** (compact) car that Aston Martin has made for many years, and at only €100,000, it is ²_____ (affordable) Aston Martin ever. The V8 is ³_____ (important) car in the company's history because it will compete with rivals like the Porsche 911. They do not expect to sell as many units as Porsche, but are sure that the V8 Vantage will be ⁴_____ (popular) car they have ever made. At the top of the range at Geneva was the Bugatti Veyron from the VW Group. With a top speed of about 400 kph, this was ⁵_____ (powerful) car on display. But with a price tag of $1 million, it was also ⁶_____ (expensive), and they only plan to make 300 units.

③ Irregular forms

Complete the text with the superlative form of the adjectives in brackets.

One of ¹the **best-looking** (good-looking) concept cars at the show is the Mitsubishi Nessie 4x4. In general, 4x4 SUVs* have ²_____ (bad) figures for CO_2 emissions of any kind of car, but the Nessie is different. It has a new hydrogen engine, which will give it ³_____ (good) CO_2 emissions figure possible – 0%. And with its powerful engine and 4x4 design, the Mitsubishi Nessie will be able to handle ⁴_____ (bad) driving conditions with ease.

*SUV = Sports Utility Vehicle

④ Review

Read the sentences and correct the mistakes.

1 In 2001, we had ~~the most best~~ results ever.   the best
2 Remington is the most old gunmaker in the US.   _____
3 Wal-Mart is the company the largest in the world.   _____
4 London is the most biggest city in England.   _____
5 That was the worse presentation I have ever heard.   _____
6 The GTX2 is the product most successful we have ever made. _____
7 They say the Bangkok Oriental is the better hotel in the world. _____
8 Intel's latest chip is the most smallest processor they have ever made. _____

Make sentences with the superlative using the notes and your own ideas.

1 good decision/you have ever made Studying economics was the best decision I have ever made.
2 expensive thing/you own   _____ .
3 nice city/in your country   _____ .
4 interesting part/your job   _____ .
5 boring part/your job   _____ .
6 big company/in your country   _____ .
7 famous person/in your country   _____ .
8 rich person/in your country   _____ .

49 *too* and *not … enough*

a *too* and *not … enough* with adjectives

We can use use *too* + adjective when we are talking about a problem:

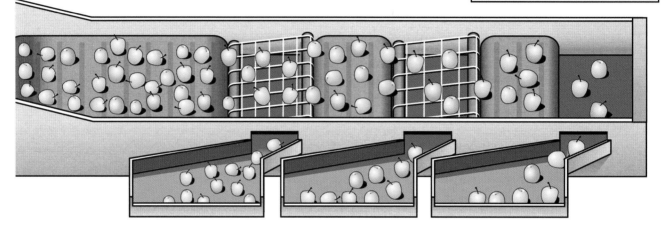

QUALITY CONTROL

These apples are 90g.	*These apples are 115g.*	*These apples are 145–160g.*
They are not OK.	*They are OK.*	*They are not OK.*
There is a problem.		*There is a problem.*
They are too small.	*No problem.*	*They are too big.*

We can also use *not* + adjective + *enough* to talk about problems like this:
The 90g apples are not big enough. The 160g apples are not small enough.

❗ Remember that the adjective comes before the word *enough*, not after it.
wrong: *Turn on the heater, please. It is ~~not enough warm~~ in here.*
right: *Turn on the heater, please. It is not warm enough in here.*

b *too* and *not … enough* with adverbs

We can use *too* and *not … enough* in the same way with adverbs:
I can't understand Mrs Morales. She speaks too fast.
I can't understand Mrs Morales. She doesn't speak slowly enough.

c *too* and *not enough* with nouns

We can use *too much, too many,* and *not enough* with nouns. We use *too much* with uncountable nouns like *money, information, traffic,* etc. (see Unit 56):
There is too much traffic.

We use *too many* with countable nouns like *books, cars, apples,* etc.:
There are too many cars.

We use *not enough* with countable or uncountable nouns:
There aren't enough roads. There isn't enough space.

❗ Remember that nouns come after the word *enough*.
wrong: *I can't finish the project. I haven't got ~~time enough~~.*
right: *I can't finish the project. I haven't got enough time.*

1 *too* and *not ... enough* with adjectives

Read the text. Write two sentences for each topic with *too* and *not ... enough* and the adjectives in the box.

Our Tests A portable printer needs to be small and light – at 3.5 kg, this is neither. Noise levels were very high, print quality was OK, but very, very slow. The P3 costs $320, so, all in all, this is not a good buy.

SUMMARY:

Size	3/10	Noise	4/10		
Print quality	7/10	Speed	2/10	Price	2/10
VERDICT: **2/10**		RECOMMENDED? **NO**			

1 Size   It was too big.
         It was not small enough.

2 Noise   _____ .
         _____ .

3 Speed   _____ .
         _____ .

4 Price   _____ .
         _____ .

cheap   ~~big~~
expensive fast
noisy   quiet
slow   ~~small~~

2 *too* and *not ... enough* with adverbs

Read the sentences about Robert's presentations. Correct the mistakes by moving one word.

1 You speak quietly too.   You speak too quietly.
2 You don't prepare enough carefully.   _____ .
3 You talk fast too.   _____ .
4 You don't explain the ideas enough slowly. _____ .
5 You finish your talks early too.   _____ .
6 You don't answer the questions enough clearly. _____ .

3 *too* and *not enough* with nouns

Complete the text with *too much*, *too many*, or *not enough*.

There is one problem that many of the world's big cities share – terrible traffic.

From Athens to London, the cause of the problem is the same: there are ¹too many cars and there are ²not enough roads. Every morning, millions of people spend ³_____ time sitting in traffic jams. And at the end of the journey, they still have a problem because there are ⁴_____ places to park.

Many people use their cars because public transport is bad. At busy times you can wait for hours because there are ⁵_____ buses. When the bus finally arrives, it goes very slowly because there is ⁶_____ traffic on the streets. The metro is just as bad. Between 8.00 and 9.00 in the morning there is ⁷_____ space on the trains because there are ⁸_____ people on them.

In some cities, like London, there is now a 'congestion charge' – car drivers have to pay every time they enter the city. This has been very successful. In the past, there was ⁹_____ money to improve public transport. Now the money from the congestion charge is spent on trains and buses, so public transport is better and the streets are emptier.

Using *too* or *not ... enough*, say why you don't do these things.

Why don't you ...
1 buy a very big yacht? I am not rich enough. They are too expensive.
2 retire now? _____ .
3 buy a big apartment in New York? _____ .
4 run the company you work for? _____ .
5 get a holiday home in Alaska? _____ .
6 only work six hours a day? _____ .

50 Pronouns and possessives
I, me, my, mine

ⓐ Subject and object pronouns

We use subject pronouns to talk about the subject of a sentence and object pronouns to talk about the object:

Subject pronouns	I	you	he	she	it	we	they
Object pronouns	*me*	*you*	*him*	*her*	*it*	*us*	*them*

In statements, subject pronouns come before the verb:
*I work in Venezuela for Mr Garcia. **He** owns the company.*

In statements, object pronouns come after verbs or prepositions:
After verbs: *Peter phoned **me** and he wants **you** to call **him**.*
After prepositions: *I spoke to **her** briefly about it and she'll either send it to **you** or to **me**.*

ⓑ Possessives: *my, your, his*, etc.

We use these words to talk about things that belong to us:

my	*your*	*his*	*her*	*its*	*our*	*their*

This is my Porsche.

Are these your keys?

Peter is the Sales Manager. His desk is in the corner.

Sara is the secretary. Her desk is by the window.

This is a great product. Let me tell you about its features.

Vera and I work in Production. This is our office.

Bob and Dan work in R&D. Their office is on the fourth floor.

! Be careful with spelling.

it's = it is	*This is my new computer. It's great.*
its = belonging to it	*I really like its design.*
they're = they are	*Bob and Dan are away. They're in Australia.*
their = belonging to them	*Their office is free.*

ⓒ Possessives: *mine, yours, his*, etc.

When we do not want to repeat a noun, we can use the following words to show possession:

mine	*yours*	*his*	*hers*	*ours*	*theirs*

A: *Whose pen is this? Is it **yours**?*   (*yours* = your pen)
B: *No, **mine** is blue. Ask Jane. Maybe it's **hers**.*   (*mine* = my pen, *hers* = her pen)

1 Subject and object pronouns

Complete the sentences with the words in the box.

| I | ~~you~~ | you | he | him | her | it | ~~it~~ | we | us | they |

1 A: I saw the new catalogue this morning.
  B: Really? Do you think it looks nice?
2 A: Did the technician come to fix Ms Lawson's air conditioning?
  B: Yes, _____ came to fix _____ for _____ yesterday.
3 A: Did the sales reps tell Mr Low about you and me?
  B: Yes, _____ told _____ about _____ last week.
4 A: I really need a lift to the station. Can you help?
  B: No problem. _____ can take _____ there. _____ can leave at 5.00.

2 Possessives: *my, your, his,* etc.

Complete the dialogues with one word from each box.

| ~~their~~ | my | his | your | her |

| name | ~~hotel~~ | colleague | mobile | address |

A: I need to talk to John and Sally. Are they back from Germany yet?
B: No, they're still there.
A: Do you know the name of ¹ their hotel ?
B: No, I don't know where they're staying, but you can send John an email. I've got
² _____ _____ .
A: I really want to talk to Sally. Has she got ³ _____ _____ with her?
B: Yes, I think so. I'll get the number and you can phone her.

Alex: Pierre, I'd like you to meet ⁴ _____ _____ , Nora Watson.
Pierre: Hello, Nora. Nice to meet you.
Nora: I'm sorry, I didn't catch ⁵ _____ _____ .
Pierre: I'm Pierre Leblanc.
Nora: Nice to meet you, Pierre.

3 Possessives: *mine, yours, his,* etc.

Read the sentences and correct the mistakes.

1 Janet says this isn't her file. Is it ~~your~~?   Is it yours?
2 No, that's not my jacket. The mine is on the chair. _____
3 It's OK – we've got our tickets and they've got they're. _____
4 The problem is that their products are cheaper than the ours. _____
5 Are these yours keys or Mr Henderson's? _____
6 Maria knows my husband, but I don't know his. _____

Complete the sentences with your own ideas. Each sentence must finish with an object pronoun (*me, you, him, her,* etc.)

1 Mrs Gunnarson probably knows the answer. Why don't you _____ ?
2 I like our new assistant. What do you think _____ ?
3 He told me his name, but I _____ .
4 Some of the questions were hard and I couldn't _____ .
5 My boss is friendly and open, and you can always _____ .

Now complete the sentences in a way that is true for you.

6 Janet's boss is very demanding, but my boss isn't.
                 but mine is very relaxed.
7 Our competitors' products are very _____ , but _____ .
8 Our offices are very _____ , but _____ .
9 My journey to work is _____ , but _____ .

51 Reflexive pronouns
myself, yourself

PRESENTATION **ⓐ Form**

Look at the table showing how we make *myself, yourself,* etc.:

I pay for *myself*.	It pays for *itself*.
You pay for *yourself*.	We pay for *ourselves*.
He pays for *himself*.	You pay for *yourselves*.
She pays for *herself*.	They pay for *themselves*.

ⓑ Use

We use these reflexive pronouns when the person doing an action is also the object:

Jake is the owner of a large private company.
Zara is his secretary. He pays her $200 a month.
He pays himself $15,000 a month.

More examples:

Don is studying on the computer. He is teaching himself English.
Carla received her first pay rise. She bought herself a new car.

ⓒ by myself, etc.

by myself, by himself, etc. means *alone*:
Franz has no family. He lives by himself.

Myself can also mean *with no help from other people*:
Nobody helps me with the exhibitions. I do all the work myself.
You don't need a builder to paint the door. You can do it yourself.

ⓓ each other

If I do something to you, and you do the same thing to me, we can use *each other*:

I am writing to Catherine.	*I saw Zoltan at the conference.*
Catherine is writing to me.	*Zoltan saw me at the conference.*
We are writing to each other.	*We saw each other at the conference.*

PRACTICE **① Form**

Complete the sentences with *myself, yourself, himself,* etc.

1 Joanna is in hospital. She hurt herself at work yesterday.
2 Don't worry about me. I can look after ＿＿＿＿＿ .
3 Henri and Paul are self-employed. They work for ＿＿＿＿＿ .
4 The system overheated and shut ＿＿＿＿＿ down.
5 Peter, we want you to tell us a little about ＿＿＿＿＿ .
6 He came to the factory to see for ＿＿＿＿＿ how bad the damage was.
7 Sal and I have a family business. We pay ＿＿＿＿＿ $2,000 a month each.
8 We would like you and Mr Stone to make ＿＿＿＿＿ available for interview on the 23rd.

❷ Use

Choose the correct option from the words in *italics*.

1 My boss doesn't like travelling. He sends *me/~~myself~~* to meet important clients.
2 I don't like being late. I give *me/myself* lots of time for journeys.
3 This invoice is for Mr Turing. Please fax it to *him/himself*.
4 Hello, I'd like to introduce *me/myself*. My name is Enrico Real.
5 We never had any IT training. We taught *us/ourselves* to program.
6 Paul and Saffron need this information. Could you give it to *them/themselves*?

❸ *by myself*, etc.

Rewrite the words in *italics* with the words in the box.

~~himself~~	by himself	herself	ourselves
~~by ourselves~~	by herselfyourself	by yourself	by herself

1 He doesn't use an accountant. He does all his tax *without any help*. himself
2 Ali and I work *alone*. by ourselves
3 Did you write this report *without any help?* ⎯⎯⎯⎯
4 She is divorced now, and she lives *alone*. ⎯⎯⎯⎯
5 We don't have any secretaries here. We type our letters *without any help*. ⎯⎯⎯⎯
6 He spends lots of time thinking and planning and likes to be *alone*. ⎯⎯⎯⎯
7 She's the kind of manager who likes to do everything *without any help*. ⎯⎯⎯⎯
8 David is busy, so you will have to go to the meeting *alone*. ⎯⎯⎯⎯

❹ *each other*

Look at the pictures. Complete the sentences with *each other* or *themselves*.

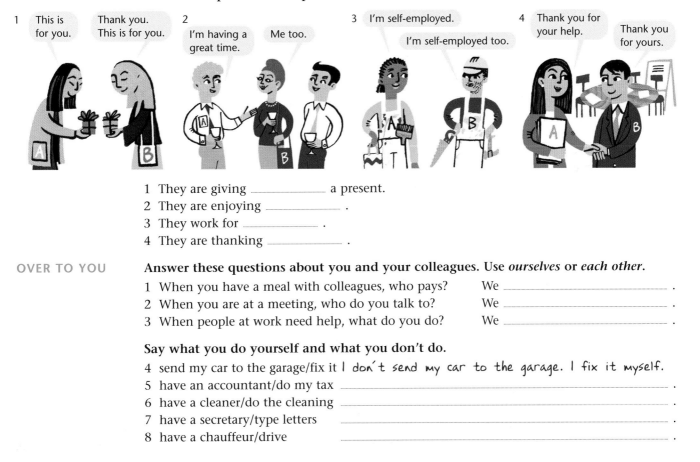

1 This is for you. / Thank you. This is for you.
2 I'm having a great time. / Me too.
3 I'm self-employed. / I'm self-employed too.
4 Thank you for your help. / Thank you for yours.

1 They are giving ⎯⎯⎯⎯ a present.
2 They are enjoying ⎯⎯⎯⎯ .
3 They work for ⎯⎯⎯⎯ .
4 They are thanking ⎯⎯⎯⎯ .

OVER TO YOU

Answer these questions about you and your colleagues. Use *ourselves* or *each other*.

1 When you have a meal with colleagues, who pays?   We ⎯⎯⎯⎯ .
2 When you are at a meeting, who do you talk to?   We ⎯⎯⎯⎯ .
3 When people at work need help, what do you do?   We ⎯⎯⎯⎯ .

Say what you do yourself and what you don't do.

4 send my car to the garage/fix it I don't send my car to the garage. I fix it myself.
5 have an accountant/do my tax ⎯⎯⎯⎯ .
6 have a cleaner/do the cleaning ⎯⎯⎯⎯ .
7 have a secretary/type letters ⎯⎯⎯⎯ .
8 have a chauffeur/drive ⎯⎯⎯⎯ .

PRESENTATION   **ⓐ**   *who* and *that*

We can use *who* or *that* to join two sentences or parts of a sentence. We use *who* or *that* to talk about people:

I know a woman. She works for HSBC.
*I know a woman **who** works for HSBC.* or *I know a woman **that** works for HSBC.*

ⓑ   *which* and *that*

We can use *which* or *that* to join two sentences or parts of a sentence. We use *which* or *that* to talk about things:

We make heating panels. They use solar power.
*We make heating panels **which** use solar power.* or *We make heating panels **that** use solar power.*

❗ The words *who*, *which*, and *that* replace the subject (*she, the car,* etc.). Do not repeat the subject.

wrong: *I know a woman who ~~she works~~ for HSBC.*
right: *I know a woman **who** works for HSBC.*
wrong: *We make heating panels which ~~they use~~ solar power.*
right: *We make heating panels **which** use solar power.*

ⓒ   *with*

We can use *with* to mean *who has, that has,* or *which has*:

My colleague is the woman over there who has long black hair.
*My colleague is the woman over there **with** long black hair.*

I've got a mobile phone which has a colour screen.
*I've got a mobile phone **with** a colour screen.*

PRACTICE   **①**   *who* and *that*

Read the job advertisements. Make sentences with the information in bold. Say what the companies want using *who* or *that*.

1
Wanted – Bilingual secretary. Must speak French and English. For further information reply to G K Hetherington, 18 Market Square

2
Wanted Sales assistant for our busy weekend fashions sales. **If you can work at weekends**, please contact us on 01927 34521 to find out more about joining our busy team

3
Tour Guides required for London-based travel company. **If you know London well**, and would like to show foreign visitors around London's sights, write to the Personnel Manager, Capital Travel

4
In-house Language Trainer needed for Japanese Bank. **Must have at least three years' experience of teaching English to executives**. For further details please contact

5
Holiday Representatives needed by busy Ibiza resort. Applicants **must have a good knowledge of Spanish**

6
Programmer required by small logistics company. **Must know C++ and Java**. Excellent salary and conditions. Please apply with CV and covering letter to

1 They are looking for a secretary **who speaks French and English.**
2 They are looking for ....
3 They ....
4 ....
5 ....
6 ....

② *which* and *that*

Make sentences with *which* or *that*. Use a word or phrase from each of the three columns.

A dictionary	motorbike	says what words mean
A studio	letter	travels on water
An email	phone	has one main room
A jetski	meeting	goes from one computer to another
An AGM	flat	takes place every year
A mobile	book	works almost anywhere

1 **A dictionary is a kind of book that says what words mean.**
2 A .... is a kind of ....
3 ....
4 ....
5 ....
6 ....

③ *with*

Look at the details of things that people have lost. Write down what they say at the lost property office.

1 Item: suitcase	2 Item: file	3 Item: keyring
Features: two red straps	Features: a label saying 'Tax letters'	Features: five keys and a small torch

4 Item: wallet	5 Item: a pair of glasses	6 Item: mobile phone
Features: €60 and a gold credit card	Features: black frames	Features: blue and white cover

1 **I've lost a suitcase with two red straps.**
2 ....
3 ....
4 ....
5 ....
6 ....

•VER TO YOU

Complete the sentences with *who, which, that,* or *with.*

1 I have a boss **who treats me very well.**
2 I've got a colleague ....
3 I know some people ....
4 I've got a computer ....
5 I'd like a job ....
6 I don't know anyone ....
7 I like people ....
8 I'd like a house ....

53 Articles (1)
a, an, the

PRESENTATION **a** *a or an?*

We use *a* with singular nouns that begin with a consonant sound:

a business	*a director*	*a gate*	*a company*	*a fax*	*a house*

We use *an* with singular nouns that begin with a vowel sound:

an assistant	*an executive*	*an idea*	*an office*	*an overdraft*	*an upgrade*

We also use *an* with adjectives that begin with a vowel sound:
   an interesting suggestion, an honest answer

! It is the first sound of the word, not the letter, that is important.
We use *an* with these words: *an hour   an MP   an MBA   an MEP   an NGO*
We use *a* with these words: *a USP   a university   a UN resolution   a Euro*

b *a* and *the*

We use *a* or *an* with singular nouns. We use *a* or *an* when we talk about an unspecified noun
for the first time:
   I have bought a modem and an anti-virus program.
We only know that she has bought one modem, not two or three. It is one of many in the
shop. We know she bought only one anti-virus program, not two or three.

The next time we talk about the same noun, we often use *the*:
   The modem cost $30 and the anti-virus program cost $45.

We also use *the* when the speaker and listener both know what the speaker is talking about:
   I'm going to the canteen – I'll be back in twenty minutes.

c No article

We usually use no article when we are talking about:
   uncountable nouns in general (see Unit 56)   *Money is important.*
   abstract nouns in general   *Happiness is important.*
   plural countable nouns in general (see Unit 56) *Computers are cheap these days.*

But when we talk about particular nouns we use *the*:
   Can you pay back the money I gave you last week?

PRACTICE **1** *a or an?*

Complete the dialogue with *a* or *an*.

Lars: Is Daniel going away next year?
Inga: Yes he's planning to do ¹ *an* MBA.
Lars: You know that if he goes, I'll need ² _____ new assistant.
Inga: That won't be ³ _____ problem. I know you can't run ⁴ _____ office like this with no
       help. But I don't know who.
Lars: I've got ⁵ _____ idea. Do you remember Karin?
Inga: Yes, she went to work in ⁶ _____ hospital in Africa.
Lars: That's right. She's working for ⁷ _____ NGO in Ghana, but I know she only had ⁸ _____
       one-year contract. I'll send her ⁹ _____ email – she can come for ¹⁰ _____ interview.

② *a* and *the*

Complete the dialogues with *a* or *the*.

Guest: Hello. I've got ¹ a room on the fourth floor and I'd like to change rooms, please.

Clerk: Is there a problem with ² _____ room, sir?

Guest: Yes. The problem is that ³ _____ room is very noisy.

Clerk: I'm very sorry. Let me look ... I can give you ⁴ _____ suite on the sixth floor.

Guest: Will it be quiet?

Clerk: Yes, sir. ⁵ _____ suite is very quiet and it also has ⁶ _____ nice view of ⁷ _____ sea.

Lars: I want to order ⁸ _____ projector and ⁹ _____ digital camera – is that OK?

Hans: What are they for?

Lars: I'm giving ¹⁰ _____ presentation and I need ¹¹ _____ projector for my talk.

Hans: When are you giving ¹² _____ presentation?

Lars: Next week.

Hans: How much are they?

Lars: ¹³ _____ projector is $1,680 and ¹⁴ _____ digital camera is $590.

Hans: That sounds OK, but make sure you keep ¹⁵ _____ receipt.

③ No article

Choose the correct option from the words in *italics*.

1 *Digital cameras/~~The digital cameras~~* are getting cheaper these days.
2 Can you use *mobile phones/the mobile phone*s on planes?
3 Did you look at *tools/the tools* in the catalogue?
4 The price of *oil/the oil* changes from week to week.
5 *Success/The success* usually comes after a lot of hard work.
6 *Freedom/The freedom* is important to everybody.

OVER TO YOU

Write sentences about some of your possessions and give details about them.

1 two new things you have at home
   say where you bought them

   I've got a TV and an MP3 player.
   I got the TV from a department store and I got the MP3 player from the Internet.

2 two things you use at work
   say what you use them for

   _____
   _____
   _____

3 two things you had ten years ago
   say what happened to them

   _____
   _____
   _____

4 two qualifications you have
   say where you studied for them

   _____
   _____
   _____

54 Articles (2)
a, an, the

PRESENTATION **ⓐ a, an, or no article**

We use *a* or *an* with jobs and professions:
  A: *What do you do?*   B: *I'm **an** architect.*
  A: *What does your father do?*   B: *He's **a** lawyer.*

When we talk about business sectors, we do not use an article:
  A: *What do you do?*   B: *I'm in computers.*

ⓑ Places

We use *the* when a place name has a noun like *republic, union, kingdom, state, coast,* etc.:

the United Kingdom	*the former Soviet Union*	*the Dominican Republic*
the United States	*the west coast*	*the east coast*	*the south coast*

We use *the* for rivers, canals, seas, oceans, groups of islands, and mountains:

the Seine	*the Suez Canal*	*the Mediterranean*	*the Atlantic*	*the Seychelles*	*the Alps*

We use *the* for hotels and restaurants:

the Oriental	*the Ritz*	*the Fat Duck*	*the Tour d'Argent*	*the Intercontinental*

Most cities, countries, and continents do not have an article:

London	*Berlin*	*France*	*Germany*	*Africa*	*Europe*

Streets and roads do not have an article:

Oxford Street	*Madison Avenue*

We use *the* for roads with letters and numbers:

the M25	*the N17*	*the A4*	*the B4134*

Airports, stations, and harbours do not have an article:

Charles de Gaulle Airport	*Paddington Station*	*Sydney Harbour*

ⓒ No article

We do not use an article for *breakfast, lunch,* or *dinner*:
  Let's have dinner at the Fat Duck.

We do not use an article in these expressions:

go to work/be at work/be away from work
go to hospital/be in hospital
go to university/go to school
go by bus/by car/by taxi/by plane
go home/stay at home/be at home

We do not use an article with names of people or companies:
  Bill Gates is the Chairman of Microsoft.

1 *a, an,* or no article

Complete the text with *a, an,* or Ø (no article).

THE CLIPPER YACHT RACE

The Clipper Round-The-World Yacht Race is an international sporting event that gives amateurs the chance to sail round the world. In the next race, which starts in September, ten identical boats will compete in a 30,000-mile race around the world.

FAQs

Can anyone join?

Yes, anyone can join. In the past we have had [1]_____ traffic warden, [2]_____ engineer, [3]_____ artist, and [4]_____ mechanic. Other crew members have been in [5]_____ sales and [6]_____ farming, so your background is not important.

What about emergencies?

Most crews will have [7]_____ doctor or [8]_____ nurse, or someone with medical experience. Each boat will also have [9]_____ full-time professional captain.

How much will it cost?

The total cost for the whole race is £28,000. Shorter sections start at £6,000.

2 Places

Complete the text with *the* or Ø (no article).

THE JOURNEY

The race will start in [1]_____ UK, and the boats will sail across [2]_____ Atlantic Ocean to [3]_____ Brazil. After a change of crew, they will sail round [4]_____ Cape of Good Hope to [5]_____ South Africa. The yachts will then sail to [6]_____ west coast of Australia, staying in [7]_____ Freemantle Harbour from 17 December to 1 January.

They will then race north via [8]_____ Singapore and on past [9]_____ Philippines towards [10]_____ China. After crossing [11]_____ North Pacific they will go down [12]_____ west coast of [13]_____ USA to [14]_____ Panama Canal. They will race across [15]_____ Caribbean, and in the final part they will cross [16]_____ Atlantic Ocean again and finish the race in [17]_____ England.

3 No article

Complete the text with *a* or Ø (no article).

FAQs (CONT)

Can I just do a part of the race?

Yes, if you can't be away from [1]_____ work for eight months, you can do one or more parts of the race. For example, you can sail from Australia to China and then go [2]_____ home by [3]_____ plane from Beijing.

Are the boats comfortable?

Not very. But you will have [4]_____ bed and storage space. There are toilets and there is [5]_____ small kitchen where you can cook [6]_____ lunch or [7]_____ dinner.

Who runs the race?

The race is organized by [8]_____ Robin Knox-Johnson, the head of [9]_____ Clipper Ventures plc.

Answer the questions with information about you.

1 What towns or cities (in your own country) have you lived in?
I have lived in Munich, Freiburg, and Stuttgart.

2 What countries have you visited?
I have visited _____ .

3 What big hotels have you stayed in?
I have stayed in _____ .

4 Where do people from your country go for skiing holidays?
They go _____ .

5 Where do people go for beach holidays?
They go _____ .

PRESENTATION **ⓐ** **this, that, these, those**

Look at the way we use these words:

This car is cheap.

That car is expensive.

These cars are cheap.

Those cars are expensive.

ⓑ Dates and times

We often use *this* and *these* to refer to times:
*I want to come and see you **this afternoon**.*
*Peter is leaving for America **this evening**.*
*We're having a lot of problems with suppliers **this year**.*
*Everything is so expensive **these days**.*

ⓒ No noun

We can use *this, that, these,* or *those* without a noun:
this = *this person* or *thing*
that = *that person* or *thing*
these = *these people* or *things*
those = *those people* or *things*

    A: *Who is the woman talking to Brian?*
    B: ***That's** Roberta. (that = that person)*

I think we have the wrong keys. **These** are yours and **those** are m
(*these* = these keys, *those* = those keys)

ⓓ Common expressions

We use ***This is*** on the telephone:
    A: *Good morning, Pearson Enterprises.*
    B: *Good morning. **This is** Mr Jackson. Could I speak to Helen Simms, please?*

We introduce people with ***This is***:
*Irene, I'd like you to meet our new Finance Manager. Irene, **this is** Elena.*

We can respond to something someone says with ***that***:
    A: *We've won the contract!*   B: ***That's** great.*
    A: *The computer isn't working.*   B: ***That's** strange.*
    A: *Thank you very much.*   B: ***That's** OK.*

PRACTICE

① *this, that, these, those*

Complete the dialogue with *this*, *that*, *these*, or *those*.

A: How much is ¹this radio?
B: It's $189. But ²_____ radios here behind me are cheaper.
A: I see. What about ³_____ radio by the window?
B: You mean the red one – next to ⁴_____ CD players?
A: Yes.
B: ⁵_____ one costs $65.

② Dates and times

Complete the sentences with the words from the box.

this morning	this afternoon	today	this week	this month	these days

1 I'm free on Tuesday and Thursday _____ , but next week I'm very busy.
2 Twenty years ago PCs cost a fortune, but _____ they are very good value.
3 I'm not going on holiday _____ , but I may go in September or October.
4 Sally's working at home _____ , and she's coming into the office after lunch.
5 I spoke to Bob at lunch and then again at about 4.15 _____ .
6 What day is it _____ ? Is it the 15th?

③ No noun

Complete the sentences with *this*, *that*, *these*, or *those*.

1 Where do you want me to put ᵗʰⁱˢ? It's a package for Ms Duchène.
2 Who is _____ talking to Roberta? Is it Frau Müller?
3 They didn't have any white envelopes, so I bought _____ . Are they OK?
4 Look, we have the same car, but _____ one here is mine. _____ 's yours, over there by the blue Mercedes.
5 _____ are the keys I found. Are they yours?

④ Common expressions

Match sentences 1–6 to responses a–f.

1 I saw Carla today.
2 Thank you for your help.
3 The train will be delayed by two hours.
4 Can I ask who is calling?
5 We haven't met.
6 They want €5,000 to repair the car.

a Sorry – John, this is Jane; Jane this is John.
b That's terrible. We will miss the meeting.
c Yes, this is Madeleine Ford.
d That's OK. It's a pleasure.
e That's not possible. She's in New York.
f That's too much. Go to another garage.

OVER TO YOU

You are sitting next to a colleague at a conference. Write down what you say beginning with *This*, *That*, *These*, or *Those*. You want to ...

1 point out someone you know on the other side of the room That's the Finance Director.
2 introduce your colleague to someone _____ .
3 say that you think the conference is very boring _____ .

Your boss says these things to you. Think of a reply beginning *That's* ...

4 You must come and work on Sunday. That's great! I love working at weekends.
5 I am not going to give you a pay rise this year. _____ .
6 We are going to make you a Director. _____ .
7 We are sending you to China for two years. _____ .
8 We lost 2.5 million last year. _____ .

this, that, these, those 115

56 Nouns (1)
countable and uncountable

PRESENTATION **ⓐ Countable and uncountable nouns**

Most nouns are countable – we can count them. For example, we can say *one pen, two pens, three pens,* etc. Countable nouns have a singular form and a plural form:

Singular	Plural
a customer	*two, three, four, five customers*
a book	*two, three, four, five books*
a meeting	*two, three, four, five meetings*

Some nouns are uncountable – we cannot count them. For example, we cannot say *two advices, three advices, four advices,* etc. Uncountable nouns are always singular:

Your **advice is** always very helpful.
Platinum costs more than gold.
That **money** on the table **is** for you.

! When we talk about an uncountable noun in general, we do not use *the*.
Coffee has more **caffeine** than **tea**.

However, we often use *some* with uncountable nouns. We do not use *a* or *an*.
I'm going to buy **some wine**.

We also use *some* with plural countable nouns. We do not use *a* or *an*.
We need **some tables** and **chairs**.

ⓑ Categories of noun

The following nouns are usually uncountable and singular:

Liquids:	Gases:	Small grains:	Solid substances:	Fabrics:	Some foods:
water, oil, petrol, wine, tea, milk	*air, oxygen, carbon dioxide*	*rice, sand, salt, pepper, coffee*	*gold, silver, wood, glass, steel*	*silk, cotton, nylon*	*butter, cheese, bread, pasta, flour*

We'll need **some tea** and **some coffee** for the meeting this afternoon.
I bought **some silk** on my business trip to China.
Oil always floats on **water**.

1 **Countable and uncountable nouns**

Complete the sentences with *a, an,* or *some.*

1 I am taking some customers out to lunch.
2 Can you talk to Alice? She needs _____ help.
3 I've got _____ good book about American companies.
4 I've got _____ important meeting in Berlin next week.
5 Franz left _____ books for you – they're in my office.
6 Can we have _____ meeting some time next week?
7 I am going to give you _____ advice.
8 Herr Kleist is talking to _____ customer.

2 **Countable and uncountable nouns, and categories of noun**

Complete the dialogues with *a, an,* or *some.*

A manager of an office complex is talking to a builder.

Manager: Can you come and do the repairs tomorrow?
Builder: Yes – can I just check which jobs we are doing?
Manager: There's ¹a wall by the garage that needs repairing.
Builder: OK, I've got ²_____ sand and I can get ³_____ cement later today.
Manager: Good, we've got ⁴_____ bricks so we don't need any more.
Builder: I've got ⁵_____ cement mixer, and I'll bring ⁶_____ petrol for it. The only other thing I'll need is ⁷_____ water.
Manager: That's no problem – the garage has ⁸_____ tap. And don't forget that there are ⁹_____ windows that need fixing.
Builder: OK. I'll take the measurements and I can order ¹⁰_____ glass when I know what size they are.

Alain is talking to Marie about a small party they are organizing.

Alain: Is everything ready for the party?
Marie: Yes I think so. We've got ¹¹some wine and Laure is bringing ¹²_____ cheese.
Alain: And I've got ¹³_____ biscuits. What about soft drinks?
Marie: We've got ¹⁴_____ water – fizzy and still – and I've also got ¹⁵_____ orange juice.
Alain: Have you checked the room?
Marie: Yes, it's fine – there's ¹⁶_____ big table for the food and drink, and there's ¹⁷_____ air conditioner, so it won't be too hot.
Alain: That's good. I've got ¹⁸_____ box of wine glasses in the car – I'll go and get them.
Marie: OK, see you in ¹⁹_____ minute.

What will you need for these activities? You are going to ...

1 build a wall   I'll need some sand and a few bags of cement.
2 give a party   _____.
3 go on a car long journey _____.
4 have an afternoon meeting _____.
5 cook dinner for some colleagues _____.

Write sentences about your likes and dislikes.

6 tea/coffee   I like tea and coffee. I prefer tea.
7 beer/cider   _____.
8 English food/French food _____.
9 red wine/white wine _____.
10 pasta/rice   _____.

57 Nouns (2)
countable and uncountable

ⓐ Common uncountable nouns

The following common nouns are uncountable, so we use a singular verb with them:

accommodation	*equipment*	*insurance*	*money*	*research*	*travel*
advertising	*furniture*	*luck*	*news*	*room*	*weather*
cash	*information*	*luggage*	*progress*	*traffic*	*work*

The cash is in the safe.
That information is very interesting.
The news doesn't sound good.
The weather was bad at that time of year.

ⓑ Singular or plural?

Uncountable nouns are singular. But words with a similar meaning may be countable and plural:
Uncountable: *The equipment is on the lorry.*
Countable: *The photocopiers are on the lorry.*

Uncountable: *My luggage is very heavy.*
Countable: *My suitcases are very heavy.*

We can often use *a bit of* or *a piece of* with uncountable nouns. These can be singular or plural:
I've got one piece of luggage that is very heavy.
My colleague has got two pieces of luggage that are very heavy.

ⓒ *a*, *an*, *some*, and *any*

❗ We do not use *a* or *an* with uncountable nouns.
wrong: *I have got ~~an information~~ for you.*
right: *I have got some information for you.*

We often use *some* or *any* (see Unit 59) with uncountable nouns.
We use *some* in positive sentences:
I've got some information about their latest plans.

We use *any* in negatives and often in questions:
Have you got any equipment you don't need?
I don't want the photocopier in my office. There isn't any room.

We do not need to use *some* or *any* when we are talking in general:
Money does not always make people happy.

① Common uncountable nouns

Complete the sentences with the words in the box.

accommodation   insurance   information   luggage   ~~news~~   progress

1 Can you turn on the TV? I think the **news** is on.
2 If you are young and have a fast car, the _____ is expensive.
3 You should talk to Caroline – she has got some interesting _____ .
4 The project is going well and we are making a lot of _____ .
5 _____ in Tokyo is expensive, especially in hotels in the city centre.
6 At the airport, you must keep your _____ with you at all times.

② Singular or plural?

Complete each pair of sentences with the words in the box.

accommodation/rooms   ~~office chairs~~/~~furniture~~   money/US dollars   traffic/cars and lorries   suitcases/luggage

1 a The **furniture** is here in reception.
   b The **office chairs** are here in reception.
2 a _____ causes pollution.
   b _____ cause pollution.
3 a Is your _____ heavy?
   b Are your _____ heavy?
4 a The _____ at the Plaza Hotel is luxurious.
   b The _____ at the Plaza Hotel are luxurious.
5 a The _____ you ordered is in the envelope.
   b The _____ you ordered are in the envelope.

③ *a, an, some,* and *any*

Complete the email. Choose the correct option from the words in *italics*.

Heinrich
I have ¹*an/some* information about your trip to the Kyoto Research Centre next week.
I tried to book you ²*a/some* room at the Sheraton, but I didn't have ³*a/any* luck. But don't worry, because I found you ⁴*a/some* accommodation at the Kyoto Research Campus, and I know it's very nice there.
Jenna has ⁵*a/some* ticket for you and she has also got you ⁶*a/some* travel insurance. You'll need to pay the taxi driver in Yen, so you'll need ⁷*a/some* cash. You can change ⁸*a/some* money at one of the banks at the airport.
Hope you have ⁹*a/some* good weather.
Best wishes
Louis

Using your own ideas, write sentences about the topics below.

1 travel   *Sometimes I find that travel is very tiring.*
2 the weather at this time of year _____ .
3 the traffic in the mornings _____ .
4 the cost of accommodation _____ .
5 any money _____ .
6 some good news _____ .
7 my car insurance _____ .
8 my work _____ .

58 Nouns (3)
singular and plural

ⓐ Plurals – spelling

Most countable nouns have plurals that end in -*s*:
> *We have an office in Lisbon.*
> *We have three offices in Madrid.*

Nouns ending in consonant + *y* add -*ies*:
> *We have one company in France.*
> *We have three companies in Italy.*

Nouns ending in -*ss*, -*x*, -*ch*, and -*sh* add -*es*:
> *I used to have one box of files.*
> *Now I have five boxes of files.*

ⓑ Irregular plurals

Some countable nouns have irregular plurals:

businessman – businessmen	*man – men*
child – children	*person – people*
half – halves	*salesperson – salespeople*
life – lives	*woman – women*

Some nouns end in -*s* but are singular:

mathematics	*economics*	*politics*	*news*

> *Mathematics is useful.*
> *The news is good!*

Some nouns are always plural:

assets	*scissors*	*glasses*	*premises*	*trousers*
clothes	*earnings*	*headquarters*	*savings*	*valuables*

> *Our headquarters are in New York.*
> *Her clothes are very nice.*

ⓒ Groups

Some nouns can refer to groups of people:

board	*company*	*group*	*Hitachi*	*staff*	*team*

These are usually singular:
> *Siemens is a large German company.*
> *Real Madrid is a very successful football team.*

However, we can use the plural if we are thinking more about the people in the group:
> *Bertelsmann are having a big party next week.*
> *The staff are very unhappy about the pay cut.*

1 Plurals – spelling

Complete the information from a business directory with the plural form of the words in brackets.

LOCKTON SOUTH TRADE DIRECTORY

Allensons, 16 Forth Bridge Street.
Electrical ¹ *supplies* (supply). Retailer of electrical
² .... (cable),
³ .... (switch), and security ⁴ .... (alarm).

PartyMania, 22 Elson Road.
Hire of ⁵ .... (glass) for
⁶ .... (wedding) and
⁷ .... (party). Catering service on request.

Gill Ironmongers, 3 Medway Passage.
DIY equipment. Large range of ⁸ .... (paint) and
⁹ .... (varnish), paint
¹⁰ .... (pad) and
¹¹ .... (brush). Also have ¹² ....
(workbench) for sale/hire.

Transon Office Assist, Unit 8 Lockton Industrial Park.
Wide range of ¹³ ....
(service) for small local
¹⁴ .... (business). Can make ¹⁵ ....
(photocopy) and send/receive
¹⁶ .... (fax). Can print/deliver publicity leaflets to local ¹⁷ ....
(address).

2 Irregular plurals

Read the sentences and correct the mistakes.

1 Do you have any ~~childs~~?   *any children*
2 Japanese businessmens work very long hours.   ....
3 Do you think that politics are interesting?   ....
4 Our headquarters is in Seattle.   ....
5 We are going to move to new premise in the summer. ....
6 A lot of the clotheses we sell are made in China. ....
7 You can't be an accountant if your maths aren't good. ....
8 The new safety laws will save hundreds of lifes. ....

3 Groups

Choose the correct option from the words in *italics*.

1 Hitachi *is*/~~are~~ one of the biggest companies in the world.
2 I like doing business with Renault – *they are/it is* very friendly.
3 Huaxin has a 13.9% interest in SBDG, which *is/are* a subsidiary of Swire Pacific.
4 The staff *is/are* collecting money for a leaving present for Annie Taylor.
5 AGL *owns/own* over 22,000 kilometres of the natural gas distribution system in New South Wales.

Say what you like or dislike about your job. Write sentences beginning with the phrases in the box. Put them into the 'Good' column or the 'Bad' column.

| My colleagues   The hours   The pay   The facilities   The building |
| My boss   The canteen   The opportunities |

Good
My colleagues are friendly.

Bad

59 *some* and *any*

a **Positive and negative**

In positive sentences, we often use *some* with plurals and uncountable nouns (see Unit 57):
We have got some new brochures.
I'd like some information about your prices.

In negative sentences, we often use *any* with plurals and uncountable nouns:
The meeting room doesn't have any windows.
We haven't got any time.

With singular countable nouns we can use *a* or *an*:
There's a message for you on the answerphone.

b **Questions**

With most questions, we use *any*:
Are there any messages for me?

But if the question is a request or an offer, we usually use *some*:
Could I have some coffee?
Would you like some milk?

c **Polite offers**

We often use *if ... any* when we make polite offers:
Let me know if you need any help.
Please contact me if you need any more information.
If you have any questions, give me a call.

d **Pronouns**

We can also use *some* and *any* on their own, when it is not necessary to repeat the noun:
A: *Why are you ordering twenty boxes of paper?* B: *Because we haven't got any.* (paper)
A: *Shall I stop here for some petrol?* B: *Yes, I think we probably need some.* (petrol)

1 **Positive and negative**

Complete the sentences with *a*, *an*, *some*, or *any*.

1 I'm worried because we haven't got **any** new orders.
2 I'll send you _____ price list today.
3 Bob has _____ interesting news for you.
4 There are _____ letters for you to sign.
5 Nowadays we don't have _____ problems with the unions.
6 I can't find _____ information about their suppliers.
7 I work in _____ office in London Road.
8 Franz has _____ new ideas he wants to discuss.
9 We don't do _____ work at weekends.
10 We bought _____ shares in HSBA in 2002.

② Questions

Make questions from the notes using _some_ or _any_.

1 Have/you/got/letters/for/me?
   Have you got any letters for me?
2 Would/you/like/wine/sir?
   _____?
3 Is/there/new/information/available?
   _____?
4 Could/I/have/help/please?
   _____?
5 Did/he/give/Ms Smith/tea?
   _____?
6 you/have/experience/in/this/field?
   _____?

③ Polite offers

Rewrite the sentences with _if_ and _any_.

1 You may have some questions. If you do, please call me.
   Please call me _if you have any questions._
2 You may have some problems. If you do, please let me know.
   Please let me know _____.
3 You may need some further information. If you do, please contact me.
   Please contact me _____.
4 You may have some comments or questions. If so, please do not hesitate to contact me.
   Please do not hesitate to contact me _____.

④ Pronouns

Complete the sentences with _some_ or _any_.

1 A: There isn't any paper in the printer.
   B: I know. We need to order _some._
2 I'm looking for information on travel to Singapore, but I can't find _____ .
3 A: Do you need any Euros for your trip?
   B: No, thanks. I've got _____ .
4 Could you give me a bit of help? I really need _____ .
5 They want someone with experience of sales, but I haven't got _____ .

OVER TO YOU

Complete each sentence in two ways. Use (a) a singular countable noun, and (b) a plural noun or an uncountable noun.

1 At the office, we have got _a canteen._
   some parking spaces for visitors.
2 At the office, we haven't got _____ .
   _____ .
3 At work, I would really like to have _____ .
   _____ .
4 At work, I wouldn't like to have _____ .
   _____ .
5 When I go on business trips, I take _____ .
   _____ .
6 When I go on holiday, I don't take _____ .
   _____ .

60 *something* and *anything*

ⓐ *something* **and** *anything*

We use *anything* and *something* in place of a noun. We usually use *something* in positive sentences. We use *anything* in negative sentences and some questions:

A: *Do you know **anything** about the presentation today?*
B: *Yes, it's on **something** to do with marketing.*

ⓑ **People and places**

We talk about people and places in the same way.
We use *anyone/anybody* and *someone/somebody* to talk about people:

A: *Do you know **anyone** who works in Cairo?*
B: *No, but I know **somebody** with an office in Luxor.*

We use *anywhere/somewhere* to talk about places:

A: *Are you going **anywhere** this weekend?*
B: *Yes, I'm going **somewhere** with Mark.*

ⓒ *anything*, **etc. + adjective**

We often use an adjective after *something, anything, someone, anyone, somewhere,* and *anywhere*:

A: *Do you know **anywhere** good to stay in London? (= a place that is good)*
B: *No, but I think Kira knows **somewhere** nice. (= a place that is nice)*

A: *Did you meet **anyone** new at the conference? (= a new person)*
B: *Yes, I met **someone** very interesting. (= an interesting person)*

ⓓ *no-* **and** *every-*

We can use the prefixes *no-* and *every-* to talk about things, people, and places:

no-	*every-*
nothing	*everything*
no one	*everyone*
nobody	*everybody*
nowhere	*everywhere*

*I know **everyone** in the office. (= all the people)*
*There is **nowhere** to eat in the building. (= no places)*

① *something* **and** *anything*

Complete the dialogues with *something* or *anything*.

1 A: Is there _____ else you need to know?
   B: Yes, there is _____ – can you tell me how long the holidays are?
2 A: Has the post arrived?
   B: Yes, but there isn't _____ for you. There's _____ for Mr Dawson.
3 A: Could we go to a different restaurant? I don't like _____ on this menu.
   B: Really? There must be _____ you like.
4 A: Is there _____ else to pay? What about the air conditioning?
   B: No, it doesn't cost _____ at all. It's free.

② People and places

Complete the sentences with *anyone*, *someone*, *anywhere*, or *somewhere*.

1 There's ~someone~ waiting for you at Reception.
2 I can't find that file, but I know it's here _____ .
3 Do you know _____ who earns more than $1m?
4 I didn't like the party because I didn't know _____ .
5 I want to talk to _____ about fleet cars.
6 I'm not going _____ on holiday this year.
7 _____ called and left a message for you.
8 I'm not sure where their Head Office is. I think it's _____ in Brazil.

③ *anything*, etc. + adjective

Complete the dialogues with a word from each box.

anyone	~someone~	tropical	more colourful
anyone	somewhere	~dynamic~	exciting
something	something	suitable	outside
somewhere		young	

Wanted
Promotions Manager
Must be

A: What sort of person are you looking for to run the department?
B: We're looking for ¹ ~someone dynamic~ and full of energy and ideas.
A: Isn't there ² _____ in the company?
B: No, there's no point looking in-house. We have to look
   ³ _____ .

A: We can't have a black and white photo on the cover. It's a
   travel brochure for 18 to 25-year-olds.
B: No, I agree. I think we need ⁴ _____ .
   Lots of bright blues and greens.
A: Yes, maybe we could have ⁵ _____ , like
   the Seychelles.
B: I'm not sure ⁶ _____ really thinks about
   places like that. Maybe the cover should show ⁷ _____
   _____ like jet-skiing or hang-gliding.

Sunlight Sunlight
Sunlight Sunlight

④ *no-* and *every-*

Complete the sentences with the words in the box.

everyone   everywhere   everything   nothing   nobody

1 Getting money is not a problem – there are cash machines _____ .
2 It's a completely free service – it costs _____ .
3 We will do _____ possible to make sure your stay is a success.
4 It's a mystery why he resigned – _____ knows why he did it.
5 If there are any changes, I will keep _____ informed by email.

OVER TO YOU

**You are talking to a colleague about a one-day conference you went to last week.
Complete the sentences using *something*, *anyone*, *nowhere*, etc.**

1 I stayed ~somewhere cheap~ .
2 I met _____ .
3 I didn't go _____ .
4 I didn't learn _____ .
5 I heard _____ .
6 In the evening, I went _____ .

much and *many*

a **Asking about quantities**

We use *How much* and *How many* to ask about quantities.
We use *How much* with uncountable nouns (*time, money, water, sand, gold,* etc.):
 A: *How much money is there in the account?*   B: *About $300.*

We use *How many* with plural countable nouns (*chairs, people, books, offices,* etc.):
 A: *How many people are coming to the presentation?*   B: *About 200.*

! We use *How much + to be* to ask about price.
A: *How much is* the 512MB SD card?   B: It's €75.
A: *How much are* the 128MB cards?   B: They're €30.

b **Small and large quantites**

We use *not much* and *not many* to talk about small quantities.
We use *not much* with uncountable nouns:
 There's not much money in the account.
We use *not many* with plural countable nouns:
 We have not got many vacancies at the moment.

We can use *a lot of* with countable or uncountable nouns to talk about large quantities:
 The company has got a lot of problems.   *It needs a lot of help.*

! We do not normally use *much* with nouns in positive sentences.
wrong: *I have ~~much work~~ to do.*   right: *I have a lot of work to do.*

c ***a little* and *a few***

We use *a little* and *a few* to talk about small quantities.
We use *a little* with uncountable nouns:
 I need a little time to finish this report.
We use *a few* with countable nouns:
 I need a few minutes to finish this report.

We can use *very little* or *very few* to express a very small quantity:
 I can't pay this bill – there is very little money in the account.
 We have a problem – we have very few orders at the moment.

1 **Asking about quantities**

Rewrite the sentences with *How much* or *How many*.

1 What amount of paper do you want to order?   How much paper do you want to order ?
2 What number of people work for you? .... ?
3 What is the price of a DX14? .... ?
4 What number of complaints were there? .... ?
5 What is the price of the two big chairs? .... ?
6 What amount of time do we have left? .... ?
7 What amount of petrol do you use? .... ?
8 What number of emails did you get? .... ?
9 What is the price of a small apartment? .... ?
10 What amount of cash have you got? .... ?

2 Small and large quantities.

Choose the correct option from the words in *italics*.

If you want to reduce your electricity bills, it makes sense to make your own power.

For example, you can save ¹*much/a lot of* money by installing a wind turbine. There are ²*much/a lot of* different models available, and some, like the Southwest Whisper H80, can be installed without ³*much/many* difficulty.

Most turbines simply need an open site with ⁴*much/a lot of* wind, and can produce about 20% to 30% of an average household's electricity needs. The power comes directly into the house and at night, when you aren't using ⁵*many/much* appliances and don't need ⁶*much/many* electricity, the extra power is stored in batteries for later use.

3 *a little* and *a few*

Complete the sentences with *very little*, *a little*, *very few*, or *a few*.

1 Let's have a meeting – I've got a few ideas to talk about.
2 We're selling .... tickets because they are too expensive.
3 Hurry up – we've got .... time left.
4 Olga's got your air tickets, and she's got .... cash for your trip as well.
5 Everybody loves working at this company, and .... people leave.
6 I've got a long holiday in May and .... days in June too.

OVER TO YOU

Make sentences about your company and your country with the words in the box.

a lot of   a few   a little   (not) much   (not) many   very few   very little

In your country ...

1 are there any women in Parliament? No, there are very few women in Parliament.
2 are there any high-tech companies? ....
3 are there any people on unemployment benefit? ....
4 is there any oil, gas, or coal? ....
5 is there any gold, silver, or platinum? ....

In your company ...

6 are there any women in senior positions? ....
7 are there any part-time workers? ....
8 is there any valuable equipment? ....
9 is there any cash kept overnight? ....

62 Numbers (1)
large numbers, dates

a **Large numbers**

Look at the table:

100	a hundred	10,000	ten thousand	1,000,000	a million
1,000	a thousand	100,000	a hundred thousand	1,000,000,000	a billion

If a large number includes a number from 1 to 99 we use *and*:
256	*two hundred **and** fifty-six*
51,324	*fifty-one thousand, three hundred **and** twenty-four*
256,324	*two hundred **and** fifty-six thousand, three hundred **and** twenty-four*

When we write large numbers, we put commas before every set of three numbers:
  21,275   1,251,372

b **Numbers or words?**

When we use a number that is a real amount or quantity (for example, the price of something), we usually say the full number:
  The population of Christchurch is one hundred and seventy thousand (170,000).
  The latest Range Rover costs ninety thousand euros (€90,000).

When we use a number that is a code or reference (for example, a telephone number), we usually say the individual figures:
  The product code is TR563844. (T-R-five-six-three-eight-four-four)
  You can phone me on 081 6234. (oh-eight-one-six-two-three-four)

c **Dates**

We write and say dates in two ways:
We write: *10 September 2005* or *10/09/05*
We say: *the tenth of September, 2005* or *September the tenth, 2005*

When we talk about a year we usually divide it into two parts:
  1975: *I was born in nineteen seventy-five.*
  2030: *I will retire in twenty thirty.*

! For the first ten years of the 21st century, most people say *two thousand and*.
  2001: *two thousand and one*
  2005: *two thousand and five*

1 **Large numbers**

Write the numbers in words.

1 243,955   Two hundred and forty-three thousand, nine hundred and fifty-five.
2 6,439   ....
3 9,082,375   ....
4 3,609,438   ....
5 500,000   ....
6 18,500,050   ....

2 Numbers or words?

Look at the numbers that are circled. Write them in words.

@2005 Google – Searching 8,058,044,651 web pages

See page 187

H.R 3103

Tel: 01748 884200

Title: *To amend the International Revenue Code of 1986 to improve portability of health insurance coverage.*

I'll be on flight DR426 arriving at 22.20

3 Dates

Match the dates with the pictures. Write the dates in words.

> 20 July 1969   ~~1 May 1844~~   16 December 2004   25 January 1924   5 May 1912

1 Samuel Morse sent the first telegraphic message on 1 May 1844.
   The first of May, eighteen forty-four.

2 Apollo 11 landed on the moon on ....

3 The first Winter Olympics opened in Chamonix, France on ....

4 The Millau bridge was opened on ....

5 The Soviet Communist Party newspaper Pravda was first published on ....

OVER TO YOU

Estimate the answers to these questions. Write the numbers in a and the number in words in b.

1 How much is a two-bedroom apartment in your town/city centre?
   a £200,000   b *Two hundred thousand pounds*

2 How much did your car cost?
   a ....   b ....

3 How much do you spend every month?
   a ....   b ....

4 How much do the top executives at your company earn?
   a ....   b ....

5 How much do the most junior people at your company earn?
   a ....   b ....

6 What is the population of your country?
   a ....   b ....

63 Numbers (2)
decimals and fractions

PRESENTATION **ⓐ Decimals**

For decimals, we use a point (.). We do not use a comma (,). After the decimal point, we say the individual figures:

He finished the race in 10.34 seconds. (ten point three four seconds)
The standard rate of VAT is 17.5%. (seventeen point five per cent)

If we are talking about money we say the name of the currency and not the word *point*. After the decimal point we use the whole number (of cents, pence, etc.):

$3.50 *Three dollars fifty.* or *Three dollars and fifty cents.*

€5.99 *Five euros ninety-nine.* or *Five euros and ninety-nine cents.*

£18.42 *Eighteen pounds forty-two.* or *Eighteen pounds and forty-two pence.*

ⓑ Fractions and percentages

Look at the way we say fractions and percentages:

$^1/_4$	*a quarter*	25%	*twenty-five per cent*
$^1/_3$	*a third*	33.33%	*thirty-three point three three per cent*
$^1/_2$	*half*	50%	*fifty per cent*
$^2/_3$	*two-thirds*	66.66%	*sixty-six point six six per cent*
$^3/_4$	*three-quarters*	75%	*seventy-five per cent*

For other fractions we say *a fifth, a sixth, a seventh, an eighth, two fifths*, etc.:

$^1/_5$ *a fifth*	$^1/_6$ *a sixth*	$^1/_7$ *a seventh*	$^2/_5$ *two fifths*

ⓒ Dimensions

Look at the way we ask and answer questions about dimensions:

How long is it?   *It's 39 cm long.*
How wide is it?   *It's 31 cm wide.*
How high is it?   *It's 16 cm high.*
How much does it weigh? *It weighs 8.5 kg.*

DIMENSIONS & WEIGHT	
Overall length in mm	390
Overall width in mm	310
Overall height in mm	160
weight in kg	8.5

We often use the word *by* with dimensions:

I need a new piece of glass – it needs to be 28.5 cm by 14.7 cm.

1 Decimals

Complete the dialogue with the numbers in the box. Use a calculator if you need to.

| ~~5.52~~ | ~~17.5~~ | 23.74 | ~~47.48~~ | 53 | ~~€9.28~~ | €86.07 | €491.84 | €577.91 |

Johann: Hello, this is Mr Andersen. I'm calling about an order I placed for carpets.

Bill: Hello, Mr Andersen. I've got all the details here. The two rooms downstairs are [1]_____ square metres each so that makes [2] **47.48** square metres. And you're having the same carpet for the stairs, aren't you?

Johann: Yes, that's right.

Bill: OK, well we will only need [3] **5.52** square metres for the stairs, so if we add that up it comes to a total of [4]_____ square metres exactly.

Johann: Can you give me a price?

Bill: Yes – the carpet costs [5] **€9.28** a square metre so that comes to [6]_____ for the two rooms and the stairs. Then we add on the VAT at [7] **17.5%**, which is [8]_____ , and that makes a total of [9]_____ .

Now write down the numbers and prices in words.

1 _____
2 forty-seven point four eight
3 five point five two

4 _____
5 nine euros twenty-eight
6 _____

7 seventeen point five per cent
8 _____
9 _____

2 Fractions and percentages

Look at the pie chart. It shows sales of a company's products in different markets. Complete the sentences with the fractions in the box.

| a fifth | a quarter | half | three quarters |

1 We make **half** of our sales in Germany.
2 We make _____ of our sales in France.
3 We make _____ of our sales in Western Europe.
4 We make _____ of our sales in Argentina.

Global sales
France 25%
Argentina 20%
Australia 3%
Other 2%
Germany 50%

3 Dimensions

Complete the dialogue with the words in the box.

| high | ~~how much~~ | long | weigh | weighs | wide |

Check-in clerk: I'm sorry sir, you can't take this bag as cabin luggage.

Traveller: What's the problem? [1] **How much** does it [2]_____ ?

Check-in clerk: It [3]_____ more than 10 kg and it should be less than 6 kg.

Traveller: OK. I'll put some of the books in my main bag.

Check-in clerk: No, the bag is too big. The rules say that a bag can only be 55 cm [4]_____ , 40 cm [5]_____ , and 20 cm [6]_____ .

Hand baggage:
1 piece weighing up to 6 kg in total.
Maximum dimensions 55x40x20 cm.

OVER TO YOU

Think about how you spend your day. Write sentences using fractions or percentages to describe how you spend your time.

1 Working — I spend a third of my day working.
2 Sleeping _____ .
3 Relaxing _____ .
4 Eating _____ .
5 Travelling to work _____ .

PRESENTATION ⓐ **Place**

We use these prepositions to say where something is:

at   in   on   next to   opposite   between   in front of   behind   above   below

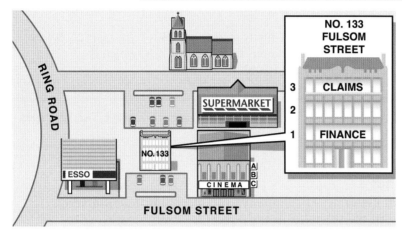

I'm *at* work at the moment. The office is *in* Fulsom Street, just off the ring road. It's *at* number 133, *between* the ABC cinema and the Esso petrol station. There's a small car park *in front of* the building, and there's another one *behind* it, *next to* the supermarket and more or less *opposite* the church. I'm *on* the second floor, so I can take you to the Claims Department, which is *above* me on the third floor. Then we can go to the Finance Department, which is *below* me on the first floor.

ⓑ **Direction**

We use these prepositions to talk about movement or direction:

from, to
The lorry is going *from* London *to* Munich.

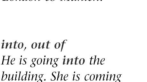

into, out of
He is going *into* the building. She is coming *out of* the building.

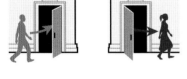

onto, off
They are putting the wood *onto* the lorry. They are taking the boxes *off* the lorry.

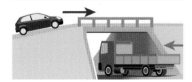

over, under
The car is going *over* the bridge. The lorry is going *under* the bridge.

up, down
He is going *up* the stairs. She is coming *down* the stairs.

along, across
He is walking *along* the road. She is walking *across* the road.

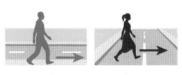

round, through
The lorry is going *round* the town. The car is going *through* the town.

ⓒ **Useful phrases**

Look at the prepositions we use with these useful phrases:

at a conference	*in a meeting*	*on holiday, on business*
at work, at home, at the office	*(get) in touch*	*on + telephone number*
at this address	*in London, Singapore, etc.*	*on the left, on the right*

1 Place

Choose the correct option from the prepositions in *italics*.

1 Ohinemuri Estate is *in/at/into* the Karangahake Gorge, *between/through/across* Paeroha and Waihi.

2 We are *onto/in/at* St Louis, *along/next to/between* the airport.

3 The offices of Metroland are located *at/into/on* 419 Madison Avenue, *onto/in/at* Albany, New York.

4 We are *in/to/on* the city centre, *across/between/over* the new Starbucks and HSBC bank, and *opposite/next/in front* the tube station.

2 Direction

Complete the text with the prepositions in the box.

along   down   from   round   through   ~~to~~   to   up

YELLOWSTONE NATIONAL PARK

Tourists come [1] to Wyoming [2] _____ all over the world to see Yellowstone National Park. Yellowstone was first explored by John Colter, who passed [3] _____ in 1808, and it became the world's first National Park in 1872.

Most visitors go straight [4] _____ the Old Faithful Geyser. This blows every 75 minutes and sends over 20,000 litres of boiling water 45 metres [5] _____ in the air. In between eruptions, visitors can go [6] _____ the other attractions or follow one of the trails [7] _____ the Firehole River.

The other main sight is the Grand Canyon of the Yellowstone River, where a pair of powerful waterfalls drop [8] _____ into a 300-metre-deep canyon.

3 Useful phrases

Complete the dialogue with *in*, *at*, or *on*.

Bob: Hi, Jan. What sort of sales department is this? Where is everybody?
Jan: Well, Anna's [1] at a conference [2] _____ Paris, and Janie's [3] _____ a meeting.
Bob: Is Ken [4] _____ a business trip again? I can't get [5] _____ touch with him.
Jan: No, he's [6] _____ holiday.
Bob: Isn't Laura here?
Jan: No, she's [7] _____ home today, but she'll be back [8] _____ work tomorrow.

Say where these things are in your town and how you get there from your place of work.

1 the nearest bank The nearest bank is in Corn Street, opposite the cinema. You go along the A134 to Witney, go through the town, up the hill, and it's on the right.

2 the nearest cash machine _____

3 the nearest place to get a good coffee _____

4 your favourite restaurant _____

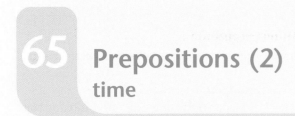

65 Prepositions (2)
time

ⓐ Prepositions

We use these prepositions to talk about time:

in	*1998, 2001, 2028*
	January, February, March ...
	the near future
	the spring, the summer, the autumn, the winter
	in the morning, in the afternoon, in the evening
on	*Monday, Tuesday, Wednesday ...*
	Monday morning, Tuesday afternoon
	the 22nd
	Friday 13th
	Christmas Day, New Year's Day
at	*6.15, 7.00, 9.30*
	the weekend
	midday, midnight
	Christmas, New Year, Easter

ⓑ No preposition

With some expressions, we do not use a preposition:

today, tonight
this morning/afternoon/evening
this weekend, this week
yesterday
yesterday morning/afternoon/evening
last night
the day before yesterday
three days ago
last week/month/year
tomorrow
tomorrow morning/afternoon/evening
the day after tomorrow
next week/month/year

ⓒ *from*, *to*, and *for*

We can talk about periods of time with *from*, *to*, and *for*:
Sasha came to London on Monday.
Sasha left on Thursday.
We can say:
   *Sasha was in London **from** Monday **to** Thursday.*

Or we can count the number of days and say:
   *Sasha was in London **for** four days.*

❶ Prepositions

Complete the email with *in*, *on*, or *at*.

> From: HR Department   To: All staff
>
> **Subject: Christmas arrangements**
>
> Because Christmas Day is ¹at the weekend (as it was ² _____ 2002), there will be special office
>
> hours ³ _____ Christmas. We will be closed ⁴ _____ Monday 27 December and we will re-open for
>
> business ⁵ _____ 8.30 ⁶ _____ Wednesday.
>
> In addition, all staff will have an extra half-day free ⁷ _____ Friday 24 December. The office will
>
> close ⁸ _____ midday to make holiday travel arrangements easier.
>
> We will need to keep some departments open ⁹ _____ New Year's Day. We will email details of
>
> these arrangements ¹⁰ _____ the near future.

2 No preposition

Complete the dialogue with *in, on, at,* or Ø (no preposition).

A: I'm calling to see if you have the sales figures for the first quarter. Have you got the results from Eastern Europe?

B: Yes, Kasia faxed them to me ¹_____ a couple of days ago. I had some questions, but she's going to send me the answers ²_____ tomorrow afternoon.

A: Good. What about Spain?

B: Nothing yet. I phoned Manuel ³_____ Monday and he's going to send them ⁴_____ this evening.

A: So when will you have everything?

B: Everything will be ready ⁵_____ the 18th.

A: OK then, I think we should have a meeting ⁶_____ next week to talk about them.

3 *from, to,* and *for*

Look at the pictures and complete the sentences with *from, to,* and *for*.

1 a The conference went on from 1 April to 4 April.
   b The conference went on for four days.
2 a She will be in Rome _____ .
   b She will be in Rome _____ .
3 a The course will last _____ .
   b The course will last _____ .
4 a He stayed in the USA _____ .
   b He stayed in the USA _____ .

OVER TO YOU

Complete the sentences with information about you.

1 I was born in 1970.
2 I started school _____ .
3 I left school _____ .
4 I started work _____ .

Look at your diary for the next week or so. Complete the sentences.

5 I am having an English lesson _____ .
6 I am having a meeting _____ .
7 I am going out _____ .
8 I am not working _____ .

66 Prepositions (3)
noun + preposition, preposition + verb, preposition + noun

PRESENTATION

a Noun + preposition

Look at these common noun + preposition combinations:

advantage of	The *advantage of* the new model is that it is easy to repair.
advice *about/on*	Can you give me some *advice about* DVD software?
application for	We had fifty *applications for* the job.
cause of	Do they know the *cause of* the accident?
cheque for	Please send me a *cheque for* $150.
cost of/price of	The *cost of* spare parts seems very high.
demand for	*Demand for* oil is still rising.
difference between	What is the *difference between* the two models?
experience of	Do you have any *experience of* working abroad?
example of	Can you give me an *example of* what you mean?
fall in/decrease in	We are not expecting a *fall in* interest rates.
interest in	We have no *interest in* buying the company.
invitation to	Thank you for the *invitation to* the party.
(your) letter of	Thank you for your *letter of* 18 May.
reply to/answer to	Where is his *reply to* my letter?
rise in/increase in	We are expecting a *rise in* interest rates.
trouble with/problem with	We're having a lot of *trouble with* the new IT system.

b Preposition + verb

When there is a verb after a preposition it takes the *-ing* form:

He didn't show any interest in working for us.
Do you have any experience of running a large department?

c Preposition + noun

Look at these common preposition + noun combinations:

by accident	Sorry. I deleted your files *by accident*.
by air/by car/by train (but on foot)	I prefer to travel *by train*.
by credit card	Can I pay *by credit card*?
by post	I can't fax it so I'll send it *by post*.
by return	Please send payment *by return*.
for lunch	What would you like *for lunch*?
for sale (used for houses, cars, etc.)	Is that house *for sale*?
in charge of	Who is *in charge of* this department?
in debt	He is *in debt* – he owes over $10,000.
in a hurry	Quick! I'm *in a hurry*.
in my opinion	*In my opinion*, this is a great idea.
on business	She's in Lima *on business*.
on foot	I sometimes go to work *on foot*.
on the phone	He's not free; he's *on the phone*.
on sale (= in the shops now)	The new Nokias are *on sale* now.
on strike	The factory is shut and the workers are *on strike*.
on time	In Japan, trains usually arrive *on time*.
out of date	We can't sell this milk – it is *out of date*.
out of order	Call the technician. The water cooler is *out of order*.
out of stock	We have no copies of Tomb Raider 5. We're *out of stock*.

1 Noun + preposition

Complete the puzzle with the missing words. Find the key word, which is a machine invented by Charles Babbage in the nineteenth century.

1 We are looking for someone with at least three years' _____ of working in the Middle East.
2 Thank you for the _____ to the launch party next month.
3 There is still strong _____ for oil, so the price is high.
4 The 379 QR Inkjet provides excellent quality at half the _____ of a laser printer.
5 We don't take credit cards, so please send us a _____ for $390.65.
6 Thank you for your _____ of 3 June.
7 What is the _____ between advertising and public relations?
8 If there is a _____ in interest rates, it will cost more to borrow money.

The key word is: _____

2 Preposition + verb

Complete the sentences with the verbs in the box.

> buying   flying   leaving   setting   ~~taking~~   working

1 The advantage of taking the train is that you'll get there faster.
2 Super-jumbos like the Airbus A380 will bring down the cost of _____ .
3 She is very independent and has many years' experience of _____ for herself.
4 I know Jake resigned, but did he give a reason for _____ his job?
5 The bank manager is going to give me some advice about _____ up my own business.
6 We have no interest in _____ new software for our network.

3 Preposition + noun

Rewrite the sentences with a preposition + noun combination.

1 Peter's in Athens for work. Peter's in Athens on business.
2 The firemen aren't working. The firemen are _____ .
3 They're selling their London office. Their London office is _____ .
4 The lift still isn't working. The lift is still _____ .
5 Ulrika's calling someone. Ulrika's _____ .
6 Yes, we take plastic. Yes, you can pay _____ .

Complete the sentences with your own ideas.

1 At the moment there is a strong demand for aluminium.
2 I would like an invitation _____ .
3 I can't tell the difference _____ .
4 I sometimes give people advice _____ .
5 I buy some things by cheque and other things _____ .
6 There's pasta or fish. What would you like to have _____ ?
7 Why are you running? Are you _____ ?
8 I prefer to travel _____ .

67 Prepositions (4)
adjective + preposition

PRESENTATION

ⓐ Adjective + preposition

Look at these common adjective + preposition combinations:

afraid of	I travel by train because I am **afraid of** flying.
angry about	The passengers were **angry about** the long delay.
capable of	The A11 is **capable of** storing 500 gigabytes of data.
different from	My new boss is very **different from** my old one.
excited about	We are very **excited about** the new store which is opening.
famous for	Florence is **famous for** its art.
interested in	We would be **interested in** setting up a new company in Poland.
pleased with	We are very **pleased with** your work.
popular with	The new model is very **popular with** our customers.
proud of	We are very **proud of** winning the Retailer of the Year competition.
satisfied with	I am **satisfied with** the progress you are making.
suitable for	Our furniture is **suitable for** small offices.
worried about	Consumers are **worried about** chemicals in food.

ⓑ Adjective + choice of preposition

Sometimes the same adjective can be followed by different prepositions:

angry with someone	The customer was **angry with** the sales assistant.
angry about something	The customer was **angry about** the poor service.
responsible for something	As HR Manager, I am **responsible for** recruiting new staff.
responsible to someone	I am **responsible to** Mr Hasan – he is my boss.
good at something	Anna was **good at** maths and decided to study it at university.
good for something	The publicity will be **good for** business.
kind of someone	It's very **kind of** you to help us.
kind to someone	She's a great boss and she's very **kind to** new employees.
sorry for doing something	I'm **sorry for** sending you the wrong information.
sorry about something	I'm very **sorry about** the delay.

ⓒ Preposition + verb

When a verb comes after the adjective + preposition we use the *-ing* form:
- Are you **interested in applying** for the job? (not: ~~to apply~~)
- Juan is **responsible for booking** air tickets. (not: ~~to book~~)
- I don't think Hans is **capable of doing** the job. (not: ~~to do~~)

PRACTICE

❶ Adjective + preposition

Complete the text with a word from each box.

capable	~~excited~~	famous	satisfied	suitable

~~about~~	for	for	of	with

New this month

Cookery expert Donna Francis was very [1]excited about the latest Panasonic Bread-maker available in the Kitchen Appliances department from July. 'It's a fantastic machine,' she says. 'Try it and you'll never be [2]_____ _____ shop bread again! It's [3]_____ _____ making all sorts of bread – from pizzas to naan bread – and it's very easy to use.'

Panasonic is [4]_____ _____ its high quality electronic equipment, and the SD 253 is a great machine. It is quite large, so it is not really [5]_____ _____ small kitchens.

2 Adjective + choice of preposition

Complete the sentences with a preposition.

1 I am very sorry about the problems with the contract.
2 We are sorry _____ causing any inconvenience.
3 It is very kind _____ you to show us round the factory.
4 Some people don't like my boss, but he is always very kind _____ me.
5 I'm not very good _____ giving presentations because I get nervous.
6 If the euro goes down in value it will be good _____ exports.
7 Please stop shouting and tell me what you are angry _____ .
8 I lost the contract, so the boss is angry _____ me.

3 Preposition + verb

Complete the dialogue with a preposition and the -ing form of the verbs in brackets.

Salesman: Sorry for keeping you waiting, sir. Can I help you?
Customer: Hello, I'm from Talbot Systems. I'm responsible [1] for reorganizing (reorganize) our delivery service and I am interested [2]_____ (buy) some new vans.
Salesman: Can you tell me a little more about what you need?
Customer: Well, I'm looking for something that is capable [3]_____ (carry) small or medium loads – about 1,500 kg.
Salesman: Well, we have a good range of medium-sized vans.
Customer: OK. I'm worried [4]_____ (get) something that will be unreliable.
Salesman: Our VW and Ford vans come with three years' free servicing, so you won't get big bills from the garage. And the latest VW also has free satellite navigation, which is great if you have drivers who aren't very good [5]_____ (read) maps.
Customer: OK, let's go and have a look at what you've got.

OVER TO YOU

Write some things you might say at a job interview using the words below and a preposition.

1 responsible   In my current job, I am responsible for running the IT department.

2 interested   _____ .
3 not interested   _____ .
4 good   _____ .
5 not very good   _____ .
6 pleased   _____ .
7 popular   _____ .
8 suitable   _____ .

68 Prepositions (5)
verb + preposition

PRESENTATION **ⓐ Verb + preposition**

Look at these common verb + preposition combinations:

agree with	*No. I don't **agree with** you. I think you're wrong.*
apply for	*Are you going to **apply for** that new job?*
belong to	*This isn't my car. It **belongs to** the company.*
deal with	*I design clothes and my partner **deals with** the money and contracts.*
depend on	*We may have the party in the garden – it **depends on** the weather.*
listen to	*You must **listen to** the instructions carefully.*
look forward to	*I **look forward to** meeting you on Monday.*
rely on	*Ken will definitely be here at 9.30. You can always **rely on** him to be on time.*
speak to	*I'd like to **speak to** Mr Ling, please.*
talk to	*I'd like to **talk to** Mr Ling, please.*
wait for	*I'll **wait for** you in Reception. See you in five minutes.*
write to	*You must **write to** the bank today.*

! In British English there is no preposition after *meet* or *phone*.
I met Juanita in Madrid last week. (not: ~~met with~~)
Can you phone Mr Martinez this afternoon? (not: ~~phone to~~)

ⓑ Verb + choice of preposition

Sometimes the same verbs can be followed by different prepositions:

complain about	*I am writing to **complain about** the noise from your restaurant.*
complain to	*If there is a problem, **complain to** the manager.*
look at	***Look at** this newspaper article – it's very interesting.*
look for	*I can't find my keys. Can you help me **look for** them?*
pay by	*I haven't got any cash. Can I **pay by** credit card or cheque?*
pay for	*How much did you **pay for** your flight?*
think about	*I'll **think about** your offer. I'll give you my answer tomorrow.*
think of	*What do you **think of** your new boss?*
work for	*Elena is my boss and she owns the company. I **work for** her.*
work with	*Maria is my colleague. I **work with** her.*

ⓒ Verb + object + preposition

These common verbs can be followed by an object + preposition:

borrow something from	*The company **borrowed** $3.2m **from** the bank.*
congratulate someone on	*I want to **congratulate** you **on** your promotion. Well done.*
lend something to	*The bank **lent** $3.2m **to** the company.*
prevent someone from	*This software will **prevent** people **from** making copies of the disk.*
provide someone with	*When you come for the interview, we will **provide** you **with** meals and accommodation.*
spend something on	*We don't **spend** money **on** TV advertising.*
thank someone for	*I am writing to **thank** you **for** helping us last week.*

❶ Verb + preposition

Say if the sentences are right or wrong and correct the mistakes.

1 I am going to apply for the job.   *right*
2 I ~~look forward at~~ hearing from you.   *wrong   look forward to*
3 You are meeting Ms Vernes tomorrow afternoon.
4 Give the report to Youssef, because he deals for all the
    clients from Iran.
5 Hello, is that Parmatal? Could I speak at Mr Benedetti,
    please?
6 Who do these keys belong in?
7 Yes, I agree on you – it's a very good idea.
8 Please could you be quiet? I'm trying to listen to
    the announcement.

❷ Verb + choice of preposition

Complete the puzzle with the missing words. Find the key word which is the name of a profession.

1 Could you have a look _____ these figures and tell me if they are
    correct?
2 I can't decide now. I need some time to think _____ the problem.
3 If you have a problem with your manager, you should complain
    _____ one of the directors.
4 My colleagues are great and I enjoy working _____ them.
5 What do you think _____ John's proposal? Is it a good idea?
6 We pay a lot _____ petrol in this country because taxes are so
    high.
The key word is: _____

❸ Verb + object + preposition

Complete the sentences with a word from each box.

| borrowed   congratulate   lend   provide   ~~spent~~   thank |

| for   from   on   ~~on~~   to   with |

1 Some telecoms companies are in trouble because they *spent* billions *on* 3G licences.
2 The company had a cash flow problem so it _____ some money _____ the
    bank.
3 I would like to _____ you all _____ working so hard this year. I am very
    grateful.
4 I'm just going to buy a card to _____ Caroline _____ her engagement.
5 Franz's car is in the garage, so I'm going to _____ mine _____ him for a week.
6 When you start working here, we will _____ you _____ a uniform.

Say what you can do in these situations. Use the word in brackets.

What can you do when you ....

1 buy something that doesn't work? (complain) *You can complain to the manufacturer.*
2 have a personal problem? (talk) _____ .
3 need $20,000 for a new car? (borrow) _____ .
4 have no cash on you? (pay) _____ .
5 can't find a job? (work) _____ .
6 miss a train? (wait) _____ .
7 don't know someone's number? (phone) _____ .
8 win the lottery? (spend) _____ .

Expressions with *make* and *do*

PRESENTATION **ⓐ** *make* and *do*

Look at the main meanings of the verbs *make* and *do*.
make = manufacture or create:
  *We **make** these radios in China.*
  *The printer **is making** a lot of noise.*

do = perform a job, activity, or action:
  A: *What **are** you **doing** at the moment?*
  B: *I'm writing a report on last week's trip.*

We also use *do* in two special questions:
  *How **do** you **do**? = Nice to meet you.*
  *What **do** you **do**? = What is your job?*

ⓑ **Expressions with *make* and *do***

We use *make* in these expressions:	We use *do* in these expressions:
make an appointment	*do business (with someone)*
make an arrangement	*do a course*
make a difference	*do an exam*
make a list	*do someone a favour*
make a mistake	*do the filing, the accounts*
make money	*do your homework*
make a noise	*do some work*
make a phone call	*do well/badly*
make a profit/loss	
make progress	

PRACTICE **❶** *make* and *do*

Match questions 1–6 with answers a–f.

1 What are you making?
2 What do you do?
3 How do you do?
4 Is Mary still very busy?
5 Are you doing anything on Friday?
6 What does your husband do?

a How do you do?
b Yes, she's still got a lot to do.
c I'm making a table for a client.
d I'm a designer.
e He's an engineer.
f No, and I'm free all weekend.

❷ *make* and *do*

Complete the sentences with *make* or *do*.

1 We **make** the components at our Augsburg factory.
2 What are we going to _____ about this problem?
3 What does he _____ for a living?
4 We are going to _____ a film for the new advertising campaign.
5 Come over tonight and I'll _____ supper.
6 Could I miss today's meeting, please? I've got so much to _____ .

❸ Expressions with *make* and *do*

Complete the email with the words in the box.

~~make~~	make	make	made	do	doing	doing

Don

I'd like to ¹**make** an appointment to see you about staffing this August – I have ² .... a list of who will be here and who will be away, and we are going to have a problem.

As you know, I am ³ .... business in Korea from 2–14 August. Sally will be on holiday for the first two weeks, and Jane is ⁴ .... a three-week IT course starting at the end of July. This means that there will be nobody here to ⁵ .... the filing, typing, and general administrative work.

I know it will be expensive to hire someone extra, but it would ⁶ .... a big difference to the department, and I would be happy to ⁷ .... all the arrangements. Bob

❹ Expressions with *make* and *do*

Complete the puzzle with the missing words. Find the key word which is the name of a mobile phone company.

1 The market is very competitive, and it is very hard to .... money.

2 Could I borrow your mobile? I need to make a .... call.

3 I'm sorry, I have made a .... The total is €23.36, not €21.36.

4 Could you .... me a favour? I need a lift to the station.

5 We bought the company for $3.2m and sold it for $4.5m, so we made a .... of $1.3m.

6 The printer is making a terrible .... Can you send someone to fix it?

7 Our income was $1.5m, but our expenses were $2m, so we made a .... of $500,000.

8 At the end of the course you will have to do an ....

The key word is : ....

OVER TO YOU

Answer the questions with your own ideas. Use an expression with *make* or *do* in each answer.

1 How are you getting on with your English?

I'm making a lot of progress. or My teacher says I'm doing very well.

2 What was your last exam or test result like?

....

3 Why can't you come out for a drink tonight?

....

4 What would you like to study in the future?

....

5 How did your company do last year?

....

6 What do you have to do before you can see a doctor?

....

7 What is one advantage of having a mobile phone?

....

8 What happens if you buy shares high and sell them low?

....

PRESENTATION **ⓐ** *have* and *have got*

We can use *have* or *have got* to mean *possess*. We only use *have got* in the present tense:
> *I've got a new job.*
> *I've got a bad headache.*
> *I haven't got any money.*

In other tenses (past and future), we use *have*:
> *He had a good job a few years ago.*
> *I had a bad headache yesterday.*
> *Will you have enough money?*

ⓑ **Expressions with *have* or *have got***

We can use *have* or *have got* with these nouns to make common expressions:

have a good idea	*have experience*
have a meeting	*have a question, have any questions*
have a point	*have an advantage/a lot of advantages*
have a feeling	*have time (to do something)*
have a problem/a lot of problems	*have the money (to do something)*
have a complaint	*have the chance (to do something)*
have a degree/an MBA	*have a day/week/month (to do something)*
have a suggestion	

ⓒ **Activities with *have***

We use *have* to talk about these activities:

have a party	*have a bad day*
have a shower	*have second thoughts (about something)*
have lunch	*have a go (= try)*
have a meal/sandwich	*have a word/a chat (with someone)*
have a cup of coffee	*have a look at*
have a good time/a hard time	*have difficulty (with something)*

We do not use *have got* to talk about activities. Compare:
> *I have got a shower.* (There is a shower in my house. It is in my bathroom.)
> *I am having a shower.* (I am in the shower. I am having a wash.)

PRACTICE **❶** *have* and *have got*

Choose the correct option from the words in *italics*.

1 I *had/~~had got~~* a bad headache this morning, but it's gone now.
2 *Have you/Have you got* a message for me?
3 I haven't got the information today, but I *will have/will have got* it tomorrow.
4 He went home early yesterday because he *doesn't get/didn't have* any meetings.
5 Before I came to America, I *had/had got* a house in England.
6 In the 1930s, many European countries *had/had got* economic problems.

2 Expressions with *have* or *have got*

Complete the conversation with the words in the box.

> degree   experience   feeling   meeting   idea   ~~problem~~
> question   suggestions   time   a week

Dave: As you know, Herr Fischer in Luxembourg has had an accident and will be off work for six months. That means we've got a ¹ problem. We need to find someone to replace him, and fast. Has anyone got any ² _____ ?

Ken: Why don't we advertise for someone?

Dave: We haven't got ³ _____ . There's a very important conference in Luxembourg on the 18th, and it's the 10th today, so we've only got ⁴ _____ or so to find a new manager.

Oliver: I have an ⁵ _____ . How about Petra? She's very competent.

Dave: That's a very good idea.

Ken: Excuse me, I have a ⁶ _____ .

Dave: Yes, Ken, what is it you want to know?

Ken: Sorry, I haven't met Petra. Who is she?

Dave: Well, she's quite new here, but she's got a lot of ⁷ _____ in sales and marketing. She's also got a ⁸ _____ in modern languages and an MBA.

Ken: How would she feel about moving so quickly?

Oliver: I can't be sure, but I have a ⁹ _____ she would really like the job. In fact, I've got a ¹⁰ _____ with her later on today. I can ask her if you like.

3 Activities with *have*

Look at the pictures. Say what the people are doing with the words in the box.

> a bad day   a chat   ~~a cup of coffee~~   a party   a shower   lunch

1 He is having a cup of coffee.
2 They _____ .
3 He _____ .
4 Sarah and Karen _____ .
5 She _____ .
6 Jonas and Elka _____ .

OVER TO YOU

Write sentences about yourself or your work using the words below and *have* or *have got*.

1 problems   We had problems with our new software last week.
2 experience   _____ .
3 degree   _____ .
4 a meeting   _____ .
5 lunch   _____ .
6 a good time _____ .
7 the money to _____ .
8 a word with _____ .

Expressions with *get*

PRESENTATION   **a**   **Meanings of** *get*

We use *get* to mean *receive*:
>*If you buy five items you get a discount.*
>*I got your letter yesterday.*

We use *get to* to mean *arrive at*:
>*I'll phone you when I get to the hotel.*
>*She got to the meeting at 10.30.*

We use *get* + comparative adjective to mean *become* or *change* in some way:
>*The economy is slowly getting better.*

Often we repeat the comparative:
>*The economy is getting better and better.*

b   **Expressions with** *get*

There are many common expressions with *get*:

get back to someone (= reply)	*I don't know the answer, but I'll check and get back to you.*
get drunk	*A lot of people got drunk on champagne at the office party.*
get to know someone	*He seems serious, but he's good fun when you get to know him.*
get married/divorced	*We plan to get married in June.*
get ready (= prepare)	*The presentation is at 10.00, so you have an hour to get ready.*
get the sack (= lose your job)	*Tony got the sack because he was always late for work.*
get started (= begin)	*We have a lot of work, so we should get started.*
get together (with someone)	*Let's get together for a drink after work.*
get in touch (with someone)	*If you need more information, please get in touch.*
get into (financial) trouble	*The company got into trouble when several bills were not paid.*

c   **Two- and three-part verbs with** *get*

There are many two- and three-part verbs with *get*:

get away (= leave)	*I'm hoping to get away from work early on Friday.*
get in (= arrive)	*My flight to Paris gets in at 10.45.*
get on with someone	*I get on with my colleagues very well.*
get on with something	*I can't talk now – I need to get on with this report.*
get over something (= recover from)	*It took a long time for Alain to get over losing his job.*
get round to (doing) something	*I haven't read the report yet – I'll get round to it later.*
get up	*I have to get up at 05.00 to catch the early flight to Brussels.*

I get on with my colleagues.

Be quiet, I'm trying to get on with my work.

① Meanings of *get*

Rewrite the sentences with *get*.

1 Your letter arrived yesterday. I got your letter yesterday.
2 My salary is about £3,000 a month. I _____ .
3 Order today and we will send you a free gift. Order today and you _____ .
4 Computers are becoming cheaper and cheaper. Computers _____ .
5 The market is expanding. The market _____ .
6 He arrived at work late. He _____ .

② Expressions with *get*

Complete the sentences with a suitable word to make an expression with *get*.

1 My boss is getting married next month. The wedding is on the 20th.
2 I can't decide now, but I am interested and I will get _____ to you as soon as I can.
3 I'm new here, but I'm getting to _____ a few people and I feel at home.
4 Let's get _____ for lunch one day next week and discuss the proposal.
5 We have a lot to discuss in today's meeting, so let's get _____ right away.
6 Getting _____ at the office party is not a good idea.
7 I want to prepare my notes and get _____ for the presentation.
8 Thanks for your contact details – I will get in _____ when I have some news.
9 You may get into _____ if you don't pay your tax bill.
10 She stole some money from the company, so she got the _____ .

③ Two- and three-part verbs with *get*

Replace the words in *italics* with the verbs in the box.

get away	get over	get on with	get up	~~get in~~

1 Do you know what time the trains from London *arrive* this evening? get in
2 I go to bed early and *get out of bed* at 6.00 in the morning. _____
3 It took the company a long time to *recover from* the loss of the contract. _____
4 Do you *have a good relationship with* your new secretary? _____
5 The traffic will be bad, so I'd like to *leave* early this afternoon. _____

Write sentences about yourself using the words in the box. Put the sentences in the Personal/Home column or the Work/Office column.

~~get a new car~~	~~get married~~	get angry	get up	get to work	get home
get on with	get together	get to know			

Personal/Home
My sister got married three years ago.

Work/Office
I'm going to get a new company car next month.

PRESENTATION **ⓐ Expressions with *give***

Here are some common expressions with *give*:

give a presentation   give someone a discount (= a lower price)
give someone my regards   give someone a refund (= return their money)
give someone a call/ring   give someone a reference (for a job)
give someone an opportunity/a chance   give someone an idea
give notice (= say when you will
leave your job)

ⓑ Expressions with *take*

Here are some common expressions with *take*:

take a photo (of someone/something)   take care (of someone/something)
take time (to do something)   take action (= do something)
take ten minutes/two hours   take place (= happen)
take advantage of someone   take part in (an activity)

Note the way we use *take* to ask and answer questions about time:
A: *How long does it take you to get to work?*   B: *It takes me twenty minutes by car.*

ⓒ Two-part verbs with *give* and *take*

Look at these common two-part verbs:
give up (= stop doing something)
give away (= let someone have something for free)
take over (= take control of a company or organization)
take up (= occupy time or space)
take on (= employ)
I gave up smoking when they made the office a no-smoking zone.
We gave away 1,000 copies of the new book to bookshops and journalists.

PRACTICE **① Expressions with *give* and *take***

Complete the puzzle with the missing words. Find the key word.

	1				
1	N	O	T	I	C	E

1 After the trial period, employees must give one month's **notice**.
2 If the goods are faulty, we will replace them or give you a full
   ....
3 .... me a ring when you get to the airport.
4 The Frankfurt Motor Show will take .... in September.
5 If you see Hiroshi, please give him my .... – he's an ol
   friend of mine.
6 If you want to .... a photo, you can use my digital
   camera.
7 We will give you a .... of 10% on orders of 40 or more
8 My previous employer says that she will give me a ....

The key word is: ....

② Expressions with *give* and *take*

Complete the text with the words in the box.

| action | ~~advantage~~ | call | opportunity | part | place | presentations | half an hour |

Thurgau High-Tech Business Park, Switzerland
Central European Location

Many international companies are coming to the high-tech Business Park in Thurgau, Switzerland to take

[1] **advantage** of its excellent facilities.

The authorities have taken [2] _____ to make sure that Thurgau is attractive to new businesses. There are low

tax rates and special discounts which give new companies the [3] _____ to save money.

Advanced telecommunications mean that you can take [4] _____ in meetings or give [5] _____ over the

Internet, saving time and money.

If you need to travel, the Business Park is close to Zurich. It only takes [6] _____ to get to Zurich Kloten-Airport,

and Thurgau is only 160 km from Stuttgart, where high-tech conferences regularly take [7] _____ .

For more information, please give us a [8] _____ on 329 43 43 43, or contact us at www.withurgau.ch.

---

③ Two-part verbs with *give* and *take*

Complete the texts with the two-part verbs in the box which mean the same as the phrases in brackets.

| ~~give up~~ | give away | take on | take over | take up |

Dart Software has announced that is going to [1] **give up** (stop) developing Internet browser software. Company chairman Dan Brooker explained: 'We all know that the big companies [2] _____ (let people have) their browsers for free, but we can't do that. It [3] _____ (uses) too much of our budget and we can't afford it.'

A leading supermarket is going to [4] _____ (buy) the Dalton chain of corner shops. It is planning to open 250 extra stores and will [5] _____ (employ) 1,000 new workers.

OVER TO YOU

Make true sentences about yourself or your company using expressions with *give* or *take* and the words below.

1 ring   I'm going to give my colleague in Austria a ring this afternoon.
2 presentations I _____ .
3 give up   I _____ .
4 time   It _____ .
5 discounts   We _____ .
6 place   Our _____ .
7 action   We _____ .

Appendix 1 – Spelling rules

1 Verbs

With most verbs in the present simple, we add -s to the verb in the 3rd person, and make no other changes:

I/you/we/they run	he/she/it runs

With verbs that end in -o, -ch, -ss, -sh, and -x, we add -es:

I/you/we/they go	he/she/it goes
I/you/we/they teach	he/she/it teaches
I/you/we/they miss	he/she/it misses
I/you/we/they rush	he/she/it rushes
I/you/we/they fix	he/she/it fixes

With verbs that end in a consonant + -y, we remove the -y and add -ies:

I/you/we/they try	he/she/it tries

2 Nouns

Most nouns just add -s to make the plural form:

pen	pens

Nouns ending in -ch, -ss, -sh, and -x add -es in the plural:

match	matches
class	classes
dish	dishes
box	boxes

Nouns ending in a consonant + -y drop the -y and add -ies:

party	parties

Nouns ending in a vowel + -y add -s:

day	days

3 -ing form

With most verbs, we add -ing to the verb and make no other changes:

build	building
try	trying

With one-syllable verbs that have a short vowel sound, and end in a consonant, we double the consonant and add -ing:

sit	sitting
run	running

If the vowel sound is long, we do not double the consonant:

read	reading
speak	speaking

If the verb ends in a silent -e, we delete the -e and add -ing:

take	taking
drive	driving

4 Past tense, regular verbs

With most regular verbs, we add -ed to form the past tense:

look	looked
stay	stayed

If the verb ends in a silent -e, we just add -d:

like	liked
behave	behaved

If the verb ends in a consonant + -y, we remove the -y and add -ied:

try	tried
deny	denied

If the verb has a short vowel sound and ends in a consonant, we double the consonant:

stop	stopped
ban	banned

Appendix 2 – Irregular verbs

Verb	Past tense	Past participle
be	was, were	been
become	became	become
begin	began	begun
bleed	bled	bled
blow	blew	blown
break	broke	broken
bring	brought	brought
build	built	built
buy	bought	bought
choose	chose	chosen
come	came	come
cost	cost	cost
cut	cut	cut
deal	dealt	dealt
dig	dug	dug
do	did	done
drive	drove	driven
eat	ate	eaten
fall	fell	fallen
feel	felt	felt
find	found	found
fly	flew	flown
forget	forgot	forgotten
get	got	got
give	gave	given
go	went	gone
grow	grew	grown
have	had	had
hear	heard	heard
hold	held	held
keep	kept	kept
know	knew	known
lay	laid	lay
lead	led	led
learn	learnt/learned	learnt/learned
leave	left	left
lend	lent	lent
let	let	let

Verb	Past tense	Past participle
lie	lay	lain
light	lit	lit
lose	lost	lost
make	made	made
mean	meant	meant
meet	met	met
pay	paid	paid
put	put	put
read	read	read
ring	rang	rung
rise	rose	risen
run	ran	run
say	said	said
see	saw	seen
sell	sold	sold
send	sent	sent
set	set	set
sit	sat	sat
speak	spoke	spoken
spell	spelt/spelled	spelt/spelled
spend	spent	spent
stand	stood	stood
steal	stole	stolen
take	took	taken
teach	taught	taught
tear	tore	torn
tell	told	told
think	thought	thought
throw	threw	thrown
understand	understood	understood
wear	wore	worn
win	won	won
wind	wound	wound
write	wrote	written

Verbs from this list are also irregular when they have a prefix, e.g. *mistake – mistook – mistaken; withstand – withstood – withstood.*

Answer key

1   *to be* (1)

EXERCISE 1

2 We   5 She
3 They   6 He
4 It

EXERCISE 2

2 It is in Paris.   5 It is in Dubai.
3 They are in New York.   6 He is in Sydney.
4 She is in Rome.

EXERCISE 3

2 's   5 're
3 'm   6 're
4 're

OVER TO YOU (Sample answers only)

Surname: Petersen
First name: Gustav
Nationality: Norwegian
Age: 22
Status: single
Occupation: Graphic Designer

My name is Gustav Petersen and I am from Norway.
I am 22 and I am single.
I am a graphic designer.

2   *to be* (2): questions and negatives

EXERCISE 1

2 Are we on the same flight?   5 Are they in Tokyo?
3 Is Mme Strens free?   6 Am I late?
4 Is the conference in July?

EXERCISE 2 (Long forms are also correct)

2 I'm afraid she isn't free at the moment. She's in a meeting.
3 I'm sorry, they aren't in the office today. They're in London.
4 I'm afraid we aren't open on Saturday. We're open from Monday to Friday.

EXERCISE 3

2 No, they aren't.   5 Yes, he is.
3 No, we aren't.   6 Yes, I am.
4 Yes, she is.

OVER TO YOU (Sample answers only)

1 Is your boss American?   No, she isn't.
2 Is your boss from Iceland?   No, she isn't.
3 Is your Head Office in London?   No, it isn't.
4 Are you a doctor?   No, I'm not.
5 Are you from Paraguay?   No, I'm not.
6 Are you married?   Yes, I am.

3   *have* and *have got*

EXERCISE 1

2 has got/'s got   6 has got/'s got
3 has got/'s got   7 have got/'ve got
4 have got/'ve got   8 have got/'ve got
5 has got/'s got

EXERCISE 2

3 hasn't got   6 Have (you) got
4 haven't got   7 haven't got
5 Have (we) got   8 Have (you) got

EXERCISE 3

2 Have (you) got   9 have got/'ve got
3 have   10 Have (you) got
4 have got/'ve got   11 haven't got
5 have got/'ve got   12 Have (you) got
6 have (you) got   13 haven't
7 has got/'s got   14 have got/'ve got
8 has got/'s got

OVER TO YOU (Sample answers only)

2 I've got a TV, but I haven't got an Ipod.
3 I've got a car, but I haven't got a motorbike.
4 I've got Windows XP, but I haven't got Quark.
5 I've got a suit, but I haven't got a cashmere coat.
6 I've got a tennis racket, but I haven't got a football.
7 I've got an MBA, but I haven't got a PhD.
8 I've got a brother, but I haven't got a sister.

4   Present simple (1)

EXERCISE 1

3 wrong – lives   6 wrong – looks
4 wrong – agree   7 wrong – work
5 right   8 right

EXERCISE 2

2 fixes   6 watches
3 flies   7 mixes
4 goes   8 tries
5 finishes

EXERCISE 3

2 watches   12 talk
3 listens   13 spends
4 reads   14 goes
5 arrives   15 come
6 has   16 tell
7 opens   17 is
8 replies   18 works
9 works   19 says
10 make   20 enjoy
11 have

EXERCISE 4

2 makes
3 employs
4 uses
5 come

6 distributes
7 sells
8 owns

OVER TO YOU (Sample answers only)

1 I work for a bank in London.
2 I live in a flat in Docklands and I am single.
3 In the evenings, I go out with friends or have people to dinner.
4 My company specializes in lending money to entrepreneurs.

5 Present simple (2): questions and negatives

EXERCISE 1

2 Do you work for Sotheby's?   Yes, I do.
3 Does your boss travel to New York a lot? No, he doesn't.
4 Do your colleagues like the new office? Yes, they do.
5 Do you work at weekends?   No, we don't.
6 Does your company operate in Europe? Yes, it does.

EXERCISE 2

2 doesn't work
3 don't give
4 don't know
5 doesn't come
6 don't advertise
7 don't want
8 don't use

EXERCISE 3

3 wrong – don't like
4 wrong – doesn't eat
5 wrong – does your colleague/do your colleagues
6 wrong – do you want
7 right
8 wrong – does he travel

OVER TO YOU (Sample answers only)

2 Do you live near the place you work? Yes, I do.
3 Do you come from Spain?   No, I don't.
4 Do you speak Arabic?   Yes, I do.
5 Do you work for yourself?   Yes, I do.
6 Do you drive to work?   Yes, I do.

6 Questions

EXERCISE 1

2 Do you pay
3 B: Yes, I do.
4 Does your colleague want
5 Do you come
6 Does he want
7 A: Do you live here?
8 Do American companies pay

EXERCISE 2

2 How do you spell your name?
3 What is your mobile number?
4 When does the next talk start?
5 Why do you like big cities?
6 Where do you come from?
7 Who do you work for?

EXERCISE 3

2 How do you do?   5 How is he?
3 What do you do?   6 What's it like?
4 Who do you work for?

OVER TO YOU (Sample answers only)

1 What's your name?
2 Where do you come from?
3 Where do you live?
4 What do you do?
5 Who do you work for?
6 What's your number?
7 What's your email address?
8 When do you finish work?

7 Present continuous (1): *I am doing*

EXERCISE 1

2 are trying   5 are meeting
3 is helping   6 am finishing
4 is working

EXERCISE 2

2 Anna is leaving the manager's office.
3 Someone is taking away a computer.
4 David is turning off the lights.
5 Klaus is driving out of the car park.
6 Two men are waiting at the back door.

EXERCISE 3

2 Markus and Ingrid are newsreaders. This week they are making a commercial in New York.

3 Sue is a nurse. This week she is attending a conference in Paris.

4 Johannes is a lorry driver. This week he is doing a language course in Seville.

5 Franz is a chef. This week he is playing golf with friends in La Manga.

6 Bob is a builder. This week he is sailing in the South of France.

OVER TO YOU (Sample answers only)

Right now

1 I am working in the study.
2 I am wearing a dark suit.
3 No, I am not listening to the radio.
4 Yes, I am working at a desk.
5 I am writing with a blue pen.

Current projects

1 I am doing a course in DTP.
2 I am learning Spanish.
3 I am designing a new magazine.
4 They are producing other journals.
5 It is expanding into South America.

8 Present continuous (2): questions and negatives

EXERCISE 1

2 Are you looking for something?   Yes, I am.
3 Is the photocopier working yet?   No, it isn't.
4 Are they having a meeting?   Yes, they are.
5 Is Gina working with you?   Yes, she is

EXERCISE 2

2 Who is Hans having lunch with?
3 What are you eating?
4 Where is Olga giving the presentation?
5 Who are you phoning?
6 What's Herr Braun doing?

EXERCISE 3

2 Pierre is not talking to Alain or Michel.
3 Alain is not holding a glass of wine.
4 Anna is not wearing a red dress.
5 Marie is not leaving the party.
6 Pierre is not talking to Laure or Marie.

Names:

1 Marie   5 Pierre
2 Anna   6 Gina
3 Alain   7 Laure
4 Michel

OVER TO YOU (Sample answers only)

2 Where are you going?
3 What are you drinking?
4 Who are you talking to?
5 Why are you calling?
6 How are you feeling?

9 Present simple or present continuous (1)

EXERCISE 1

2 take
3 am having
4 don't work
5 is having
6 gets
7 am calling
8 use

EXERCISE 2

2 I work for Honda.
  We manufacture cars.
  At the moment we are developing a new hydrogen car.
3 I work for Danzig Telecom.
  We install mobile phone systems.
  At the moment we are building a new telecoms system in India.
4 I work for Gravis Books.
  We publish books and magazines.
  At the moment we are producing a new encyclopedia.

EXERCISE 3

2 are selling
3 look
4 are giving away
5 is
6 are offering
7 is
8 tastes
9 costs
10 are cutting

OVER TO YOU (Sample answers only)

I work for JB Accounting. We are a small accountancy firm and we look after clients in the local area.
At the moment I am preparing the tax returns for my clients. It is a very busy time of year and everyone is working very hard.

Present simple or present continuous (2): actions and states

EXERCISE 1

1 b action
2 a action
  b state
3 a state
  b state

EXERCISE 2

2 belongs
3 look
4 likes
5 know
6 believe
7 look like
8 loves
9 thinks
10 hate
11 seems
12 know
13 want

EXERCISE 3

3 right
4 wrong – Klaus wants
5 wrong – You don't seem
6 wrong – Do you like
7 right
8 wrong – I feel
9 right
10 right

OVER TO YOU (Sample answers only)

Possessions: I have a nice car and a lovely house.
I want a new MP3 player and some new clothes.
Likes and dislikes: I like classical guitar music, but I don't like modern classical music.
Opinions: People like our products and we believe in them.
Appearance: At work I look smart and wear expensive suits. At home I look relaxed and wear jeans.

 Past simple (1): regular verbs: *I worked*

EXERCISE 1

3 past
4 past
5 present
6 past
7 present
8 present

EXERCISE 2

2 graduated
3 decided
4 moved
5 rented
6 worked
7 designed
8 called
9 used
10 added
11 started
12 ordered
13 expanded
14 entered
15 manufactured

EXERCISE 3

3 at
4 on
5 Ø
6 in
7 Ø
8 in
9 at
10 in

OVER TO YOU (Sample answers only)

2 I studied Mechanical Engineering.
3 I liked Physics.
4 I disliked Chemistry.
5 No, I didn't.
6 Yes, I worked in a hospital.
7 I graduated in 2002.
8 I started my first job in September 2002.

Past simple (2): regular verbs: questions and negatives: *Did I ...?, I didn't ...*

EXERCISE 1

2 Did you want
3 Did you attend
4 Did the payment arrive
5 Did you stay
6 Did you post
7 Did they change
8 Did she travel

EXERCISE 2

2 Why did she travel to Venice?
3 When did she arrive?
4 Where did she stay?
5 What tourist sights did she visit?
6 When did she return to Brazil?
8 She travelled to attend the IWT conference.
9 She arrived on 18 June.
10 She stayed at the Palazzo Hotel.
11 She visited the Doge's Palace and the Campanile.
12 She returned to Brazil on 21 June.

EXERCISE 3

2 didn't stay
3 didn't look at
4 didn't use
5 didn't visit
6 didn't order

OVER TO YOU (Sample answers only)

1 I worked for a big organization.
2 I worked in the Import-Export Department.
3 The working day started at 7.30.
4 The working day finished at 4.00.
5 No, I didn't enjoy the work.
6 Yes, I liked the people.
7 I didn't like the filing.
8 No, but I earned some money.
9 I stayed for two months.

13 Past simple (3): irregular verbs

EXERCISE 1

2 was
3 Did you have
4 had
5 were
6 was
7 Did you have
8 didn't have
9 weren't
10 were

EXERCISE 2

2 got
3 forgot
4 left
5 met
6 brought
7 put
8 found
9 wasn't
10 made
11 didn't know
12 didn't have
13 rang
14 drove
15 paid
16 thought
17 set
18 began
19 took
20 became
21 went
22 meant
23 didn't have
24 felt
25 grew
26 saw
27 came

EXERCISE 3

2 didn't know
3 didn't have
4 didn't pay
5 didn't feel
7 Did, have
8 did, ring
9 did, bring
10 Did, set

OVER TO YOU (Sample answers only)

1 In 2000, I bought a new house.
2 Five years ago, I got a new job.
3 Last year, I went to Austria.
4 Last summer, I didn't have any time off.
5 Last week, I met some colleagues from Japan.

14 Past continuous: *I was doing*

EXERCISE 1

2 we were working
3 they were not expecting
4 it was raining
5 Was the train waiting
6 he was travelling

EXERCISE 2

1 was coming
2 weren't working
3 was going
4 was thinking
5 were having
6 wasn't going

EXERCISE 3

2 fell
3 was fixing
4 was mending
5 broke
6 burned

OVER TO YOU (Sample answers only)

2 While we were having a meeting last week, Caroline came in to say hello.
3 While I was looking for a job, I heard about a vacancy in Ethiopia.
4 While we were having a skiing holiday in Austria, I fell and broke my arm.
5 While I was going home from work last week, I ran out of petrol.
6 While I was travelling to New York in 1998, I met a famous pop star on the plane.

15 Used to: *I used to do*

EXERCISE 1

3 The factory used to be in Charentes.
4 The unions used to be powerful.
5 I used to live in Kuwait too.
6 Did you use to work with Alain?
7 I didn't use to have a long journey to work.
8 Factories used to be very dangerous.
9 It used to take a long time to travel to the USA.
10 We didn't use to need IT specialists.

EXERCISE 2

3 There used to be a lot of accidents.
4 The workers used to go on strike.
5 Relationships between the management and workers used to be bad.
6 They didn't use to run training courses.
7 The management didn't use to communicate well.
8 The mine didn't use to be profitable.

EXERCISE 3

2 It used to be difficult to travel to, but now it has good transport links.
3 It used to have social problems, but now it is a popular area.
4 It used to have poor housing, but now it has skyscrapers and luxury flats.
5 It used to have no facilities, but now it has a university, an airport, and an exhibition centre.

OVER TO YOU (Sample answers only)

2 I used to be an accountant, but now I am a film producer.
3 I used to work for Mr Davos, but now I work for myself.
4 I used to earn $30,000, but now I earn $60,000.
5 I used to want to be a Company Director, but now I want to win an Oscar.

16 Future (1): *I will*

EXERCISE 1
2 I won't be able
3 Everything will be
4 will the economy start

5 our prices will rise
6 interest rates will go up

EXERCISE 2
2 will grow
3 will become
4 won't continue
5 will export
6 will start
7 won't be

8 will cost
9 will become
10 will have
11 will increase
12 will lead

EXERCISE 3
2 I'll use another one.
3 I'll send it today.
4 I'll come next week.

5 I'll have a word with her.
6 I'll take another route.

OVER TO YOU (Sample answers only
2 I think they will rise next year.
3 I don't think the Democrats will win next time.
4 I think the Labour party will win.
5 I think it will become more unpredictable.
6 I think they will rise.
7 I think I will get married and have children.
8 Yes, but I don't think I will move to the country.

17 Future (2): *I am doing*

EXERCISE 1
3 wrong – You're seeing
4 wrong – What are you doing
5 right
6 wrong – Tanya is seeing

7 wrong – I'm not doing
8 wrong – are you leaving
9 right
10 right

EXERCISE 2 (Full forms are also correct)
2 you're staying
3 I'm meeting
4 are we doing
5 We're doing
6 you're giving
7 you're having

8 he's taking
9 am I getting
10 Pauline Freyer is coming
11 she's driving
12 Where are we staying
13 You're staying

EXERCISE 3
2 goes
3 don't change
4 does it get
5 arrives

6 departs
7 does it arrive
8 gets

OVER TO YOU (Sample answers only)
2 I'm seeing John Davis on the 21st.
3 I'm going to London on Friday afternoon.
4 Bob is sending me some papers next week.
5 Jane is coming over for a meeting on the 27th.
7 We are going to Amanda's house at the weekend.
8 We are going sailing on Sunday.
9 I'm playing tennis on Friday.
10 I'm seeing Anna on Sunday morning.

18 Future (3): *I am going to do*

EXERCISE 1
2 are we going to do
3 is going to look after
4 are going to help
5 is going to ring

6 am not going to send
7 Who is going to look after
8 is going to collect

EXERCISE 2
2 c
3 a
4 e

5 b
6 g
7 d

EXERCISE 3
2 are going to be
3 is going to have
4 are going to build

5 are going to come
6 are going to buy
7 are going to provide

EXERCISE 4
2 She is going to write a cheque.
3 They are going to order lunch.
4 He is going to answer the phone.
5 They are going to paint the office.
6 He is going to change the tyre.

OVER TO YOU (Sample answers only)
2 I am going to hire two new assistants.
3 I am going to start a new project.
4 I am going to go to Monaco in September.
6 We are going to bring out a new model in September.
7 We are going to hire 500 new workers.
8 We are going to open a subsidiary in Germany.

19 Future (4): *I am going to do, I will do,* or *I am doing*

EXERCISE 1

2 are going to
3 'll
4 are going to
5 is going to

6 are going to
7 will
8 is going to

EXERCISE 2

3 'm having
4 are starting
5 will be
6 will learn
7 am staying

8 won't have to
9 'll see
10 'll make
11 am coming
12 'll give

EXERCISE 3

2 am having
3 will be
4 will recover
5 'll give

6 going to reach
7 'm not doing
8 'll send

OVER TO YOU (Sample answers only)

Plans
  2 I'm going to take over a new department in October.
  3 The company is going to appoint a new director.
Predictions
  5 I think interest rates will fall.
  6 I think the government will try to raise taxes.
Arrangements
  8 I am having a meeting with Tom to get the designs.
  9 I am seeing Mr Lopez in Madrid next week to discuss the latest sales figures.

20 Present perfect (1): *I have done*

EXERCISE 1

2 has taken
3 have relocated
4 have made

5 have ordered
6 have lost

EXERCISE 2

2 a He is going to take off his tie.
  b He has just taken off his tie.
3 a The plane is going to land.
  b The plane has just landed.

EXERCISE 3

2 have just resigned
3 has just finished
4 have just announced

5 has just exploded
6 have just fallen

EXERCISE 4

3 right
4 right
5 right
6 wrong – We arrived

OVER TO YOU (Sample answers only)

2 Janet has taken over the department.
3 I have moved house.
4 I have just started learning French.
5 Lara Bright has got married.

21 Present perfect (2): questions and negatives

EXERCISE 1

2 d
3 f
4 g
5 h

6 a
7 b
8 e

EXERCISE 2

a 7
b 3
c 4
d 5

e 2
f 8
g 6
h 9

EXERCISE 3

2 A: Have you ever used Linux?
  B: No, I've never used Linux.
3 A: Have you ever fired anyone?
  B: No, I've never fired anyone.
4 A: Has you boss ever been to London?
  B: No, he's never been to London.

EXERCISE 4

2 A: Have you ever been to China?
  B: Yes, I have.
  A: When did you go there?
  B: I went there last July.
3 A: Have you ever worked in South America?
  B: Yes, I have.
  A: Where did you work?
  B: I worked in Brazil in the 1990s.

OVER TO YOU (Sample answers only)

2 Have you ever been to England?   Yes, I have.
3 Have you ever worked abroad?   Yes, I have.
4 Have you ever given a presentation
  in English?   No, I haven't.
5 Have you ever met the head of
  your company?   Yes, I have.
6 Have you ever flown First Class?   Yes, I have.
7 Have you ever missed a plane?   No, I haven't.
8 Have you ever run a large department?   Yes, I have.

22 Present perfect (3): *already, yet*

EXERCISE 1
2 have already agreed
3 have already discussed
4 has already made
5 has already written
6 have already seen
7 have already said

EXERCISE 2
2 They haven't finished the main stadium yet.
3 They haven't built the Olympic Village yet.
4 They haven't constructed the new railway yet.
5 They haven't planted the Olympic Park yet.

EXERCISE 3
2 Have you received, yet
3 Have you seen, yet
4 Have they signed, yet
5 Have you moved, yet

EXERCISE 4
2 Have you spoken, yet
3 have already reached
4 has not arrived yet
5 have already had lunch
6 have not finished it yet

OVER TO YOU (Sample answers only)
2 I have already had a best-selling product.
3 I have already organized our main conference.
4 I have already run two large projects.
5 I have already been in charge of an international project.
7 I haven't run my own department yet.
8 I haven't worked abroad yet.
9 I haven't met the chairman yet.
10 I haven't retired yet.

 ## 23 Present perfect (4): *for, since*

EXERCISE 1
2 has been
3 was
4 went on

EXERCISE 2
2 He has owned the school for five years.
3 It has been in Durban for four years.
4 He has had the Cessnas for seven years.
5 He has had the helicopters for a year.
6 He has been at the school for two years.

EXERCISE 3
2 We have been in our new offices since the 19th.
3 Laura has had a Powerbook since May.
4 I have known Mr Ng since 2001.
5 We have had broadband since July.

EXERCISE 4
2 How long has he had that Mercedes?
3 How long has Peter had an assistant?
4 How long have you been unemployed?
5 How long have you known about their plans?
6 How long has Maria been ill?

OVER TO YOU (Sample answers only)
2 I am a general manager.
   I have been a general manager for three years.
3 I have an Audi.
   I have had an Audi since 2004.
4 I am divorced.
   I have been divorced for three years.

 ## 24 Present perfect (5): present perfect or past simple

EXERCISE 1
2 has just bought
3 took
4 appointed
5 sold
6 have just risen

EXERCISE 2
2 have
3 worked
4 have never been
5 Have you had
6 went
7 have already offered
8 haven't made
9 How long has she known
10 has been
11 took
12 have known
13 worked

EXERCISE 3
2 have been
3 got
4 has already phoned
5 arrived
6 haven't seen
7 didn't see
8 ordered

OVER TO YOU (Sample answers only)
2 Liz has taken a job with the BBC.
3 Paul has left.
4 We've moved to a new building.
6 I haven't ordered the materials for the new building.
7 I have discussed the new plans with the contractor.
8 I have set up a meeting with the architect.
10 I have shown an ability to communicate well.
11 I have never had any problems with colleagues.
12 I have always reached my targets.

25 Present perfect continuous: *I have been doing*

EXERCISE 1

2 How long has he been running his own company?
He has been running his own company for five years.
3 How long have they been looking for new drugs?
They have been looking for new drugs for five years.
4 How long have they been testing the drug for hepatitis?
They have been testing the drug for hepatitis for three years.
5 How long have they been waiting for a licence?
They have been waiting for a licence for two months.

EXERCISE 2

2 How long have you known Xavier?
3 My boss has been away for two weeks.
4 I have been learning English for three years.
5 How long have you been living in the States?
6 *The Times* newspaper has belonged to Mr Murdoch since 1976.
7 We have been working on this project since last July.
8 Interest rates have been falling since last year.

OVER TO YOU (Sample answers only)

2 How long have you been working for them?
3 How long have you been married?
4 How long have you been working with her?
5 How long have you been doing that?
7 I have been living in Berlin for two years.
8 I have been working for them for six months.
9 I have been working in this department for two months.

26 Passive (1): *is done, are done*

EXERCISE 1

1 is
2 are, are
3 am, are
4 is, are
5 are, are

EXERCISE 2

2 manufactured
3 received
4 appointed
5 checked
6 grown
7 given
8 sent
9 spent
10 met

EXERCISE 3

2 are produced
3 are grown
4 are picked
5 are taken
6 are cooled
7 are packed
8 are transported
9 are flown
10 are sold
11 are imported
12 are repackaged
13 are exported

OVER TO YOU (Sample answers only)

2 We are not allowed to smoke anywhere in the building.
3 We are expected to complete our projects on time.
4 We are paid once a month.
5 We are never asked to work at weekends.
6 We are sent spam every day.

27 Passive (2): *was done, were done*

EXERCISE 1

2 was directed
3 was written
4 was established
5 was not made
6 were added

EXERCISE 2

2 were joined
3 was produced
4 were ordered
5 were received
6 were solved
7 were sold
8 were bought
9 was dominated
10 was designed
11 was launched
12 were ordered

EXERCISE 3

2 Where was your last conference held?
3 The project was delayed for three months.
4 In 2004, Abbey National was taken over by Banco Santander.
5 Rubber was introduced to Malaysia after 1900.
6 The London Eye was built in 1999.

OVER TO YOU (Sample answers only)

1 I was born in Italy.
2 My company was founded in 1886.
3 My department was set up in 2002.
4 My boss was appointed last year.
5 I was promoted in 2005.

28 Ability and permission: *can, could*

EXERCISE 1
2 can deal with figures
3 can use a PC
4 can't see
5 can't hear
6 can organize your work well
7 can deal with people
8 can explain things well

EXERCISE 2
2 could
3 couldn't
4 can't
5 can
6 couldn't
7 could
8 can't

EXERCISE 3
2 You can smoke here.
3 You can't use your mobile.
4 You can't take any photos.
5 You can't turn right.
6 You can't drink the water.
7 You can park here.
8 You can leave the building here.

OVER TO YOU (Sample answers only)
2 I can play the guitar, but I can't play the piano.
3 I can use Microsoft Word, but I can't use Excel.
4 I can play tennis, but I can't sail.
5 I can work alone, but I can't work with lots of other people.
6 I can wear a blue or grey suit, but I can't wear jeans.

29 Requests and offers: *Could you ...?, Shall I ...?, Would you like me to ...?*

EXERCISE 1
2 Could I speak to Jane Grace, please?
3 Could you hold on a minute, please?
4 Could you take a message for me?
5 Could you ask her to ring Mr Baxter urgently?
6 Could I have your number?

EXERCISE 2
2 Could I have a coffee, please?
3 Could you take this report to Hans, please?
4 Could I use your phone, please?
5 Could I have a mineral water, please?

EXERCISE 3
2 I'll give you a lift. or Shall I give you a lift?
3 I'll send you a new one. or Shall I send you a new one?
4 I'll come another day. or Shall I come another day?
5 I'll send you an email. or Shall I send you an email?
6 I'll give him a message. or Shall I give him a message?

EXERCISE 4
2 Would you like a receipt?
3 Would you like me to send you the details?
4 Would you like to come to dinner?
5 Would you like to think about it?
6 Would you like me to send them a reminder?

OVER TO YOU (Sample answers only)
1 Could I have the wine list, please?
  Could I have another bottle of water, please?
2 Could you post this for me, please?
  Could you get me Mr Davis's file, please?
3 Could you take a message for me, please?
  Could you call back later, please?
4 Could I have an aisle seat, please?
  Could you tell me what gate we go from, please?
5 Shall I bring you the menu, sir?
6 Would you like me to pay those bills for you?
7 Shall I give her a message?
8 Would you like a free upgrade to Business Class?

30 Suggestions: *Why don't you ...?, Let's ..., What about ...?*

EXERCISE 1
2 Why don't you get a new Mac?
3 Why don't you send them a reminder?
4 Why don't you ask Bill to come to the meeting?
5 Why don't you leave now?
6 Why don't you take the train tomorrow?
7 Why don't you come to the conference?
8 Why don't you write to the CEO?

EXERCISE 2
2 How about inviting some important clients?
3 Why don't we have it at a nice hotel?
4 Let's hire a good after-dinner speaker.
5 What about having the conference in Paris?
6 How about getting different caterers this year?
7 Why don't we try to save money this year?
8 Let's ask the staff for their ideas.

EXERCISE 3
2 I suggest that you advertise more.
3 I suggest that you design some new ones.
4 I suggest that you find new suppliers.
5 I suggest that you give them new incentives.
6 I suggest that you move to new premises.

OVER TO YOU (Sample answers only)
2 What about giving them a free CD player?
3 How about organizing a competition?
4 Let's offer free servicing for a year.
5 What about paying their road tax?
6 How about offering interest-free credit?
7 Let's let the showrooms have big discounts.
8 Why don't we include air conditioning?

Units 28–30 **Answer key** 161

31 Advice: *if I were you, should, ought to*

EXERCISE 1

2 If I were you, I'd find out about the company.

3 If I were you, I'd prepare some questions.

4 If I were you, I wouldn't ask about holidays.

5 If I were you, I wouldn't argue about the salary.

6 If I were you, I'd arrive on time.

7 If I were you, I wouldn't complain about your last boss.

8 If I were you, I'd explain why you want the job.

EXERCISE 2 (in all sentences, *ought to* or *ought not to* can replace *should* or *shouldn't*)

A 2 I think he should take off his T-shirt.

B 1 I think he should get a better ladder.

   2 I think he should come down immediately.

EXERCISE 3

3 You shouldn't go home so early.

4 You should communicate more.

5 You shouldn't criticize so much.

6 You should praise the staff more.

OVER TO YOU (Sample answers only)

2 I think he should move closer to work.

3 I think we should ask for our money back.

4 I don't think we should accept it.

5 I don't think he should go.

6 I think she ought to make a reservation.

7 I think he should resign.

8 I don't think you should apologize.

32 Uncertainty: *may, might*

EXERCISE 1

3 wrong – might not pass

4 right

5 right

6 wrong – might have to

EXERCISE 2 (*may* is also possible)

2 might run

3 might be able

4 might have

5 might look

6 might cost

EXERCISE 3 (either *may* or *might* is possible)

2 They may lose some of their staff.

3 They may waste a lot of time moving.

4 They may have problems recruiting.

6 They might get cheaper premises.

7 They might save money on rent.

8 They might find bigger offices.

EXERCISE 4

2 Our market share will probably increase next year.

3 Inflation may go down next year.

4 The dollar might go up next year.

5 The cost of living probably won't fall next year.

6 There may be tax rises next year.

OVER TO YOU (Sample answers only)

2 I might see some friends.

3 I might get an important promotion.

4 I might get another job.

5 Taxes might go down.

6 We might open an office in New York.

7 It might be a bestseller.

8 My assistant might leave.

33 Obligation (1): *must, mustn't, needn't*

EXERCISE 1

3 wrong – You mustn't

4 wrong – he must

5 right

6 wrong – what time must we

7 right

8 wrong – must check

EXERCISE 2

2 must

3 must

4 mustn't

5 must

6 must

7 mustn't

EXERCISE 3

2 needn't

3 needn't

4 mustn't

5 needn't

6 mustn't

7 needn't

OVER TO YOU (Sample answers only)

1 You must get that report finished by tomorrow.

2 You must show me the figures Sally sent.

3 You needn't bring anything to the party.

4 You must tell me if you have a problem.

5 You must stop drinking.

6 You mustn't drive like that.

7 You must keep your receipts.

8 You must declare all your income.

34 Obligation (2): *have to, don't have to, can't*

EXERCISE 1
3 right
4 wrong – I have to
5 right
6 right

EXERCISE 2
2 She has to type letters.
3 She has to do the filing.
4 She has to go to meetings.
5 She has to make appointments.
7 Do you have to arrange accommodation?
8 Do you have to prepare timetables?
9 Do you have to organize speakers?
10 Do you have to give presentations?

EXERCISE 3
2 have to
3 don't have to
4 doesn't have to
5 don't have to
6 have to
7 can't
8 can't
9 have to
10 can't
11 have to

OVER TO YOU (Sample answers only)
2 You don't have to eat the food. You can't use a phone.
   You have to wear a seat belt.
3 You don't have to have your licence with you. You can't
   drink and drive. You have to have insurance.
4 You don't have to advertise on TV. You can't say anything
   that is not true. You have to make the product look
   exciting.

35 Imperative: instructions and directions

EXERCISE 1
2 Take the lift to the fourth floor. Turn right out of the lift.
   Go down the corridor and it's on your left.
3 Turn left out of the lift. Go down the corridor. Take the
   first turning on your right and it's the second room on
   your left.

EXERCISE 2
2 don't arrive
3 Don't forget
4 Don't cross
5 Prepare
6 listen
7 Give
8 Finish
9 don't ask

EXERCISE 3
2 you tell
3 you fill
4 you click
5 you choose
6 you confirm
7 you give

OVER TO YOU (Sample answers only)
2 Talk politely before you start talking about business.
3 Wear suitable clothes.
4 Know your product well.
5 Speak the language of the country if you can.
7 Don't ask personal questions.
8 Don't stand too close to colleagues.
9 Don't shout or act aggressively.
10 Don't forget to be polite.

36 Zero conditional: *if you work ..., you get*

EXERCISE 1
2 collect, get
3 mix, get
4 light, explodes
5 explodes, turns

EXERCISE 2
3 wants
4 is
5 get
6 use
7 has
8 suggest
9 chooses
10 check
11 don't have
12 carry
13 offer
14 doesn't want
15 visit
16 stops
17 crashes
18 means

OVER TO YOU (Sample answers only)
2 I sometimes help a colleague.
3 I generally feel good on Monday.
4 we sometimes get a pay rise.
5 I always get extra money.
6 I generally feel quite nervous.
7 I sometimes go home early.
8 I often travel Business Class.

37 Conditional 1: *if you work ..., you will get*

EXERCISE 1

2 wrong – if your order is
3 right
4 right
5 right
6 wrong – if you order

EXERCISE 2

3 get
4 will put
5 have
6 will supply
7 won't need
8 are
9 call
10 will they be able
11 give
12 will tell

EXERCISE 3

2 let, need
3 is, don't disturb
4 see, tell
5 phone, order
6 Work, is

EXERCISE 4

2 if
3 when
4 if
5 If
6 If

OVER TO YOU (Sample sentences only)

2 If I have some free time at the weekend, I'll do some work on the house.
3 If I need some cash, I'll go to the cash machine.
4 If I don't feel well next week, I'll make an appointment with the doctor.
5 If I go abroad next year, I'll need a new passport.
6 If I buy a new car, I'll get a diesel.

38 Conditional 2: *if you worked ..., you would get*

EXERCISE 1

3 wrong – if you lost
4 right
5 wrong – didn't have
6 right
7 wrong – if we had
8 wrong – She would be

EXERCISE 2

2 If we served meals, we would need a lot of cabin crew.
3 If we didn't use the Internet, we would need a lot of offices.
4 If we weren't reliable, people wouldn't come back to us.
5 If we issued tickets, we would need a lot of office staff.
6 If our flights weren't cheap, they wouldn't be popular.
7 If we didn't have a great safety record, people wouldn't feel safe with us.

EXERCISE 3

2 If Amy isn't better tomorrow, she will take the day off and she will stay at home.
3 We would buy the house if we had the money, but it's too expensive for us.
4 I would travel to Australia if I had three months' holiday, but I only have three weeks.
5 Peter will come to the party if he has time. He will ring and tell us when he knows.
6 If we don't book quickly, the hotel will be full, so we should book a room today.

OVER TO YOU (Sample sentences only)

2 I would earn more money.
3 something happened to our pension scheme.
4 someone tried to trick me.
5 I would join them.
6 I was unhappy at work.
7 I would run the department myself.
8 I felt too ill to come to work.

39 *-ing* or infinitive (1)

EXERCISE 1

2 installing
3 returning
4 getting
5 starting
6 working
7 hearing

EXERCISE 2

2 to use
3 to pay
4 to lower
5 to have
6 to do

EXERCISE 3

2 to sell
3 to buy
4 using
5 to cut
6 to buy
7 selling
8 to keep
9 to buy
10 to have

OVER TO YOU (Sample answers only)

you
2 having to work at weekends.
3 to get a new car.
4 to going away next week.
5 to live in London.

your work
6 dealing with customers.
7 doing the accounts.
8 to have a more responsible job.
9 to earn more.
10 to start a new project in September.

40 -ing or infinitive (2)

EXERCISE 1

3 wrong – a taxi to take
4 right
5 wrong – rang to invite
6 wrong – reps to sell
7 right
8 wrong – a passport to travel

EXERCISE 2

2 to store
3 to promote
4 to collect
5 to cut
6 to manufacture

EXERCISE 3

2 for dealing
3 of doing
4 in watching
5 at speaking
6 before leaving

EXERCISE 4

2 to get
3 to do
4 starting
5 to earn
6 to get
7 working
8 organizing
9 finding out
10 playing
11 organizing
12 playing

OVER TO YOU (Sample answers only)

2 I am very good at dealing with people.
3 I am bad at following orders.
4 I am responsible for organizing major publicity events.
5 I am interested in sailing and golf.

41 Verbs + infinitive

EXERCISE 1

2 to check the contracts.
3 Paula to write the report again.
4 Georg to leave early.
5 Tim to apply for a promotion.
6 Frieda to do a course on presentations.

EXERCISE 2

2 right
3 wrong – Jan wants you to
4 wrong – I told you
5 wrong – Would you like me
6 right
7 wrong – Do they allow you
8 right

EXERCISE 3

2 He lets them watch TV in the evenings.
3 He lets them relax in the swimming pool.
4 He makes them eat very small meals.
5 He makes them work out in the gym.
6 He makes them have cold showers.

OVER TO YOU (Sample answers only)

2 to use his laptop.
3 to go on trips abroad.
4 to make coffee.
5 to do a training course.
6 have a few days off.
7 use the phone for personal calls.
8 work very hard.

42 Adjectives: -ing and -ed

EXERCISE 1

1 bored
2 surprised
3 tired
4 annoyed
5 disappointed
6 interested
7 confused
8 excited

Key word: Budapest

EXERCISE 2

2 boring
3 interesting
4 confusing
5 disappointing
6 exciting
7 annoying
8 frightening

EXERCISE 3

2 thrilled
3 exhausting
4 fascinated
5 boring
6 exciting

OVER TO YOU (Sample answers only)

2 I was surprised to hear from Sue after all this time.
3 I was tired after my long day.
4 I was confused by the new traffic system.
5 I was excited about getting the new modem.
6 Some of my colleagues are very interesting.
7 My work can be tiring at times.
8 My journey to work is quite relaxing.
9 Learning English is interesting.
10 Travelling on business is entertaining.

43 Adjectives and adverbs (1)

EXERCISE 1
Good
  2 The instructions are simple.
  7 The screen is bright.
  8 There is excellent customer support.
Bad
  3 The price is high.
  4 It is not reliable.
  5 It has a small hard disk.
  6 It uses expensive batteries.

EXERCISE 2
  2 suddenly   5 badly
  3 immediately   6 silently
  4 carefully   7 slowly

EXERCISE 3
  2 slowly   6 carefully
  3 carefully   7 quickly
  4 glad   8 serious
  5 simple

OVER TO YOU (Sample answers only)
  2 They are very helpful.   5 I type badly.
  3 It is very boring.   6 I speak English fluently.
  4 I dress smartly.

44 Adjectives and adverbs (2)

EXERCISE 1
  2 My boss never goes home early.
  3 Our company is growing fast.
  4 Peter is a fast learner.
  5 You work hard, so you will get a rise.
  6 The early train leaves at 6.13 a.m.

EXERCISE 2
  1 daily   3 quarterly
  2 friendly   4 monthly

EXERCISE 3
  2 well   6 good
  3 good   7 well
  4 well   8 good
  5 well

EXERCISE 4
  2 it smells really nice   6 it looks fine
  3 it sounds terrible.   7 you don't look very happy
  4 they sound OK   8 it looks boring
  5 Does it look all right?

OVER TO YOU (Sample answers only)
  2 He is very friendly.
  3 I sometimes get to work very early.
  4 We have monthly meetings.
  5 It looks very modern.
  6 I speak English quite well.

45 Adverbs of frequency: *always, sometimes, never,* etc.

EXERCISE 1
  2 She hardly ever contacts the office during the holidays.
  3 She sometimes forgets birthdays and other family occasions.
  4 She often spends time on her hobbies at weekends.
  5 She never works from home at weekends.
  6 She sometimes arrives early for work.
  7 She always eats and works at the same time.
  8 She hardly ever has time to relax in the evening.

EXERCISE 2
  2 Our meetings are always useful.
  3 José hardly ever takes time off.
  4 Mr Jackson has always worked for us.
  5 Do you usually drive to work?
  6 Pierre is hardly ever late for meetings.
  7 I sometimes fly Business Class.
  8 Anna always gets to work a little early.
  9 My boss doesn't usually check my work.
 10 The CEO is hardly ever here.

EXERCISE 3
  2 three times a week
  3 twice a day
  4 twice a year
  5 once a year
  6 once a month
  7 once a day

OVER TO YOU (Sample answers only)
  3 I come to work by car every day.
  4 I hardly ever fly Business Class.
  5 I have meetings once a week.
  6 I am never early for work.
  7 I am never late for work.
  8 I go out with friends once a week.
  9 I take exercise three times a week.
 10 I go on holiday three times a year.

46 Comparing adjectives (1): *older than*

EXERCISE 1
2 The DX9 is lighter than the Filebox.
3 The Filebox is faster than the DX9.
4 The Filebox is brighter than the DX9.
5 The DX9 is cheaper than the Filebox.
6 The DX9 is nicer than the Filebox.

EXERCISE 2
2 quieter   5 fitter
3 prettier   6 longer
4 bigger   7 easier

EXERCISE 3
2 right   5 right
3 wrong – is better than   6 wrong – is better than
4 wrong – were worse than

OVER TO YOU (Sample answers only)
2 Spanish food is cheaper than British food.
3 The cost of living in Spain is lower than the cost of living in the UK.
4 Public transport in Spain is better than public transport in the UK.
5 British cities are nicer than Spanish cities.

47 Comparing adjectives (2): *more modern than*

EXERCISE 1
2 is younger than   6 are faster than
3 is more interesting than   7 is more difficult than
4 are more convenient than   8 is colder than
5 is more modern than

EXERCISE 2
2 Paxos is more traditional than Ibiza.
3 Paxos is more tranquil than Ibiza.
4 Paxos is more old-fashioned than Ibiza.
6 Ibiza is more exciting than Paxos.
7 Ibiza is more developed than Paxos.
8 Ibiza is more popular than Paxos.

EXERCISE 3
2 Gold is not as expensive as platinum.
3 The Empire State Building is not as tall as the Petronas Towers.
4 Italian food is not as hot as Thai food.
5 Cars are not as dangerous as motorbikes.
6 Our Internet connection at home is not as fast as the one at work.

EXERCISE 4
2 more careful   4 not as reliable
3 not as productive   5 lazier

OVER TO YOU (Sample answers only)
2 My current job is more interesting than my last job.
3 I am younger than my boss.
4 The company I work for is not as famous as Microsoft.
5 We are better than our main competitors.
6 I am more experienced than some of my colleagues.
7 I am happier than some of my colleagues.
8 I am richer now than when I was a student.

48 Superlatives: *oldest, most expensive*

EXERCISE 1
2 the cheapest   5 the cleanest
3 the biggest   6 the latest
4 the lowest

EXERCISE 2
2 the most affordable   5 the most powerful
3 the most important   6 the most expensive
4 the most popular

EXERCISE 3
2 the worst   4 the worst
3 the best

EXERCISE 4
2 the oldest gunmaker   6 the most successful product
3 the largest company   7 the best hotel
4 the biggest city   8 the smallest processor
5 the worst presentation

OVER TO YOU (Sample answers only)
2 My house is the most expensive thing I own.
3 Avignon is the nicest city in France.
4 The most interesting part of my job is going abroad.
5 The most boring part of my job is doing the filing.
6 Total is the biggest company in the country.
7 The most famous person in my country is the President.
8 I think Liliane Bettencourt, the owner of l'Oréal, is the richest person in France.

49 too and not ... enough

EXERCISE 1

2 It was too noisy.   It was not fast enough.
  It was not quiet enough.   4 It was too expensive.
3 It was too slow.   It was not cheap enough.

EXERCISE 2

2 You don't prepare carefully enough.
3 You talk too fast.
4 You don't explain the ideas slowly enough.
5 You finish your talks too early.
6 You don't answer the questions clearly enough.

EXERCISE 3

3 too much   7 not enough
4 not enough   8 too many
5 not enough   9 not enough
6 too much

OVER TO YOU (Sample answers only)

2 I am too young.
3 They are too expensive.
4 I am not experienced enough.
5 It is too cold.
6 I have too much to do.

50 Pronouns and possessives: I, me, my, mine

EXERCISE 1

2 he, it, her   4 I, you, We
3 they, him, us

EXERCISE 2

2 his address   4 my colleague
3 her mobile   5 your name

EXERCISE 3

2 Mine is   5 your keys
3 they've got theirs.   6 know hers.
4 cheaper than ours.

OVER TO YOU (Sample answers only)

1 ask her?   4 answer them.
2 of him?   5 talk to her.
3 can't remember it.
7 Our competitors' products are very cheap, but our products are high quality./ours are better.
8 Our offices are very small, but yours are very big./theirs are smaller.
9 My journey to work is long, but hers is longer./her journey is longer.

51 Reflexive pronouns: myself, yourself

EXERCISE 1

2 myself   6 himself
3 themselves   7 ourselves
4 itself   8 yourselves
5 yourself

EXERCISE 2

2 myself   5 ourselves
3 him   6 them
4 myself

EXERCISE 3

3 yourself   6 by himself
4 by herself   7 herself
5 ourselves   8 by yourself

EXERCISE 4

1 each other
2 themselves
3 themselves
4 each other

OVER TO YOU (Sample answers only)

1 We pay for ourselves.
2 We talk to each other.
3 We help each other.
5 I have an accountant. I don't do my tax myself.
6 I don't have a cleaner. I do the cleaning myself.
7 I have a secretary. I don't type letters myself.
8 I don't have a chauffeur. I drive myself.

52 Relative pronouns: who, which, that

EXERCISE 1

2 a sales assistant who can work at weekends.
3 are looking for tour guides who know London well.
4 They are looking for an in-house language trainer who has at least three years' experience.
5 They are looking for holiday representatives who have a good knowledge of Spanish.
6 They are looking for a programmer who knows C++ and Java.

EXERCISE 2

2 A studio is a kind of flat that has one main room.
3 An email is a kind of letter that goes from one computer to another.
4 A jetski is a kind of motorbike which travels on water.
5 An AGM is a kind of meeting which takes place every year.
6 A mobile is a kind of phone that works almost anywhere.

EXERCISE 3

2 I've lost a file with a label saying 'Tax letters'.
3 I've lost a keyring with five keys and a small torch.
4 I've lost a wallet with €60 and a gold credit card.
5 I've lost a pair of glasses with black frames.
6 I've lost a mobile phone with a blue and white cover.

OVER TO YOU

2 I've got a colleague with pink hair.
3 I know some people who don't have to work at all.
4 I've got a computer that keeps crashing.
5 I'd like a job that gave me the chance to travel.
6 I don't know anyone who works on a Sunday.
7 I like people who make me laugh.
8 I'd like a house with a swimming pool.

 53 Articles (1): *a, an, the*

EXERCISE 1

2 a	7 an
3 a	8 a
4 an	9 an
5 an	10 an
6 a	

EXERCISE 2

2 the	9 a
3 the	10 a
4 a	11 the
5 the	12 the
6 a	13 the
7 the	14 the
8 a	15 the

EXERCISE 3

2 mobile phones	5 Success
3 the tools	6 Freedom
4 oil	

OVER TO YOU (Sample answers only)

2 I use a computer and a scanner. I use the computer for word-processing, and I use the scanner for copying texts.
3 I had a Renault 5 and a motorbike. I sold the Renault 5, and the motorbike crashed.
4 I have an MA and an MBA. I got the MA from Oxford, and I got the MBA from Insead.

54 Articles (2): *a, an, the*

EXERCISE 1

1 a	6 Ø
2 an	7 a
3 an	8 a
4 a	9 a
5 Ø	

EXERCISE 2

1 the	10 Ø
2 the	11 the
3 Ø	12 the
4 the	13 the
5 Ø	14 the
6 the	15 the
7 Ø	16 the
8 Ø	17 Ø
9 the	

EXERCISE 3

1 Ø	6 Ø
2 Ø	7 Ø
3 Ø	8 Ø
4 a	9 Ø
5 a	

OVER TO YOU (Sample answers only)

2 I have visited Thailand, Pakistan, Italy, and the United States.
3 I have stayed in the Oriental and the Dorchester.
4 They go to France, Switzerland, and Austria.
5 They go to the Mediterranean.

55 *this, that, these, those*

EXERCISE 1

2 these	4 those
3 that	5 that

EXERCISE 2

1 this week	4 this morning
2 these days	5 this afternoon
3 this month	6 today

EXERCISE 3

2 that	4 this, That
3 these	5 These

EXERCISE 4

2 d	5 a
3 b	6 f
4 c	

OVER TO YOU (Sample answers only)

2 Heinrich, this is my assistant, Peter Marsh.
3 This conference is driving me mad!
5 That's OK. I wasn't expecting anything.
6 That's fantastic. I deserve it.
7 That's ridiculous. I can't even speak the language.
8 That's nothing. We lost 10 million the year before.

56 Nouns (1): countable and uncountable

EXERCISE 1

2 some
3 a
4 an
5 some
6 a
7 some
8 a

EXERCISE 2

2 some
3 some
4 some
5 a
6 some
7 some
8 a
9 some
10 some
12 some
13 some
14 some
15 some
16 a
17 an
18 a
19 a

OVER TO YOU (Sample answers only)

2 I'll need some wine, some soft drinks, and some sandwiches.
3 I'll need some food and a bottle of water.
4 I'll need some coffee, a pen, and some paper.
5 I'll need some pasta and some tomatoes.

LIKES AND DISLIKE

7 I prefer beer.
8 I prefer English food.
9 I don't like white wine.
10 I prefer rice to pasta.

57 Nouns (2): countable and uncountable

EXERCISE 1

2 insurance
3 information
4 progress
5 Accommodation
6 luggage

EXERCISE 2

2 a Traffic
  b Cars and lorries
3 a luggage
  b suitcases
4 a accommodation
  b rooms
5 a money
  b US dollars

EXERCISE 3

2 a
3 any
4 some
5 a
6 some
7 some
8 some
9 some

OVER TO YOU (Sample answers only)

2 The weather at this time of year is really nice.
3 The traffic in the mornings is very slow.
4 The cost of accommodation in the city centre is very high.
5 I haven't got any money to spare.
6 I've got some good news – I have got that promotion.
7 My car insurance is much more expensive this year.
8 My work is still very interesting.

58 Nouns (3): singular and plural

EXERCISE 1

2 cables
3 switches
4 alarms
5 glasses
6 weddings
7 parties
8 paints
9 varnishes
10 pads
11 brushes
12 workbenches
13 services
14 businesses
15 photocopies
16 faxes
17 addresses

EXERCISE 2

2 Japanese businessmen
3 politics is
4 headquarters are
5 new premises
6 the clothes
7 maths isn't
8 of lives

EXERCISE 3

2 they are
3 is
4 are
5 owns

OVER TO YOU (Sample answers only)

Good
The hours are good.
My boss is nice.
The canteen is cheap.
Bad
The pay is low.
The building is old.
The facilities are basic.
The opportunities are limited.

59　some and any

EXERCISE 1

2 a	7 an
3 some	8 some
4 some	9 any
5 any	10 some
6 any	

EXERCISE 2

2 Would you like some wine sir?
3 Is there any new information available?
4 Could I have some help please?
5 Did he give Ms Smith any tea?
6 Do you have any experience in this field?

EXERCISE 3

2 if you have any problems.
3 if you need any further information.
4 if you have any comments or questions

EXERCISE 4

2 any	4 some
3 some	5 any

OVER TO YOU (Sample answers only)

2 a creche, any medical facilities
3 a TV, some comfortable chairs
4 a CCTV system, any security checks
5 an iron, some books and magazines
6 a big suitcase, any work

60　something and anything

EXERCISE 1

1 anything, something
2 anything, something
3 anything, something
4 anything, anything

EXERCISE 2

2 somewhere
3 anyone
4 anyone
5 someone
6 anywhere
7 Someone
8 somewhere

EXERCISE 3

2 anyone suitable	5 somewhere tropical
3 somewhere outside	6 anyone young
4 something more colourful	7 something exciting

EXERCISE 4

1 everywhere
2 nothing
3 everything
4 nobody
5 everyone

OVER TO YOU (Sample answers only)

2 I met someone really interesting.
3 I didn't go anywhere nice.
4 I didn't learn anything new.
5 I heard something surprising.
6 I the evening, I went somewhere expensive.

61　much and many

EXERCISE 1

2 How many people work for you?
3 How much is a DX14?
4 How many complaints were there?
5 How much are the two big chairs?
6 How much time do we have left?
7 How much petrol do you use?
8 How many emails did you get?
9 How much is a small apartment?
10 How much cash have you got?

EXERCISE 2

1 a lot of	4 a lot of
2 a lot of	5 many
3 much	6 much

EXERCISE 3

2 very few	5 very few
3 very little	6 a few
4 a little	

OVER TO YOU (Sample answers only)

2 Yes, there are a few telcommunications companies.
3 Yes, there are a lot of people on unemployment benefit.
4 Yes, there is a lot of oil.
5 No, there isn't any gold, silver, or platinum.
6 Yes, there are a few women in senior positions.
7 No, there are very few part-time workers.
8 Yes, there is a lot of valuable equipment.
9 Yes, there is a little cash kept overnight.

Numbers (1): large numbers, dates

EXERCISE 1
2 Six thousand, four hundred and thirty-nine
3 Nine million, eighty-two thousand, three hundred and seventy-five
4 Three million, six hundred and nine thousand, four hundred and thirty-eight
5 Five hundred thousand
6 Eighteen million, five hundred thousand and fifty

EXERCISE 2

2005	two thousand and five
8,058,044,651	eight billion, fifty-eight million, forty-four thousand, six hundred and fifty-one
3103	three one oh three
1986	nineteen eighty-six
187	one hundred and eighty-seven
01748 884200	oh one seven four eight eight eight four two oh oh
DR 426	DR four two six
22.20	twenty-two twenty

EXERCISE 3
2 Apollo 11 landed on the moon on 20 July 1969.
   The twentieth of July, nineteen sixty-nine
3 The first Winter Olympics opened in Chamonix, France on 25 January 1924.
   The twenty-fifth of January, nineteen twenty-four
4 The Millau bridge was opened on 16 December 2004.
   The sixteenth of December, two thousand and four
5 The Soviet Communist Party newspaper Pravda was first published on 5 May 1912.
   The fifth of May, nineteen twelve

OVER TO YOU (Sample answers only)
2 €10,000, ten thousand euros
3 $3,000, three thousand dollars
4 $200,000, two hundred thousand dollars
5 £15,000, fifteen thousand pounds
6 60,000,000, sixty million

 Numbers (2): decimals and fractions

EXERCISE 1
1 23.74 twenty-three point seven four
4 53 fifty-three
6 €491.84 four hundred and ninety-one euros eighty-four
8 €86.07 eighty-six euros, seven
9 €577.91 five hundred and seventy-seven euros and ninety-one cents

EXERCISE 2

2 a quarter	4 a fifth
3 three quarters	

EXERCISE 3

2 weigh	5 wide
3 weighs	6 high
4 long	

OVER TO YOU (Sample answers only)
2 I spend a third of my day sleeping.
3 I spend a twelfth of my day relaxing.
4 I spend five per cent of my time eating.
5 I spend four per cent of my time travelling to work.

 Prepositions (1): place and direction

EXERCISE 1

2 in, next to	4 in, between, opposite
3 at, in	

EXERCISE 2

2 from	6 round
3 through	7 along
4 to	8 down
5 up	

EXERCISE 3

2 in	6 on
3 in	7 at
4 on	8 at
5 in	

OVER TO YOU (Sample answers only)
2 The nearest cash machine is in Eynsham. You go to the main road, turn left and then right, go left again, and it's down there on the right.
3 The nearest place to get a good coffee is Starbucks. Go along the High Street, turn right into Cornmarket, and it's on the right.
4 My favourite restaurant is the Chang Mai Kitchen. Go down Baker street, turn left at the lights, and it's on the left.

65 Prepositions (2): time

EXERCISE 1

2 in
3 at
4 on
5 at
6 on
7 on
8 at
9 on
10 in

EXERCISE 2

1 Ø
2 Ø
3 on
4 Ø
5 on
6 Ø

EXERCISE 3

2 from 7 August to 21 August.
  for two weeks.
3 from 1 May to 31 October.
  for six months.
4 from 1 May 2004 to 15 June 2004
  for six weeks.

OVER TO YOU (Sample answers only)

2 in 1986.
3 in 1999.
4 in 2003.
5 on Friday afternoon.
6 on Monday morning at 10.30.
7 this evening.
8 at the weekend.

66 Prepositions (3): noun + preposition, preposition + verb, preposition + noun

EXERCISE 1

1 experience
2 invitation
3 demand
4 price
Key word: Computer

5 cheque
6 letter
7 difference
8 rise

EXERCISE 2

2 flying
3 working
4 leaving

5 setting
6 buying

EXERCISE 3

2 on strike
3 for sale
4 out of order

5 on the phone
6 by credit card

OVER TO YOU (Sample answers only)

2 to the party.
3 between tap water and bottled water.
4 on what shares to buy.
5 by credit card.
6 for lunch?
7 in a hurry?
8 by plane.

67 Prepositions (4): adjective + preposition

EXERCISE 1

2 satisfied with
3 capable of
4 famous for
5 suitable for

EXERCISE 2

2 for
3 of
4 to
5 at
6 for
7 about
8 with

EXERCISE 3

2 in buying
3 of carrying
4 about getting
5 at reading

OVER TO YOU (Sample answers only)

2 I am interested in working in advertising and promotions.
3 I am not interested in doing a job that isn't challenging.
4 I am good at communicating with people.
5 I am not very good at lying.
6 My bosses have always been pleased with my work.
7 I am popular with my colleagues.
8 I think I would be suitable for this job.

68 Prepositions (5): verb + preposition

EXERCISE 1
3 right
4 wrong – deals with
5 wrong – speak to
6 wrong – belong to
7 wrong – agree with
8 right

EXERCISE 2
1 at
2 about
3 to
4 with
5 of
6 for
Key word: author

EXERCISE 3
2 borrowed, from
3 thank, for
4 congratulate, on
5 lend, to
6 provide, with

OVER TO YOU (Sample answers only)
2 You can talk to a friend.
3 You can borrow some money from the bank.
4 You can pay by credit card.
5 You can work for yourself.
6 You can wait for the next one.
7 You can phone directory enquiries.
8 You can spend it all on holidays in the Caribbean.

69 Expressions with *make* and *do*

EXERCISE 1
2 d
3 a
4 b
5 f
6 e

EXERCISE 2
2 do
3 do
4 make
5 make
6 do

EXERCISE 3
2 made
3 doing
4 doing
5 do
6 make
7 make

EXERCISE 4
1 make
2 phone
3 mistake
4 do
5 profit
6 noise
7 loss
8 exam
Key word: Motorola

OVER TO YOU (Sample answers only)
2 I did really well.
3 I've got a lot of work to do.
4 I'd like to do a course in Music.
5 We made record profits.
6 You have to make an appointment.
7 You can make phone calls from anywhere.
8 You make a loss.

70 Expressions with *have* and *have got*

EXERCISE 1
2 have you got
3 will have
4 didn't have
5 had
6 had

EXERCISE 2
2 suggestions
3 time
4 a week
5 idea
6 question
7 experience
8 degree
9 feeling
10 meeting

EXERCISE 3
2 are having a party.
3 is having a shower.
4 are having lunch.
5 is having a bad day.
6 are having a chat.

OVER TO YOU (Sample answers only)
2 I have a lot of experience.
3 I have got a degree in Maths.
4 I have an important meeting tomorrow.
5 I am having lunch with Petra on Friday.
6 I always have a good time at the company Christmas party.
7 I haven't got the money to buy another house.
8 I often have a word with colleagues if they look upset.

Expressions with _get_

EXERCISE 1
2 get about £3,000 a month.
3 will get a free gift.
4 are getting cheaper and cheaper.
5 is getting bigger.
6 got to work late.

EXERCISE 2

2 back	7 ready
3 know	8 touch
4 together	9 trouble
5 started	10 sack
6 drunk	

EXERCISE 3

2 get up	4 get on with
3 get over	5 get away

OVER TO YOU (Sample answers only)
Personal/Home
I get up early in the week.
I get home at 5.30.
I get on with my neighbours.
I get together with my old school friends once a year.
Work/Office
I never get angry with colleagues.
I get to work at about 7.45.
I would like to get to know my new boss better.

 Expressions with _give_ and _take_

EXERCISE 1

2 refund	6 take
3 Give	7 discount
4 place	8 reference
5 regards	

Key word: Investor

EXERCISE 2

2 action	6 half an hour
3 opportunity	7 place
4 part	8 call
5 presentations	

EXERCISE 3

2 give away	4 take over
3 takes up	5 take on

OVER TO YOU (Sample answers only)
2 I have to give a presentation every month.
3 I gave up smoking ten years ago.
4 It takes a lot of time to complete a tax form.
5 We give our best customers a big discount.
6 Our annual conference takes place in Geneva.
7 We have to take action on absenteeism.

Progress tests

(total = 10 marks)

Complete the sentences with *am*, *is*, or *are*.

1 Hello, my name's Jade and I .... from London.
2 My boss .... away this week.
3 A: Thanks very much.
   B: You .... welcome.
4 The new computer .... great.
5 Kristin and I .... tour guides.

Complete the sentences with *'m*, *'re*, or *'s*.

6 Mr Davis is away today. He .... in a meeting.
7 Maria is a great saleswoman. She .... also a good friend.
8 No, I .... from Canada, not America.
9 Dan and I are colleagues. We .... in the R&D department.
10 There's a message for you – it .... on your desk.

(total = 10 marks)

Complete the sentences with *am (not)*, *is (not)*, or *are (not)*.

1 A: .... Dan in the office today?
   B: No, he's at home.
2 A: Where .... Jason and Julie?
   B: They're at a conference.
3 A: .... you Spanish?
   B: Yes, I'm from Madrid.
4 I .... free at the moment. Please come back later.
5 These new computers .... expensive – they only cost $100.

Complete the dialogue with *am (not)*, *is (not)*, or *are (not)*.

Jack: Hi, Andy.
Andy: Hi, Jack. I want you to meet Pierre Longchamp – he ⁶ .... on a course here.
Jack: Nice to meet you, Pierre. I ⁷ .... Jack Daniels.
Pierre: Nice to meet you, Jack.
Jack: ⁸ .... you here with the French group?

Pierre: Yes, I ⁹ ...., but my colleagues ¹⁰ .... here today. They arrive tomorrow.

(total = 10 marks)

Complete the dialogue with *have got*, *has got*, *haven't got*, *hasn't got*, or *Have ... got?*

Malek: How's the new office, Ross?
Ross: It's fantastic – it ¹ .... lots of facilities.
Malek: ² .... you .... a place to eat?
Ross: We ³ .... a great canteen. The gym is very good, but it ⁴ .... a swimming pool.
Malek: So, no swimming for you. ⁵ .... you .... a nice place to work?
Ross: Yes, I ⁶ .... a big room on my own.
Malek: Sounds great. ⁷ .... the offices .... air conditioning?
Ross: No, they ⁸ ...., but that's OK. My office ⁹ .... a big window, and I ¹⁰ .... a really nice view of the city.

(total = 10 marks)

Complete the sentences with the present simple form of the verbs in brackets..

I ¹ .... (be) a student at London University, but I also ² .... (own) a small company that ³ .... (import) clothes from China. I mainly ⁴ .... (buy) T-shirts because they ⁵ .... (cost) very little and they ⁶ .... (be) easy to sell.

The company ⁷ .... (employ) a sales rep, and in the summer he ⁸ .... (travel) round the country and ⁹ .... (try) to sell the T-shirts at concerts and other events. When the business ¹⁰ .... (do) well, we make a few thousand pounds a year, which is great for me.

Test for Unit 5

(total = 10 marks)

Complete the dialogue with the present simple form of the verbs in brackets.

Neil: Hi, I'm Neil Brooks. Nice to meet you.

Laurens: Hello, I'm Laurens van der Schwan. How do you do?

Neil: How do you do? ¹ .... (you/come) from Holland, Laurens?

Laurens: Yes, I do. ² .... (you/know) Holland at all?

Neil: I know Antwerp a bit, but I ³ .... (not know) the other cities.

Laurens: What about you? ⁴ .... (you/live) in England?

Neil: Yes, I live in Birmingham. ⁵ .... (you/work) for this company?

Laurens: Well, this is my own company – we make office furniture. ⁶ .... (you/want) any chairs or tables?

Neil: No, thanks – we ⁷ .... (not/need) any right now.

Laurens: That's OK, I'm only joking. Now, I ⁸ .... (not/know) the name of your company – *Plaxol* is not a name that is familiar to me. ⁹ .... (you/make) office furniture too?

Neil: No, it's mainly office equipment.

Laurens: ¹⁰ .... (you/sell) your products here in Europe?

Neil: Yes, and in the USA too.

Test for Unit 6

(total = 10 marks)

Complete the dialogues with a question word.

1 A: Hello, my name is Kevin Davis.
   B: .... do you do, Mr Davis? I'm Sara Smith.

2 A: .... do you come from?
   B: I come from Argentina.

3 A: .... do you do?
   B: I'm an engineer.

4 A: Excuse me, ... is the station?
   B: Down this road and on the left.

5 A: .... does the next train leave?
   B: It leaves at 5.40.

6 A: .... do you want to work late?
   B: I've got a big report to finish.

7 A: .... do you turn this machine on?
   B: You press the red button at the side.

8 A: .... do you work with?
   B: I work with Emily and Laura.

9 A: Hello, ... are you?
   B: I'm fine thanks, and you?

10 A: .... much do these microphones cost?
   B: They cost $22 each.

Test for Unit 7

(total = 10 marks)

Complete the dialogues with the present continuous form of the verbs in brackets.

1 A: Is Ben at work this week?
   B: No, he .... (have) a few days off.

2 A: We can start the meeting when Hans arrives.
   B: Listen – that's him. He .... (come) now.

3 A: Is there a security problem at the moment?
   B: Yes, and the police .... (stop) everybody.

4 A: Is Johann still at work?
   B: Yes, he .... (work) on a new project.

5 A: The traffic is bad with the new road works, isn't it?
   B: Yes, that's why I .... (take) the train at the moment.

6 A: Is your boss away at the moment?
   B: Yes she is, so that's why Annie and I .... (look) after the office.

7 A: What's the problem with the car?
   B: I don't know, but it .... (make) a strange noise.

8 A: Do you want the window open?
   B: Yes please – it .... (get) very hot in here.

9 A: Is the technician here?
   B: Yes, he .... (fix) the machine now.

10 A: Where is Franz today?
   B: He .... (give) a talk in Brighton.

Test for Unit 8 (total = 10 marks)

Complete the dialogue with the present continuous form of the verbs in brackets.

1 A: Where's Olga?
  B: Oh, she .... (not/work) today.
2 A: Who .... (you/call)?
  B: I'm phoning Jacob from Accounts.
3 A: Is Andy in today?
  B: No, he .... (give) a talk in London.
4 A: Is the shop closed?
  B: I think so. They .... (not/answer) the phone.
5 A: What .... (you/look) for?
  B: I can't find that file on the Avery project.

Put the words in the correct order to form questions and negatives in the present continuous.

6 week/you/where/working/are/this

.... ?

7 are/we/today/coming/not

....

8 looking/what/you/are/for

.... ?

9 they/are/meeting/having/a

.... ?

10 working/my/isn't/computer

....

Test for Unit 9 (total = 10 marks)

Complete the sentences with one verb in the present simple and one verb in the present continuous.

¹ .... (work) for DRT Computer Systems. At the moment I ² .... (install) a new system in a local supermarket.

Heinrich is a film producer. He ³ .... (make) documentaries, and at the moment he ⁴ .... (make) a film about elephants in Africa.

I usually ⁵ .... (go) to work by car, but because of the road works this week, I ⁶ .... (travel) by train.

They ⁷ .... (sell) these machines at half price because there are some new models on the way, but they usually ⁸ .... (cost) $500.

I ⁹ .... (think) that Herr Fischer ¹⁰ .... (have) a meeting at the moment.

Test for Unit 10 (total = 10 marks)

Choose the correct option from the words in *italics*.

1 A: Do you know where Bill is?
  B: Yes, I *think/am thinking* he's downstairs.
2 A: Do you want the fish?
  B: No, thanks, I *don't like/am not liking* seafood.
3 A: Can I have a word with Alan?
  B: Sorry, he's out. He *takes/is taking* Joanna to the airport.
4 A: The magazine has a new cover.
  B: Really? What *does it look/is it looking* like?
5 A: *Do you know/Are you knowing* Mr Sanchez?
  B: Yes, we're old friends.
6 A: Is Harvey free?
  B: No, he *finishes/is finishing* that estimate.
7 A: *Does this pen belong/Is this pen belonging* to you?
  B: No, it's not mine.
8 A: Is Mr Abramovich really rich?
  B: Yes, he *owns/is owning* Chelsea Football Club.
9 A: Are the candidates ready?
  B: Yes, they *wait/are waiting* in Reception.
10 A: *Do you want/Are you wanting* to go for lunch?
  B: Yes, good idea.

Test for Unit 11 (total = 10 marks)

Complete the texts with the past simple of the verbs in the box.

attend	live	move	start	work

A few years ago I ¹ .... to Malaysia with my family and ² .... a new job with a car company. We ³ .... in Kuala Lumpur, about 80 miles from the factory, because my children ⁴ .... the International School in Kuala Lumpur and my wife ⁵ .... for a British bank in the city.

change	hate	like	return	travel

I ⁶ .... the job because it was interesting and the people were friendly, but I ⁷ .... the long journey to the factory. I ⁸ .... to work at 5.30 every morning, and I ⁹ .... home at 7.30 in the evening. So after two years, I ¹⁰ .... jobs, and now work for another car company in Kuala Lumpur.

(total = 10 marks)

Complete the dialogue with the past simple form of the verbs in brackets.

Wendy: Hi there, nice to see you back. ¹ .... (you/enjoy) the trip?

Jane: Yes, thanks, I ² .... (like) Brussels a lot, and the rest was OK.

Wendy: ³ .... (you/travel) by plane?

Jane: No, I ⁴ .... (not/travel) by plane this time. I ⁵ .... (want) to, but Marianne ⁶ .... (change) the reservation, so I ⁷ .... (travel) by Eurostar.

Wendy: ⁸ .... (you/stay) at the Hilton?

Jane: No, I ⁹ .... (not/stay) there – it was full, so I ¹⁰ .... (stay) at the Holiday Inn.

(total = 10 marks)

Complete the sentences with the past simple form of the verbs in brackets.

1 We .... (have) a very successful meeting last week.

2 My boss .... (go) to London yesterday.

3 .... (you/have) any problems last week?

4 Ms Schreiver .... (take) up her position in 2000.

5 We .... (leave) late, and in the end we missed the plane.

6 I .... (ring) you yesterday, but there was no answer.

7 I .... (not/know) anyone at the party last night.

8 How did you get to work yesterday? .... (you/drive)?

9 Jason's father .... (run) the family business for many years.

10 What .... (you/do) last week?

(total = 10 marks)

Complete the sentences with the past continuous form of the verbs in brackets.

1 I called the technician because the photocopier .... (not/work).

2 The trains .... (not/run) so I got a taxi.

3 What .... (you/do) when you first heard the news about the takeover?

4 I first met Alana while I .... (travel) round South America.

5 The accident happened when we .... (move) the machines to the new factory.

6 I'm sorry I was out when you called – I .... (have) lunch, I think.

7 He .... (watch) TV screens in the security office when he got the call.

8 The screen went blank while I .... (read) the licence agreement.

9 Someone stole my car while I .... (pay) for the petrol.

10 I met an old colleague when I .... (come) back from the coffee shop.

(total = 10 marks)

Complete the dialogue with *used to* and the verb in brackets.

Miner: The mine is closed now, but there ¹ .... (be) 1,000 men working here. That was in the old days. There ² .... (not/be) a museum here or any visitors.

Visitor: ³ .... (you/work) here?

Miner: Oh, yes. In those days we all ⁴ .... (have) jobs here. At the age of 16, all the boys ⁵ .... (start) in the mines, and the girls ⁶ .... (get) a job at the cotton mill. We ⁷ .... (not/choose) our careers – not like these days.

Visitor: How long ⁸ .... (you/work) in the mines?

Miner: It was a job for life – the men ⁹ .... (stay) to the age of 50 or more. But a lot of them had to stop. They ¹⁰ .... (get) sick and they couldn't work any more.

(total = 10 marks)

Make decisions with the ideas in the box and *I think I'll ...*

send them a reminder	give him a ring
go for a walk	stay late tonight	go home early

1 I need to talk to Jaime. ....
2 I'm a bit tired. ....
3 I've got a lot of work to do. ....
4 Their bill is still not paid. ....
5 I need some exercise. ....

Make predictions with *will* or *won't* and the verbs in brackets.

6 House prices may not rise very fast next year, but I'm sure they .... (fall).
7 Don't worry, we're nearly there. We .... (get) there soon.
8 Their product is expensive and very badly designed. It .... (do) well.
9 It sounds like a great job. I'm sure you .... (enjoy) it.
10 The price of oil is rising, so petrol prices .... (go up) too.

(total = 10 marks)

Complete the dialogues with the present continuous form of the verbs in brackets.

A: What time ¹ ....(you/leave)?
B: We ² .... (go) at 6.30.

A: ³ .... (you/come) to the meeting later on?
B: No, I ⁴ .... (have) the afternoon off.

A: ⁵ .... (you/see) Peter this weekend?
B: Yes, ⁶ .... (he/come) over on Saturday.

A: What ⁷ .... (you/do) tomorrow afternoon?
B: I ⁸ .... (take) Julio to the airport.

A: ⁹ .... (you/fly) to Crete tomorrow?
B: No, I ¹⁰ .... (take) the ferry tonight.

(total = 10 marks)

Rewrite the sentences with *going to*.

1 I have decided to get a new mobile.
   ....
2 What have you decided to do?
   ....
3 Where have they decided to stay?
   ....
4 We have decided to give them a 20% discount.
   ....
5 He has decided to stay with the company.
   ....
6 She has decided not to go to the conference.
   ....
7 We have decided to offer the job to Ingrid.
   ....
8 When has he decided to leave?
   ....
9 Why have you decided to cancel the meeting?
   ....
10 I have decided not to pay the bill.
   ....

(total = 10 marks)

Choose the correct option from the words in *italics*.

1 He left at 6.30, so he *will be/is being* here at about 8.30.
2 A: I need to have the day off on the 28th.
   B: OK, I *will tell/am telling* the boss when I see her.
3 A: Are you planning to see Mr Conway this week?
   B: Yes, he *will come/is coming* over this afternoon.
4 I can't see you tomorrow. I *will go/am going* to Rome for a conference.
5 A: I've got lots of extra work to do.
   B: Don't worry. I *will give/am giving* you a hand if you like.
6 A: Why are you leaving now?
   B: I *will take/am going to take* the cash to the bank.
7 A: Why are you moving your things out of the office?
   B: They *will repaint /are going to repaint* it over the weekend.
8 A: The new product looks great.
   B: Thanks. I think it *will be/is being* very popular.
9 A: I just don't understand.
   B: All right. Listen carefully and I *will explain/am explaining* it again.
10 A: Why do you need your suit tomorrow?
   B: I *will wear/am going to wear* it at my interview.

(total = 10 marks)

Complete the sentences. Put the verbs in brackets into the present perfect or the past simple.

1 Yuniko speaks English well. She .... (live) in the USA.

2 Mr Sanchez .... (call) yesterday afternoon.

3 I .... (just/send) you an email. It will arrive in a minute.

4 I .... (sell) twelve houses this year.

5 We .... (raise) all our prices two months ago.

6 Last year the company .... (make) profits of $3m.

7 Mrs Norman .... (start) working here in 1975.

8 Log onto the news! The Prime Minister .... (just/resign).

9 I know Caroline is here. I .... (just/see) her.

10 I .... (speak) to Design about the problem last week.

(total = 10 marks)

Choose the correct form of the verb: A, B, C, or D.

1 A: .... been to India before?
  B: No, this is my first visit.
    A Were you
    B Are you
    C Have you ever
    D Did you ever

2 A: Has the post arrived?
  B: No, it ....
    A didn't
    B wasn't
    C hasn't
    D has

3 Has the shop .... ?
    A shuts
    B shutting
    C has shut
    D shut

4 I'm sorry, but I .... the report. I need a few more days.
    A haven't finished
    B don't finish
    C am not finishing
    D didn't finished

5 I have never .... on the phone in English.
    A not spoken
    B spoke
    C speak
    D spoken

6 Maria doesn't work here any more – she .... the company last year.
    A left
    B leaves
    C was leaving
    D has left

7 A: Have you seen the sales figures?
  B: Yes, I .... them yesterday.
    A see
    B did see
    C have seen
    D saw

8 A: .... the parts?
  B: Yes, I ordered them yesterday.
    A Have you ordered
    B Do you order
    C Are you ordering
    D Were you ordering

9 A: What's your CEO like?
  B: I don't know. I .... him.
    A don't meet
    B doesn't meet
    C have never met
    D am not meeting

10 A: Have you sent that invoice?
  B: Yes, I ....
    A am
    B was
    C did
    D have

Test for Unit 22 (total = 10 marks)

Read the sentences and correct the mistakes in *italics*.

1 I *have finished already* my work for today.

   ....

2 Mr Stevens *doesn't see* the sales figures yet.

   ....

3 Don't worry about the invoice – we *did already paid* it.

   ....

4 *Did you phoned* Michel yet? ....

5 I don't want to discuss that problem. I *already make* my decision. ....

6 He *have already completed* the jobs you gave him.

   ....

7 They've finished the Reception Hall, but they *don't painted* the canteen yet. ....

8 *Are you received* that letter I sent yet? ....

9 I'm sorry, but the order *isn't arrived* yet. ....

10 I *am already spoken* to Mr Li – he's not coming to the meeting. ....

Test for Unit 23 (total = 10 marks)

Complete the sentences with *for* or *since*.

1 Miss Jones has worked here .... twenty years.

2 I have known Ken .... we were at Harvard.

3 We have had the new system .... January.

4 I've had the same boss .... five years.

Make questions and answers from the notes.

5 A: How long/you/work/for IBM?

   ....

6 B: I/work/IBM/2002

   ....

7 A: How long/you boss/be away?

   ....

8 B: She/be/away/three weeks

   ....

9 A: How long/they/have/an office in London?

   ....

10 B: They/have/an office in London/twenty years

   ....

Test for Unit 24 (total = 10 marks)

Complete the dialogue. Put the verbs in brackets into the present perfect or past simple.

A: How is the new building going?

B: Very well – they [1] .... (make) a lot of progress.

A: [2] .... (they/finish) it yet?

B: No, but they [3] .... (complete) all of the offices, and they [4] .... (build) the car park. So they are doing well. In fact, I [5] .... (speak) to the contractor yesterday, and I [6] .... (say) we were very happy with the work so far.

A: That's very good news. Unusual, too. I [7] .... (never/be) happy with a builder, but there's always a first time. How is the computer system getting on?

B: Different story, I'm afraid. They [8] .... (not start/yet). Anyway, I [9] .... (phone) their Managing Director last week, and I [10] .... (complain), so I think we'll see some action soon.

Test for Unit 25 (total = 10 marks)

Rewrite the sentences. Make one sentence with *for* or *since* and the present perfect simple or present perfect continuous.

1 I started waiting five minutes ago. I am waiting now.
   (wait) I have ....

2 I met Jacomina ten years ago. I know her now.
   (know) I have ....

3 Tina started working here in January. She is working here now.
   (work) Tina ....

4 We started testing the new model last May. We are testing it now.
   (test) We ....

5 My boss went away two weeks ago. He is away now.
   (be) My boss ....

Choose the correct option form the words in *italics*.

6 How long have you been *travelled/travelling* for?

7 She *has been studying/is studying* Management since January.

8 I have *been liking/liked* my job since I started.

9 They *have been speaking/are speaking* to the boss since 9 a.m.

10 I have been *trying/tried* to repair my PC for two hours.

182 **Progress tests** *Units 22–25*

Test for Unit 26 (total = 10 marks)

Rewrite the sentences with the present simple passive.

1 They make these cameras in China.
   These ....

2 We print our magazines in Hong Kong.
   Our ....

3 They grow rubber in Malaysia.
   Rubber ....

4 They pay me at the end of the month.
   I ....

5 Does the government employ you?
   Are ....

6 They don't build the engines in this country.
   The ....

7 They make the components out of aluminium.
   The ....

8 They don't give this information to the public.
   This ....

9 Does someone check the orders again?
   Are ....

10 We check our computers regularly.
   Our ....

Test for Unit 27 (total = 10 marks)

Complete the sentences with the past simple passive form of the verbs in brackets.

1 Why .... (the project/delay)?

2 Paper .... (invent) thousands of years ago.

3 The Chairman .... (appoint) in 2004.

4 Our company .... (found) in 1886.

5 I think the film .... (make) in the 1990s.

6 The Airbus A380 .... (launch) in 2005.

7 I'm sorry that you .... (not/tell) about the decision.

8 We .... (delay) because of bad weather.

9 I .... (tell) yesterday.

10 Ramirez .... (promote) last year.

Test for Unit 28 (total = 10 marks)

Complete the sentences with *can, can't, could,* or *couldn't*.

1 Amelie is bilingual. She .... speak French and English.

2 I'm sorry, but this is a non-smoking office. You .... smoke in here.

3 I tried to phone him yesterday, but I .... get through.

4 Could you speak up, please? We .... hear you at the back.

5 In the end, we .... agree on a price and the negotiations failed.

6 Mozart was a genius. He .... play the piano when he was four.

7 We wanted to buy a bigger system, but we .... afford it.

8 You're speaking too fast – I .... understand you.

9 I need an interpreter because I .... speak Chinese.

10 He .... get home because they cancelled all the trains and buses.

Test for Unit 29 (total = 10 marks)

Read the notes. Make offers and requests with the words given.

1 It is hot. Offer to open the window.
   Shall ....

2 Your boss is very busy. Offer to come back another time.
   Would ....

3 You are making coffee. Offer your colleague a coffee.
   Would ....

4 Your colleague has a file. Ask him to give it to you.
   Could ....

5 You are moving a heavy box. Ask your colleague to give you a hand.
   Could ....

6 Your colleague needs some information from Herr Fischer. Offer to phone him.
   Would ....

7 You have some sandwiches. Offer one to a colleague.
   Would ....

8 You want to use a colleague's phone.
   Can ....

9 You want to have the day off tomorrow.
   Can ....

10 You are cold. Ask a colleague to close the window.
   Could ....

Test for Unit 30 (total = 10 marks)

Rewrite the suggestions with the words given.

1 I think you should cancel the order.
   I suggest ....

2 Let's go out tonight.
   Why ....

3 Let's have another meeting next week.
   How about ....

4 Why don't we talk to them again?
   Let's ....

5 It would be a good idea for you to check your work more carefully.
   I suggest ....

6 Why don't we give them a bigger discount?
   What about ....

7 I think we should think about this again.
   I suggest ....

8 Let's have lunch.
   Why ....

9 Why don't we see what Miss Pierce thinks.
   Let's ....

10 Let's have a short break now.
   What ....

Test for Unit 31 (total = 10 marks)

Rewrite the sentences with the words in brackets.

1 You ought to get there early.
   (were) ....

2 You ought to leave now.
   (should) ....

3 It is a good idea to speak to customers politely.
   (ought) ....

4 You don't plan your work enough.
   (should) ....

5 I don't study enough.
   (more) ....

6 You ought to complain.
   (were) ....

7 You ought to wear something smart.
   (were) ....

8 If I were you, I wouldn't go to the conference.
   (don't think) ....

9 You don't relax enough.
   (more) ....

10 You complain too much.
   (so) ....

Test for Unit 32 (total = 10 marks)

Look at the notes in the table. Say what will happen if a new government comes in next year. Use *may*, *might*, *will probably*, or *probably won't*.

small chance	possible	probable
< 25%	50%	>75%
1 taxes/go down	4 economy/	8 taxes/go up
2 unemployment	get better	9 crime/
/improve	5 interest rates/	get worse
3 hospitals/	stay the same	10 inflation/
get better	6 exports/get better	go up
	7 tax laws/change	

1 ....
2 ....
3 ....
4 ....
5 ....
6 ....
7 ....
8 ....
9 ....
10 ....

Test for Unit 33 (total = 10 marks)

Complete the sentences with *must*, *mustn't*, or *needn't*.

1 You .... hurry. We have plenty of time.

2 The boss is worried about those revised figures.
   You .... finish them today.

3 We .... order any more paper. I think we have enough.

4 You .... talk to customers like that, or we will lose them.

5 My doctor says I have a heart problem and that I .... stop smoking.

6 There are lots of mistakes here – you .... check your work more carefully.

7 The meeting starts at exactly 9.30. You .... be late.

8 Thanks, but you .... come in this weekend. I think I can do the work myself.

9 That job sounds perfect for you – you .... apply for it.

10 I'm sorry, but you .... disturb Frau Muller – she's in a very important meeting.

(total = 10 marks)

Complete the dialogue with *have to, don't have to,* or *can't,* and the words in brackets.

A: [1] .... (I/wear) a uniform?

B: No, you [2] .... (wear) one, we come in our own clothes.

A: Can we smoke at our desk?

B: No, you [3] .... (smoke) in the offices at all. You [4] .... (go) outside.

A: What time [5] .... (I/arrive) in the morning?

B: At 8.30 a.m. You [6] .... (be) late. If you are late, you [7] .... (call) me and have a very good reason.

A: What if I am ill? What [8] .... (I/do)? Can I call you?

B: No, you [9] .... (visit) the doctor and get a note. But you [10] .... (do) this if you are ill for only one day.

(total = 10 marks)

Choose the correct option from the words in *italics*.

Our offices are easy to find. First, [1] *take you/take* the main road into town. [2] *Go/going* past the church and [3] *turns/turn* left. [4] *Continue/continued* for 500 metres and [5] *park/parking* your car where you can – sometimes it is difficult to find a space.

Complete the sentences with the words in the box.

Don't leave   Watch   Remember   Don't put   Go

6 .... through the security check and into the departures hall after checking in.

7 .... any sharp objects (knives, scissors, etc.) in your hand luggage.

8 .... the TV screens for flight information.

9 .... that some gates are a long way from the main hall, so give yourself time to get there.

10 .... your bags unattended at any time.

(total = 10 marks)

Complete the sentences with the present tense of the verbs in brackets.

If we [1] .... American visitors, we always [2] .... them to a traditional English pub. (take, have)

If my boss [3] .... on a business trip, she usually [4] .... the office every day. (go, contact)

If I [5] .... a lot of work, I often [6] .... it home with me. (have, take)

If you [7] .... TNT, it [8] .... (burn, explode)

If I [9] .... to work on a Monday morning, it always [10] .... a long time. (take, drive)

(total = 10 marks)

Complete the dialogue with the correct form of the verbs in brackets.

Angela: Hi, Jenny. This is Angela.

Jenny: Hi. Where are you calling from? Are you still coming to the meeting this afternoon?

Angela: Yes, I'm on a bus on my way to the station, but the traffic's very slow. If it [1] .... (not/get) any better, I think [2] .... (miss) the 12.15 train.

Jenny: Don't worry about that. If you [3] .... (not/catch) that train, there [4] .... (be) another one.

Angela: Are you sure?

Jenny: Yes, if you [5] .... (wait) a minute, I [6] .... (go) and get the timetable.

Angela: Thanks.

Jenny: Right – I thought so – there's another fast train at 12.50.

Angela: OK. Now, what time [7] .... (I/arrive) if I [8] .... (get) that one?

Jenny: Just after 2.00. Then you can just get a taxi. But if there [9] .... (not/be) any taxis, I [10] .... (come) and get you.

Test for Unit 38 (total = 10 marks)

Say if the sentences are right or wrong and correct the mistakes.

1 If I would have more time, I'd be able to finish.
  right/wrong ....

2 Would you accept the job if they offered it to you?
  right/wrong ....

3 If I were you, I wouldn't to sign the contract.
  right/wrong ....

4 If our prices were lower, we would sell more products.
  right/wrong ....

5 If there was a real safety problem with any of our
  models, we would recall them. ....
  right/wrong ....

6 I would be surprised if they agreed to these terms.
  right/wrong ....

7 If we will lost the order, the company would be in real
  trouble. *right/wrong* ....

8 If I lived in Paris, I will get a flat in the Boulevard St
  Michel. *right/wrong* ....
  ....

9 If we would place a very large order, what discount
  would you give us? *right/wrong* ....
  ....

10 If the company relocated to Scotland, I would look for
   another job. *right/wrong* ....
   ....

Test for Unit 39 (total = 10 marks)

**Complete the sentences. Put the verbs into the *-ing*
form or the infinitive.**

1 We can't afford .... (hire) a new assistant.

2 It's not worth .... (fix) the printer. It's
  cheaper to buy a new one.

3 What time do you want .... (finish) today?

4 Please ring my secretary if you would like
  .... (set up) a meeting.

5 I look forward to .... (meet) you next
  week.

6 Have you considered .... (join) the Union?

7 Please stop .... (ask) so many questions.

8 Would you mind .... (open) the window?

9 Samira has decided .... (look) for another
  job.

10 I'm afraid that they have refused .... (give)
   us a refund.

Test for Unit 40 (total = 10 marks)

**Complete the sentences. Put the verbs into the *-ing*
form or the infinitive.**

1 My boss has gone to London .... (attend)
  a conference.

2 I need to have a word with Jason before
  .... (go) to the meeting.

3 I am responsible for .... (deal) with
  customer complaints.

4 Would you be interested in .... (join) the
  team?

5 I am sure Heidi would be capable of ....
  (run) the department.

6 We are building a bigger factory ....
  (manufacture) the new model.

7 We need someone who is good at ....
  (speak) in public.

8 After .... (leave) university, Mr Ang got a
  job with a bank.

9 Janet rang .... (cancel) your meeting on
  Friday.

10 Elli has gone to the bank .... (pay in) the
   cheques.

Test for Unit 41 (total = 10 marks)

Put the words in the right order.

1 asked/boss/him/His/late/stay/to
  ....

2 I/repeat/that/to/want/you
  ....

3 join/like/to/us/We/would/you
  ....

4 advised/him/resign/She/to
  ....

5 contract/He/persuaded/sign/the/them/to
  ....

Complete the sentences with *makes* or *lets*.

6 My boss often .... us have an extra day off.

7 My boss sometimes .... me work very
  long hours.

8 My boss .... us have parties at work.

9 My boss .... us have a long lunch hour.

10 My boss sometimes .... us do jobs that
   we hate.

Test for Unit 42 (total = 10 marks)

Choose the correct option from the words in *italics*.

1 I was *tired/tiring* after the long journey home.

2 I was *annoyed/annoying* when I got a parking ticket.

3 Doing the same thing day after day can be *bored/boring*.

4 Are you *interested/interesting* in finance?

5 We were *disappointed/disappointing* when we didn't receive the Queen's Prize for Exports.

6 When the company collapsed, the director was *terrified/terrifying* of going to prison.

7 The doctor told her to take a few weeks' holiday because she was *depressed/depressing*.

8 We were *thrilled/thrilling* to hear that we had overtaken our main competitor.

9 Many people find computers *confused/confusing*.

10 The workers are all *frightened/frightening* of losing their jobs.

Test for Unit 43 (total = 10 marks)

Choose the correct option from the words in *italics*.

1 My secretary works very *efficient/efficiently*.

2 My assistant is a very *reliable/reliably* person.

3 We're going to need two *small/smalls* laptops.

4 Most of my colleagues are *nice/nicely*.

5 We have meetings *regular/regularly*.

6 I live in a *new/newly* apartment.

7 My PA speaks *fluent/fluently* Italian.

8 The new design is *attractive/attractively*.

9 The traffic is moving *slow/slowly* this morning.

10 Your handwriting is not very *neat/neatly*.

Test for Unit 44 (total = 10 marks)

Complete the sentences with the words in the box.

hard	early	fast	late	straight

1 My new laptop has a very .... processor.

2 I need to leave work .... today as I have an appointment at home at 2.30.

3 I'll go .... to the office from the airport.

4 I'm afraid I'm going to ask you to leave the company. It's a .... decision, but I have no choice.

5 You'd better be quick or you'll be .... for the meeting.

Complete the sentences with the words in the box.

casual	casually	good	well	well

6 I love the design – I think it is really ....

7 The company did .... last year and we are now the market leader.

8 A: How are you?
   B: I'm very .... , thank you.

9 My boss never wears a tie and always looks ....

10 Some of the other people in the office also dress ....

Test for Unit 45 (total = 10 marks)

Rewrite the sentences with the words in brackets.

1 I am late for work. (hardly ever)
....

2 My boss goes on holiday. (never)
....

3 I watch TV in the evening. (sometimes)
....

4 We are improving our products. (always)
....

5 Jackie helps in the office. (often)
....

Rewrite the sentences with expressions of frequency (*once a week, twice a week*, etc.)

6 We get together on Mondays and Wednesdays.
   We get together ....

7 I go to France in June and December.
   I go to France ....

8 We have a sales meeting on the last day of each month.
   We have a sales meeting ....

9 The report came out in 2003, 2004, 2005, etc.
   The report came out ....

10 I usually contact our suppliers every two weeks.
   I usually contact out suppliers ....

(total = 10 marks)

Complete the dialogue with the comparative form of the adjectives in brackets.

A: I hear you're living in London now. What's it like?

B: It's ¹ .... (good) than Oxford, at least I think so. OK, it's much ² .... (big) and ³ .... (noisy), but I like it, and I'm ⁴ .... (happy) than I was last year.

A: What's your flat like?

B: It's great. It's a bit ⁵ .... (small) than the old one, but it's ⁶ .... (nice) because it's ⁷ .... (bright) and it's in a good position, so it's ⁸ .... (easy) for me to get to work.

A: Doesn't it cost a lot?

B: No, in fact it's a bit ⁹ .... (cheap) than my old place.

A: And how's the new boss?

B: Who, Jim? He's really nice. He's a lot ¹⁰ .... (young) than old Mr Jackson. Going to work is lots of fun!

(total = 10 marks)

Read the sentences and correct the mistakes.

1 Austrian Airlines is not as bigger as British Airways.

....

2 The new model is more expensiver than the old one.

....

3 Table wine is not as nice than Champagne.

....

4 This problem is more difficult as I thought.

....

5 Porsches are more expensive that Minis.

....

6 Hamburgers are not so expensive than steak.

....

7 Motorways are dangerouser than small roads.

....

8 Taking the train is more economical as driving.

....

9 They say Chinese is more difficult as English.

....

10 The USA is more richer than India.

....

(total = 10 marks)

Complete the sentences with the superlative form of the adjective in brackets.

1 I took my clients to .... (good) restaurant in Paris.

2 This is .... (expensive) car I have ever bought.

3 *The Oriental* is .... (fine) hotel in the world.

4 Tesco is .... (big) supermarket in the UK.

5 Who is .... (rich) man in the world?

6 The Eiffel Tower is .... (famous) building in France.

7 Our new databases will provide .... (accurate) estimates.

8 We will teach you .... (effective) way of doing business.

9 Our customers are .... (important) part of our business.

10 I want to see .... (recent) financial statements.

(total = 10 marks)

Rewrite the sentences with *too* or *enough* and the words in brackets.

1 The desk is very big. It won't fit in my office. (big)
The desk is .... to fit in my office.

2 I can't afford that car. (money)
I haven't got .... to buy that car.

3 You talk so quietly that nobody can hear you. (loudly)
Nobody can hear you because you don't talk ....

4 The hotel rooms aren't quiet enough. (noisy)
The hotel rooms are ....

5 This report is bad. (good)
This report is not ....

6 I need one more hour to finish. (time)
I haven't got ....

7 There is too much traffic in London. (cars)
There are .... in London.

8 We missed the plane because we didn't arrive in time. (late)
We arrived .... to catch the plane.

9 I need more work. (work)
I haven't got .... to do.

10 We should pay the trainees more. (money)
We don't give the trainees ....

Test for Unit 50 (total = 10 marks)

Read the sentences and correct the mistakes.

1 Mr Smith is not here now, but she is coming in later.

....

2 The program will do all the calculations on it's own.

....

3 Those aren't your keys, their mine.

....

4 Is this file the yours?

....

5 I must remember to take me driving licence with me.

....

6 We don't work for them. They work for our.

....

7 I've got my tickets, but have you got your?

....

8 My office is nicer than the his.

....

9 Your clients are great, but their difficult to please.

....

10 The low price is one of it's best selling points.

....

Test for Unit 51 (total = 10 marks)

Choose the correct option from the words in *italics*.

1 At Christmas time, Herr Schmidt and I send *ourselves/each other* a card.

2 Some company directors give *himself/themselves* big bonuses.

3 John, this is the canteen – please help *you/yourself* to anything you want.

4 The training course will soon pay for *himself/itself* in lower maintenance costs.

5 Before I start, I would like to introduce *me/myself*.

6 Ken needs this information – could you send it to *him/himself*?

7 Laura, if I am not in when you get to the office, please let *yourself/you* in.

8 Can I ask *you/yourself* a question?

9 The engineer hurt *him/himself* while he was fixing the power lines.

10 My PA understands *me/myself* very well.

Test for Unit 52 (total = 10 marks)

Complete the sentences with *who, which*, or *with*.

1 Do you want a car .... air conditioning?

2 We've got a problem .... is slowing down production.

3 I've got a laptop .... a CD burner.

4 Do you know anyone .... can help me?

5 I'll send you a brochure .... describes our products and services.

6 We need someone .... speaks Japanese.

7 I met someone at the conference .... knows you.

8 I've got a cordless keyboard .... a built-in mouse.

9 I have a list of people .... are interested in attending.

10 There are some Australian wines .... are available at reasonable prices.

Test for Unit 53 (total = 10 marks)

Complete the dialogue with *a* or *the*.

Customer: I've got ¹ .... problem with ² .... computer magazine I bought from you last week.

Salesman: I'm sorry to hear that. What's ³ .... problem?

Customer: Well, ⁴ .... magazine came with ⁵ .... CD-ROM that had ⁶ .... program I really wanted. When I got back to my office, I realized that ⁷ .... CD-ROM was missing.

Salesman: I'm sorry, it happens sometimes. Have you got ⁸ .... magazine with you?

Customer: Yes, here it is.

Salesman: Thanks. Just go to ⁹ .... magazine department and get ¹⁰ .... new one.

Test for Unit 54 (total = 10 marks)

Complete the text with _a_, _an_, _the_, or Ø (no article)

Until last year, [1] .... Carla Jones was [2] .... accountant at [3] ....
WapCompNet Ltd in [4] .... London. A couple of months ago she reached the age of 40, and she decided to leave [5] .... work and travel around [6] .... world. She bought a motorbike, and began her journey in May. First she travelled through [7] .... France to [8] ....
Mediterranean, and then she crossed [9] ....
Pyrenees into [10] .... Spain. The next stage of her journey will take her across Africa.

Test for Unit 55 (total = 10 marks)

Complete the dialogue with _this_, _that_, _these_, or _those_.

Lars: John, I'd like you to meet an old colleague of mine. John, [1] .... is Peter. Peter, [2] .... is John.

John: I think we've met before. But I'm not sure where.

Peter: I think you're right. Were you at the technology conference in Barcelona [3] .... year?

John   Yes, [4] ....'s right. I remember talking to you about the new EU directives.

Peter: Yes, of course. So, what are you doing [5] .... days? Are you still with the same company?

John: Yes, I am. I'm still enjoying it, but we are very busy. I have already been to two conferences [6] .... month.

Peter: How are you enjoying [7] .... conference? Did you go to the two talks about China yesterday?

John   Yes, I thought they were very informative. What talks are you going to [8] .... afternoon?

Peter: Let's have a look at the programme. [9] .... one here looks quite interesting. What do you think, Lars?

Lars: [10] ....'s a good idea. I'll come with you.

Test for Unit 56 (total = 10 marks)

Complete the sentences with _is_ or _are_.

1 Can you hurry up – the customers .... waiting.
2 Your help .... needed now.
3 Mineral water .... often more expensive than milk.
4 Petrol .... now at record levels.
5 Our meetings .... always very useful.

Complete the sentences with _a_, _an_, or _some_.

6 I need .... advice about careers.
7 In the meeting room there is .... table and ten chairs.
8 We will send you .... brochures in the post.
9 I bought .... beautiful silk in China.
10 She gave .... amazing presentation at the conference.

Test for Unit 57 (total = 10 marks)

Complete the sentences with _a_, _some_, or _any_.

1 I need .... information from you.
2 Daniel has .... fax for you.
3 I heard .... interesting news yesterday.
4 We've had .... lovely weather recently.
5 Harriet hasn't got .... money.
6 We've still got .... cash in the bank.
7 I've got .... very heavy suitcase.
8 We don't need .... new equipment for the exhibition.
9 We are having problems and we aren't making .... progress.
10 I have got .... room on the fifth floor.

Test for Unit 58 (total = 10 marks)

Complete the dialogue with the plural of the words in brackets.

A: Home Computer Show! Good morning. Can I help you?

B: Hello, yes, I'm phoning about [1] .... (ticket) for the exhibition this weekend. Can you tell me what your [2] .... (rate) are?

A: Yes, a standard ticket is $11. But we have special
[3]............................ (pass) for [4].......................... (family),
and local [5]........................... (businessman) get 10% off.

B: Can you tell me about [6].......................... (group)?
I'm from a school, and I will be coming with two
complete [7].......................... (class). So there will be
48 [8].......................... (child), plus two [9]...........................
(teacher), making 50 [10].......................... (person) in
total.

Test for Unit 59   (total = 10 marks)

Complete the dialogues with *some* or *any*.

A: There isn't [1]........................... paper left for the
printer.

B: OK, I'll go and get [2]........................... .

A: I'm ordering some stationery. What do you need?

B: I think we need [3]........................... more files. And
could you order [4]........................... more ink
cartridges as well?

A: I'm getting [5]........................... coffee from the
canteen. Would you like anything?

B: No, thanks. I've got [6]........................... milk and tea
in the fridge.

A: We haven't got [7]........................... petrol left.

B: That's a real problem then. There aren't
[8]........................... garages open at this time of night
near here.

A: I need [9]........................... change for the parking
meter.

B: I'm sorry, I haven't got [10]........................... on me.

Test for Unit 60   (total = 10 marks)

Complete the sentences with the words in the box.

anything	something	anyone	anywhere
someone	no one	nowhere	everyone
everywhere	somewhere		

1 Let's look for that file again. I'm sure it is here
....

2 Why did you speak so quietly? .... at the
back could hear you.

3 I don't know .... about computers. Could
you show me how to play this CD-ROM?

4 I have .... important to tell you. Shall I
come to your office?

5 You'll really like working here. .... is very
friendly.

6 I've lost my keys. I don't know where they are, and
I have looked .... for them.

7 We wanted to build the factory near here, but there
was .... suitable.

8 I don't know .... who really likes their
journey to work.

9 I met .... very interesting at the
conference.

10 I don't know where the invoice is. I can't find it
....

Test for Unit 61   (total = 10 marks)

Rewrite the questions with *How much* or *How many*.

1 What does the other model cost?
How ....

2 What number of people came to the meeting?
How ....

3 What number of women work in your company?
How ....

4 What amount of time have we got?
How ....

5 What number of units do you want to order?
How ....

Complete the sentences with the words in the box.

a lot of	a few	very few	a little	very little

6 I really can't afford it. I have .... money.

7 There were .... problems with the project,
so there was a very long delay.

8 .... people wanted to come to the talk, so
we cancelled it.

9 Yes, I can see you now. I have .... time
to spare.

10 That's very interesting. Now, I just have ....
short questions to ask you, if that's OK.

(total = 10 marks)

Write down these numbers in figures.

1 sixty-two thousand, nine hundred ....

2 three hundred and ninety thousand ....

3 five hundred and forty ....

4 a hundred and twenty-five thousand ....

5 a million ....

Write these numbers in words.

6 395

....

7 3,900

....

8 18,836

....

9 387,444

....

10 5,300,000

....

(total = 10 marks)

Write the following in words.

1 $3.50

....

2 9.58 seconds

....

3 15%

....

4 €5,400

....

5 2.6 kilometres

....

6 ¼

....

7 50%

....

8 ⅔

....

9 ⅕

....

10 ¾

....

(total = 10 marks)

Look at the picture. Complete the sentences with the words in the box.

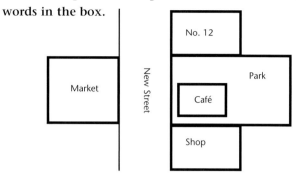

| next to | opposite | between | in | at |

1 My house is .... number 12 New Street.

2 My house is .... the park.

3 The park is .... the market.

4 The café is .... the park.

5 The park is .... the shop and my house.

Complete the text with a preposition.

My schedule for the next few days is as follows. I will be working ⁶ .... home tomorrow, and on Thursday and Friday I will be ⁷ .... a conference ⁸ .... Madrid. My secretary is ⁹ .... holiday at the moment, so if you need to get ¹⁰ .... touch, please ring me on my mobile – the number is 09797 477 556.

(total = 10 marks)

Complete the sentences with *in, on, at, from,* or Ø (no preposition).

1 I was born .... 30 May.

2 I look forward to meeting you .... the near future.

3 Demand for our products usually falls .... June and July.

4 Can I come and see you .... tomorrow afternoon?

5 I'll be in Singapore .... Monday to Thursday.

6 I'd like to finish work .... 4.30.

7 How many days do you have off .... Christmas?

8 I'm afraid I can't make the meeting .... the 12th.

9 I last saw Mr Jackson .... three weeks ago.

10 Our company was founded .... 1886.

(total = 10 marks)

Complete the sentences with a preposition.

1 Sorry, I can't stop now. I'm .... a hurry.
2 Thank you for your interest .... our company.
3 Have you sent in your application .... the job?
4 There are long delays at the airport because the pilots are .... strike.
5 Prices have dropped because of a fall .... demand.
6 We can't sell those cartons of milk – they're .... of date.
7 Did you walk or did you come .... car?
8 You need to see Jamil – he's in charge .... new accounts.
9 The trouble .... these radios is that they are not very reliable.
10 Do you have any experience .... working abroad?

(total = 10 marks)

Complete the sentences with one word from each box.

different	about
interested	in
suitable	from
popular	for
worried	with

If, like many mothers, you are [1] ....
[2] .... what your child eats, you may be
[3] .... [4] .... the new
range from First Organics. This is [5] ....
[6] .... most other baby foods because it uses
100% organic ingredients. There is a full range of meals
including 'Breakfast Carrot Purée' and 'Organic Potato
Pie' which are very [7] .... [8] ....
babies. The meals are [9] .... [10] ....
babies between six and eighteen months old but should
not be given to babies under six months.

(total = 10 marks)

Complete the sentences with a preposition.

1 Is it OK if I pay .... credit card?
2 I would like to congratulate you .... these improvements in efficiency.
3 Do you know who this pen belongs .... ?
4 We must start the meeting. We can't wait .... Eleanor any longer.
5 I look forward .... seeing you next week.
6 We may bring out the new model in May, maybe later. It depends .... the market.
7 We can borrow $500,000 .... the bank.
8 In my job, I deal .... complaints from customers.
9 We are writing .... our shareholders to explain our decision.
10 I would be grateful if you could provide me .... a reference.

(total = 10 marks)

Choose the correct option from the words in *italics*.

A: Could you [1] *make/do* me a favour?
B: Sure, what's the problem?
A: I'm trying to [2] *make/do* the accounts, but I'm just not [3] *making/doing* any progress. I think that maybe someone has [4] *made/done* a mistake somewhere.
B: OK, I'll have a look. I've just got a couple of phone calls to [5] *make/do*, and I'll be with you.

A: Are you studying Spanish now?
B: Yes, I'm [6] *making/doing* an evening course, and I'm going to be [7] *making/doing* an exam in December.
A: And is it general Spanish or business Spanish?
B: A bit of both. We do things like talking about the weather, but we also practise things like telephoning or [8] *making/doing* appointments.
A: Is it worth doing?
B: Oh, yes, I think it'll [9] *make/do* a big difference.
A: And are you a star student?
B: I don't know! Anyway, I think I'm [10] *making/doing* quite well.

(total = 10 marks)

Complete the dialogues with the phrases in the box.

a bad day	a chat	a coffee	a degree
a great time	a headache	a question
lunch	problems	time

1 A: What's the matter?
B: I'm having .... with this program.
2 A: Do you want anything to drink?
B: Yes, please. I'll have ....
3 A: Could we have .... ?
B: Sure. What do you want to talk about?
4 A: What's your problem? Why are you in such a bad mood?
B: I'm sorry, I've had ....
5 A: Are you coming to the canteen?
B: No, thanks. I've already had ....
6 A: Excuse me, I have ....
B: Yes, what is it you want to know?
7 A: Did you go to university?
B: Yes, I have .... in Economics.
8 A: Do you think you will finish on time?
B: Yes, I've still got .... to do it.
9 A: Are you enjoying your holiday?
B: Yes, we're having ....
10 A: I've got ....
B: I've got an aspirin in my bag. Would you like it?

(total = 10 marks)

Rewrite the sentences with an expression with *get*.

1 Do you *have a good relationship* with your boss?
Do you .... with your boss?
2 Let's *prepare* for the meeting.
Let's .... for the meeting.
3 It's *becoming* very hot.
It's .... very hot.
4 Please *contact me* when you are in London.
Please .... when you are in London.
5 Let's *meet socially* this weekend.
Let's .... this weekend.
6 Do you know when the train will *arrive*?
Do you know when the train will .... ?
7 I *received* your email this morning.
I .... your email this morning.
8 If his performance doesn't improve, he will *lose his job*.

If his performance doesn't improve, he will
....
9 We are disappointed about losing the contract, but we will *recover from* it.
We are disappointed about losing the contract, but we will .... it.
10 If you carry on working well, you will *be paid* a bonus at the end of the year.
If you carry on working well, you will .... a bonus at the end of the year.

(total = 10 marks)

Complete the dialogue with *give* or *take*.

A: Hi. Can I talk to you about the conference? Do you think you will be able to [1]............................ a presentation?
B: Yes, maybe. When does it [2]............................ place?
A: On the 17th and 18th. It's quite short, so it won't [3]............................ up too much of your time.
B: But that's next week! Why can't they [4]............................ us a bit more notice?
A: I know, they always do this. I'm going to [5]............................ the organizers a call. I complained last year, but this time I want them to [6]............................ action.
B: It's a bit late, but OK, I'll do it. It will [7]............................ me the opportunity to tell people about the new magazines. Have we got any copies that we can [8]............................ away? Everyone likes a free gift.
A: Yes, I'm sure we've got some. Anyway, leave it with me and I'll [9]............................ care of it.
B: What about hotels? Do you know anywhere nice to stay?
A: Yes, there's a really nice hotel I know – and they always [10]............................ us a good discount. I'll let you have the details tomorrow.

Progress tests – Answer key

1 am
2 is
3 are
4 is
5 are
6 's
7 's
8 'm
9 're
10 's

1 Is
2 are
3 Are
4 am not
5 are not
6 is
7 am
8 Are
9 am
10 are not

1 has got
2 Have (you) got
3 have got
4 hasn't got
5 Have (you) got
6 have got
7 Have (the offices) got
8 haven't
9 has got
10 have got

1 am
2 own
3 imports
4 buy
5 cost
6 are
7 employs
8 travels
9 tries
10 does

1 Do you come
2 Do you know
3 don't know
4 Do you live
5 Do you work
6 Do you want
7 don't need
8 don't know
9 Do you make
10 Do you sell

1 How
2 Where
3 What
4 Where
5 When
6 Why
7 How
8 Who
9 How
10 How

1 is having
2 is coming
3 are stopping
4 is working
5 am taking
6 are looking
7 is making
8 is getting
9 is fixing
10 is giving

1 isn't working
2 are you calling
3 is giving
4 aren't answering
5 are you looking
6 Where are you working this week?
7 We are not coming today.
8 What are you looking for?
9 Are they having a meeting?
10 My computer isn't working.

1 work
2 am installing
3 makes
4 is making
5 go
6 am travelling
7 are selling
8 cost
9 think
10 is having

1 think
2 don't like
3 is taking
4 does it look
5 Do you know
6 is finishing
7 Does this pen belong
8 owns
9 are waiting
10 Do you want

1 moved
2 started
3 lived
4 attended
5 worked
6 liked
7 hated
8 travelled
9 returned
10 changed

1 Did you enjoy
2 liked
3 Did you travel
4 didn't travel
5 wanted
6 changed
7 travelled
8 Did you stay
9 didn't stay
10 stayed

1 had
2 went
3 Did you have
4 took
5 left
6 rang
7 didn't know
8 Did you drive?
9 ran
10 did you do

1 wasn't working
2 weren't running
3 were you doing
4 was travelling
5 were moving
6 was having
7 was watching
8 was reading
9 was paying
10 was coming

1 used to be
2 didn't use to be
3 Did you use to work
4 used to have
5 used to start
6 used to get
7 didn't use to choose
8 did you use to work
9 used to stay
10 used to get

1 I think I'll give him a ring.
2 I think I'll go home early.
3 I think I'll stay late tonight.
4 I think I'll send them a reminder.
5 I think I'll go for a walk.
6 won't fall.
7 will get
8 won't do
9 will enjoy
10 will go up

1 are you leaving
2 are going
3 Are you coming
4 am having
5 Are you seeing
6 he is coming
7 are you doing
8 am taking
9 Are you flying
10 am taking

1 I'm going to get a new mobile.
2 What are you going to do?
3 Where are they going to stay?
4 We are going to give them a 20% discount.
5 He's going to stay with the company.
6 She is not going to go to the conference.
7 We're going to offer the job to Ingrid.
8 When is he going to leave?
9 Why are you going to cancel the meeting?
10 I am not going to pay the bill.

Test for Unit 19

1 will be	6 am going to take
2 will tell	7 are going to repaint
3 is coming	8 will be
4 am going	9 will explain
5 will give	10 am going to wear

Test for Unit 20

1 has lived
2 called
3 have just sent
4 have sold
5 raised
6 made
7 started
8 has just resigned
9 have just seen
10 spoke

Test for Unit 21

1 C	6 A
2 C	7 D
3 D	8 A
4 A	9 C
5 D	10 D

Test for Unit 22

1 have already finished
2 hasn't seen
3 have already paid
4 Have you phoned
5 have already made
6 has already completed
7 haven't painted
8 Have you received
9 hasn't arrived
10 have already spoken

Test for Unit 23

1 for
2 since
3 since
4 for
5 How long have you worked for IBM?
6 I have worked for IBM since 2002.
7 How long has your boss been away?
8 She has been away for three weeks.
9 How long have they had an office in London?
10 They have had an office in London for twenty years.

Test for Unit 24

1 have made
2 Have they finished
3 have completed
4 have built
5 spoke
6 said
7 have never been
8 haven't started
9 phoned
10 complained

Test for Unit 25

1 been waiting for five minutes.
2 known Jacomina for ten years.
3 has been working here since January.
4 have been testing the new model since last May.
5 has been away for two weeks.
6 travelling
7 has been studying
8 liked
9 have been speaking
10 trying

Test for Unit 26

1 cameras are made in China.
2 magazines are printed in Hong Kong.
3 is grown in Malaysia.
4 am paid at the end of the month.
5 you employed by the government?
6 engines aren't built in this country.
7 components are made out of aluminium.
8 information is not given to the public.
9 the orders checked again?
10 computers are checked regularly.

Test for Unit 27

1 was the project delayed
2 was invented
3 was appointed
4 was founded
5 was made
6 was launched
7 weren't told
8 were delayed
9 was told
10 was promoted

Test for Unit 28

1 can	4 can't
2 can't	5 couldn't
3 couldn't	6 could
7 couldn't	9 can't
8 can't	10 couldn't

Test for Unit 29

1 Shall I open the window?
2 Would you like me to come back another time?
3 Would you like a coffee? / Would you like me to make you a coffee?
4 Could you give me the file?
5 Could you give me a hand?
6 Would you like me to phone Herr Fischer?
7 Would you like a sandwich?
8 Can I use your phone?
9 Can I have the day off tomorrow?
10 Could you close the window?

Test for Unit 30

1 that you cancel the order.
2 don't we go out tonight?
3 having another meeting next week?
4 talk to them again.
5 that you check your work more carefully.
6 giving them a bigger discount?
7 that we think about this again.
8 don't we have lunch?
9 see what Miss Pierce thinks.
10 about having a short break now?

Test for Unit 31

1 If I were you, I'd get there early.
2 You should leave now.
3 You ought to speak to customers politely.
4 You should plan your work more.
5 I should study more.
6 If I were you, I'd complain.
7 If I were you, I'd wear something smart.
8 I don't think you should go to the conference.
9 You should relax more.
10 You shouldn't complain so much.

Test for Unit 32

1 Taxes probably won't go down.
2 Unemployment probably won't improve.
3 Hospitals probably won't get better.
4 The economy may get better.
5 Interest rates may stay the same.
6 Exports may get better.
7 Tax laws may change.
8 Taxes will probably go up.
9 Crime will probably get worse.
10 Inflation will probably go up.

Test for Unit 33

1	needn't	6	must
2	must	7	mustn't
3	needn't	8	needn't
4	mustn't	9	must
5	must	10	mustn't

Test for Unit 34

1 Do I have to wear
2 don't have to wear
3 can't smoke
4 have to go
5 do I have to arrive
6 can't be
7 have to call
8 Do I have to do
9 have to visit
10 don't have to do

Test for Unit 35

1	take	6	Go
2	Go	7	Don't put
3	turn	8	Watch
4	Continue	9	Remember
5	park	10	Don't leave

Test for Unit 36

1	have	6	take
2	take	7	burn
3	goes	8	explodes
4	contacts	9	drive
5	have	10	takes

Test for Unit 37

1	doesn't get	6	will go
2	will miss	7	will I arrive
3	don't catch	8	get
4	will be	9	aren't
5	wait	10	will come

Test for Unit 38

1 wrong – If I had more time
2 right
3 wrong – I wouldn't sign.
4 right
5 right
6 right
7 wrong – If we lost
8 wrong – I would get
9 wrong – If we placed
10 right

Test for Unit 39

1	to hire	6	joining
2	fixing	7	asking
3	to finish	8	opening
4	to set up	9	to look
5	meeting	10	to give

Test for Unit 40

1	to attend	6	to manufacture
2	going	7	speaking
3	dealing	8	leaving
4	joining	9	to cancel
5	running	10	to pay in

Test for Unit 41

1 His boss asked him to stay late.
2 I want you to repeat that.
3 We would like you to join us.
4 She advised him to resign.
5 He persuaded them to sign the contract.
6 lets
7 makes
8 lets
9 lets
10 makes

Test for Unit 42

1	tired	6	terrified
2	annoyed	7	depressed
3	boring	8	thrilled
4	interested	9	confusing
5	disappointed	10	frightened

Test for Unit 43

1	efficiently	6	new
2	reliable	7	fluent
3	small	8	attractive
4	nice	9	slowly
5	regularly	10	neat

Test for Unit 44

1	fast	6	good
2	early	7	well
3	straight	8	well
4	hard	9	casual
5	late	10	casually

Test for Unit 45

1 I am hardly ever late for work.
2 My boss never goes on holiday.
3 I sometimes watch TV in the evening.
4 We are always improving our products.
5 Jackie often helps in the office.
6 twice a week
7 twice a year
8 once a month
9 once a year
10 twice a month

Test for Unit 46

1	better	6	nicer
2	bigger	7	brighter
3	noisier	8	easier
4	happier	9	cheaper
5	smaller	10	younger

Test for Unit 47

1 as big as
2 is more expensive
3 is not as nice as
4 more difficult than I thought
5 more expensive than
6 not as expensive as
7 are more dangerous
8 more economical than
9 more difficult than
10 is richer

Test for Unit 48

1 the best
2 the most expensive
3 the finest
4 the biggest
5 the richest
6 the most famous
7 the most accurate
8 the most effective
9 the most important
10 the most recent

Test for Unit 49

1	too big	6	enough time
2	enough money	7	too many cars
3	loudly enough	8	too late
4	too noisy	9	enough work
5	good enough	10	enough money

Test for Unit 50

1 Mr Smith is not here now, but he is coming in later.
2 The program will do all the calculations on its own.
3 Those aren't your keys, they're mine.
4 Is this file yours?
5 I must remember to take my driving licence with me.
6 We don't work for them. They work for us.
7 I've got my tickets, but have you got yours?
8 My office is nicer than his.
9 Your clients are great, but they're difficult to please.
10 The low price is one of its best selling points.

Test for Unit 51

1	each other	6	him
2	themselves	7	yourself
3	yourself	8	you
4	itself	9	himself
5	myself	10	me

Test for Unit 52

1 with
2 which
3 with
4 who
5 which
6 who
7 who
8 with
9 who
10 which

Test for Unit 53

1 a
2 a/the
3 the
4 the
5 a
6 a
7 the
8 the
9 the
10 a

Test for Unit 54

1 Ø
2 an
3 Ø
4 Ø
5 Ø
6 the
7 Ø
8 the
9 the
10 Ø

Test for Unit 55

1 this
2 this
3 this
4 that
5 these
6 this
7 this
8 this
9 This
10 That

Test for Unit 56

1 are
2 is
3 is
4 is
5 are
6 some
7 a
8 some
9 some
10 an

Test for Unit 57

1 some
2 a
3 some
4 some
5 any
6 some
7 a
8 any
9 any
10 a

Test for Unit 58

1 tickets
2 rates
3 passes
4 families
5 businessmen
6 groups
7 classes
8 children
9 teachers
10 people

Test for Unit 59

1 any
2 some
3 some
4 some
5 some
6 some
7 any
8 any
9 some
10 any

Test for Unit 60

1 somewhere
2 no one
3 anything
4 something
5 Everyone
6 everywhere
7 nowhere
8 anyone
9 someone
10 anywhere

Test for Unit 61

1 How much does the other model cost?
2 How many people came to the meeting?
3 How many women work in your company?
4 How much time have we got?
5 How many units do you want to order?
6 very little
7 a lot of
8 Very few
9 a little
10 a few

Test for Unit 62

1 62,900
2 390,000
3 540
4 125,000
5 1,000,000
6 three hundred and ninety-five
7 three thousand, nine hundred
8 eighteen thousand, eight hundred and thirty-six
9 three hundred and eighty-seven thousand, four hundred and forty-four
10 five million, three hundred thousand

Test for Unit 63

1 three dollars fifty
2 nine point five eight seconds
3 fifteen per cent
4 five thousand, four hundred euros
5 two point six kilometres
6 a quarter
7 fifty per cent
8 two thirds
9 one fifth
10 three quarters

Test for Unit 64

1 at
2 next to
3 opposite
4 in
5 between
6 at/from
7 at
8 in
9 on
10 in

Test for Unit 65

1 on
2 in
3 in
4 Ø
5 from
6 at
7 at
8 on
9 Ø
10 in

Test for Unit 66

1 in
2 in
3 for
4 on
5 in
6 out
7 by
8 of
9 with
10 of

Test for Unit 67

1 worried
2 about
3 interested
4 in
5 different
6 from
7 popular
8 with
9 suitable
10 for

Test for Unit 68

1 by
2 on
3 to
4 for
5 to
6 on
7 from
8 with
9 to
10 with

Test for Unit 69

1 do
2 do
3 making
4 made
5 make
6 doing
7 doing
8 making
9 make
10 doing

Test for Unit 70

1 problems
2 a coffee
3 a chat
4 a bad day
5 lunch
6 a question
7 a degree
8 time
9 a great time
10 a headache

Test for Unit 71

1 get on with
2 get ready
3 getting
4 get in touch with me
5 get together
6 get in
7 got
8 get the sack
9 get over
10 get

Test for Unit 72

1 give
2 take
3 take
4 give
5 give
6 take
7 give
8 give
9 take
10 give

Index

References are to unit numbers

a, an 53, 54
a few 61
a little 61
a lot of 61
ability 28
about 66, 67, 68
actions and states 10
adjective + preposition 67
adjectives 42, 43, 44, 46, 47, 48
adjectives and adverbs 43, 44
adjectives ending in *-ly* 44
adjectives in *-ing* and *-ed* 42
adverbs 43, 44
adverbs of frequency 45
advice 31
already 22
always 45
am employed 26
am doing (future) 17
am doing (present) 7
am I? 2
am, is, are 1
any and *some* 57, 59
anybody 60
anyone 60
anything 60
anywhere 60
are doing (future) 17
are doing 7
are done 26
are going to 18
are they? 2
are we? 2
are you? 2
aren't 2
arrangements 17
articles 53, 54
asking questions 6
at 11, 64, 65, 67, 68

bad, worse 46
bad, worse, the worst 48
be (negatives) 2
be (questions) 2
be 1
between 65, 66
by 26, 27, 51, 66, 68

can 28
can I? / could I? 29

can't 28, 34
common questions 6
comparatives 46, 47
comparing adjectives 46, 47
conditionals 36, 37, 38
could 28
could you? 29
couldn't 28
countable nouns 56, 57, 61
criticizing 31

dates 62
decimals 63
decisions 16, 18
definite article 53, 54
did 12
didn't 12
didn't use to 15
dimensions 63
directions 35
do and *make* 69
doesn't have to 34
don't have to 34

each other 51
-ed and *-ing* adjectives 42
enough + noun 49
-er (older, bigger) 46
-er, -est (tall, tallest) 48
ever 21
everything 60
explaining 35
expressions of frequency 45
expressions with *do* 69
expressions with *get* 71
expressions with *give* 72
expressions with *have* 70
expressions with *make* 69
expressions with *take* 72

few 61
first conditional 37
for 65, 66, 67, 68
for and *since* 23
fractions 63
frequency 45
from 64, 65, 67, 68
future 16, 17, 18, 19, 32

gerund 39
get 71

give 72
giving advice 31
giving directions 35
giving explanations 35
giving instructions 35
going to 18
going to or *will* 19
good and *well* 44
good, better 46
good, better, best 48
group nouns 58

had 13
had to (obligation) 33
half 63
hardly ever 45
has 3
has been doing 25
has done 20, 24
has got 3, 70
have got 3, 70
have 3
have and *have got* 3, 70
have been doing 25
have done 20, 24
have got 3, 70
have to 34
house numbers 64
how about ... 30
How are you? 6
How do you do? 6
how long 23, 63
how many 61
how much 61

I suggest ... 30
I, me, my, mine, etc. 50
if + past tense 38
if a happens, b happens 36
if and imperative 37
if and *when* 37
if I were you 31
if sentences 36, 37, 38
if you work ... 36, 37
if you worked ... 38
imperative 35
imperative in *if* sentences 37
in 11, 64, 65, 66, 67
indefinite article 53, 54
infinitive 39, 40, 41
infinitive of purpose 40

infinitive or *-ing* 39, 40
-ing after adjective + preposition 67
-ing form 39, 40
-ing or infinitive 39, 40
instructions 35
interesting and *interested* 42
is doing (future) 17
is doing 7
is done 26
is going to 18
is he/she/it? 2
isn't 2

just 20

let 41
let's ... 30
little 61
long adjectives 47, 48

make 41, 69
make and *do* 69
make and *let* 41
making arrangements 17
making offers 29
making requests 29
making suggestions 30
many 61
may 32
might 32
mine, yours etc 50
modals 31, 32, 33, 34
moment of speaking 7
more ... than 47
more ... than, the most ... 48
much 61
must 33
mustn't 33
myself, yourself, etc. 51

necessity 33
needn't 33
never 21, 45
no article 53, 54
not ... yet 22
not ... enough 49
not as ... as 47
nothing 60
noun + preposition 66
nouns 56, 57, 58

numbers 62, 63

object pronouns 50
obligation 33, 34
of 66, 67, 68
offers 29
often 45
on 11, 64, 65, 66, 68
once a week 45
ought to 31
out of 64, 66

passive 26, 27
past continuous 14
past habits 15
past simple positive 11
past simple irregular 13
past simple negative 12
past simple passive 27
past simple questions 12
past states 15
percentages 63
permission 28
personal pronouns 50
place names 54
plans 18
plural nouns 57, 58
polite requests 29
possessive adjectives 50
possibility 32
predictions 18
preposition + verb 66, 67
preposition + -*ing* 40, 67
preposition + noun 66
prepositions 64, 65, 66, 67, 68
prepositions of direction 64
prepositions of place 64
prepositions of time 65
present continuous (future) 17
present continuous negative 8
present continuous or present
    simple? 9, 10

present continuous or *will?* 19
present continuous positive 7
present continuous questions 8
present perfect 20, 21, 22, 23
present perfect and past simple
    24
present perfect continuous 25
present perfect negative 21
present perfect questions 21,
    22
present perfect with *for* and
    since 23
present simple (explaining) 35
present simple (future) 17
present simple negative 5
present simple or present
    continuous? 9, 10
present simple passive 26
present simple positive 4
present simple questions 5
prices 63
pronouns 50, 51
purpose 40

quarter 63
questions 6

rarely 45
recent actions 20
reflexive pronouns 51
relative clauses 52
relative pronouns 52
relatives 52
requests 29
road names 64
routines 4, 36
second conditional 38
shall I? 29
short adjectives 46, 48
should 31
shouldn't 31
since and *for* 23

singular nouns 57, 58
some 56
some and *any* 57, 59
somebody 60
someone 60
something 60
sometimes 45
somewhere 60
states and actions 10
stative verbs 10
subject pronouns 50
suggestions 30
superlatives 48

take 72
talking about now 7, 32
talking about possibilities 32
temporary situations 7
than 46, 47
that 52, 55
the 53, 54
these 55
third 63
this 55
those 55
three times a week, etc. 45
time expressions 11, 20, 65
to 64, 65, 66, 67, 68
to be 1
too and *enough* 49
twice a week 45
two-part verbs with *get* 71
two-part verbs with *give* and
    take 72

uncertainty 32
uncountable nouns 56, 57, 61
used to 15
usually 45

verb + object + infinitive 41
verb + object + preposition 68

verb + preposition 68
verbs + gerund 39
verbs + infinitive 39, 41
verbs + -*ing* 39
verbs of liking 10
verbs of possession 10
verbs of the senses + adjectives
    44
verbs of thinking 10
very few 61
very little 61

was born 27
was doing/were doing 14
was done 27
was/were 13, 26, 27
well and *good* 44
were (if I were you) 31
were born 27
were done 27
wh – questions 6
what about ...? 30
What do you do? 6
when 37
when and *if* 37
which 52
who 52
why don't we ...? 30
why don't you ...? 30
will 16, 32, 37
will or *going to* 19
will or present continuous 19
with 52, 66, 67, 68
won't 16
would 38
would you like ...? 29
would you like me to ...? 29

yesterday 11
yet 22

zero conditional 36